FORCIBLY DISPLACED

Toward a Development Approach Supporting Refugees, the Internally Displaced, and Their Hosts

Contents

Boxes

Figures

Maps

Tables

Foreword

Today 65 million people are reportedly displaced, including 21 million refugees, many of whom have been driven from their homes by a historic rise in conflict and violence. The burden of responding to this mass movement has largely been shouldered by a handful of countries and humanitarian groups confronting an emergency that could last a generation or more.

This global crisis requires new solutions to help refugees and people in countries torn apart by conflict. Humanitarian and development partners must work more closely together in complementary ways. Development organizations such as the World Bank Group can provide longer term support as well as innovative financing solutions to help both refugees and host communities.

This ground-breaking study, *Forcibly Displaced: Toward a Development Approach Supporting Refugees, the Internally Displaced, and Their Hosts*, recommends ways to help the forcibly displaced access jobs and opportunities. Produced in partnership with the United Nations High Commissioner for Refugees (UNHCR), the study outlines how we can build resilience while supporting inclusive and sustainable growth in host countries.

The report provides insight into the scope and scale of forced displacement. While the crisis affects countries of all income levels, the fact that 95 percent of the displaced live in the developing world underscores the need to align humanitarian actions with development efforts. While refugees often endure displacement for many years, half of today's refugees have been displaced for four years or less. If we focus our efforts early, development interventions could deliver even greater impacts for refugees and their communities.

The World Bank Group is already approaching our work in new ways to strengthen our response to fragility, conflict, and violence. We are developing methods to monitor risk and anticipate forced displacement to help countries prepare. We are helping host countries improve their business climate so that the private sector can drive more rapid economic growth. We are establishing longer-term development solutions, such as providing concessional finance to middle-income countries hosting refugees.

We hope this report will improve our collective understanding of the forced displacement crisis and inspire new thinking to address this critical challenge. The World Bank Group will continue to strengthen our engagement with the United Nations, other multilateral development banks, the private sector, and civil society to address the needs of the many millions of displaced people and their host communities.

Jim Yong Kim
President
World Bank Group

Foreword

More people are living longer, healthier lives than at any time in human history. Yet, hundreds of millions remain deeply impoverished and vulnerable. Furthermore, bad governance, violence, and conflict have driven an increasing number from their homes and even to flee their country to stay alive. And, far too often, once their plight fades from the world's media, they are left to lead a precarious existence, hosted predominantly by states and communities with limited resources. Their ensuing poverty condemns generations—mostly women and children—to a life on the margins, largely denied the benefits of global progress enjoyed by so many others.

Recent crises demonstrate dramatically how the spillover effects of civil war and conflict can impact dramatically on the peace, prosperity, and security of the immediate region and even far beyond. They also underline how rapidly global solidarity for the victims can erode. This timely study presents a comprehensive analysis of forced displacement that situates this pressing issue squarely on the development agenda. It makes a compelling case for combining humanitarian and development know-how and resources to achieve lasting social and economic progress for the displaced persons of the world and the local host communities who are invariably the front line responders in every humanitarian disaster.

For the United Nations High Commissioner for Refugees (UNHCR), the search for durable solutions for refugees, internally displaced, and stateless persons remains as central to our mandate as emergency response. Enabling dignified and productive lives through development investment is key to this challenge. With the publication of this study by the World Bank Group, I am confident that its combination of analytical rigor and field-based knowledge of forced displacement can exercise significant influence on future policy and practice. Most importantly, working in a cooperative and complementary partnership as envisaged in the Secretary General's "Agenda for Humanity" report, humanitarian and development agencies can make a real difference in the lives of the world's poorest and most marginalized populations.

Filippo Grandi
United Nations High Commissioner for Refugees

Acknowledgments

This report was written by a team led by Xavier Devictor. Core team members were Caroline Bahnson, Anna Bokina, Cordelia Chesnutt, Chisako Fukuda, Nancy Kebe, Mona Niebuhr, Caroline Sergeant, Caroline Vagneron, and Neelam Verjee.

The report benefited from being formally peer reviewed by Alex Aleinikoff, Sultan Barakat, Stefan Dercon, Lynne Sherburne-Benz, and Hans Timmer. A number of advisers provided overall guidance to the team at all stages of the project. For their advice and encouragement, the team is especially grateful to Punam Chuhan-Pole, Shanta Devarajan, Saroj Kumar Jha, and Alexandre Marc.

Many people participated in the writing of the report. The main co-authors: for chapter 1, Zara Sarzin and Bernhard Metz; for chapter 2, Cordelia Chesnutt and Bledi Celiku; for chapter 3, Joanna De Berry, Helidah Ogude, Kevin Carey, and Dalia al Kadi; for chapter 4, Mona Niebuhr, with contributions from Dhiraj Sharma; for chapter 5, Taies Nezam; and for chapter 6, Stephan Massing and Julie Dana. Uri Dadush provided substantial support in conceptualizing forced displacement as a development issue. Joe Saba also provided support in articulating the collective action challenges related to forced displacement.

Tables and graphs were compiled by Zara Sarzin, who was also responsible for verifying the accuracy of statistics used or cited in the report. She benefited from the help of Michael Keenan. Caroline Vagneron oversaw the production of the entire report, together with Chisako Fukuda, Jon Walton, and Ian White. Pat Katayama, Stephen McGroarty, Abdia Mohamed, and Steve Pazdan provided support from External and Corporate Relations, Publishing and Knowledge. A team from Communications Development Incorporated, led by Bruce Ross-Larson, edited the report.

The report was written in collaboration and consultation with the United Nations High Commissioner for Refugees (UNHCR). The team would especially like to thank Louise Aubin, Theresa Beltramo, Steven Corliss, Ayaki Ito, Christina Jespersen, Preeta Law, Betsy Lippman, Ewen Macleod, Kimberly Roberson, Tammi Sharpe, and Paul Spiegel for their insights and contributions.

This task received financial support from the Office of the Chief Economist of the World Bank Group's Africa Region, the Office of the Chief Economist of the World Bank Group's Middle East and North Africa Region, and the Global Program on Forced Displacement, a World Bank Group–managed trust fund supported by Denmark, Germany, Norway, and Switzerland.

The team thanks others who have helped in preparing and writing the report and wishes to apologize to anyone inadvertently overlooked in these acknowledgments.

Abbreviations

CFF	Concessional Financing Facility (of the World Bank Group)
CIF	Climate Investment Funds
ECOWAS	Economic Community of West African States
EU	European Union
FDI	foreign direct investment
GDP	gross domestic product
IASC	Inter-Agency Standing Committee (of the United Nations)
IDMC	Internal Displacement Monitoring Centre
IDP	internally displaced person
IFFIm	International Finance Facility for Immunization
ILO	International Labour Organization
IMF	International Monetary Fund
IOM	International Organization for Migration
JIPS	Joint IDP Profiling Service
MDB	multilateral development bank
MDTF	multi-donor trust fund
OAU	Organization of African Unity
ODA	official development assistance
OECD	Organisation for Economic Co-operation and Development
OECD-DAC	Organisation for Economic Co-operation and Development—Development Assistance Committee
SAR	special administrative region
UN	United Nations
UNHCR	United Nations High Commissioner for Refugees
UNRWA	United Nations Relief and Works Agency for Palestine Refugees in the Near East

Overview

Forced displacement is emerging as an important development challenge. The reason: extreme poverty is now increasingly concentrated among vulnerable groups including people who had to flee in the face of conflict and violence, and their presence affects development prospects in the communities that are hosting them. Large movements of people are also fueling xenophobic reactions, even in high-income countries, and this could threaten the consensus that is underpinning global economic growth.

Development actors' overall objective is to help reduce poverty among both the forcibly displaced and their host communities, as part of a broader effort to achieve the United Nations' Sustainable Development Goals (SDGs). The focus is on tackling the medium-term socioeconomic dimensions of forced displacement. This is complementary to, but distinct from, the rights-based protection agenda and the urgent focus on short-term crisis responses.

To support the forcibly displaced, development actors should help reduce—even eliminate—vulnerabilities. The forcibly displaced have often acquired vulnerabilities that are specific to them, such as catastrophic losses of assets or trauma. This affects their ability to seize economic opportunities, and it can trap them in poverty. Because such vulnerabilities set them apart from other poor people in the communities where they live, broad-based poverty

reduction efforts may not suffice to relieve their plight and special interventions are needed.

To support host communities, development actors should help manage the shock caused by an inflow of forcibly displaced persons. The arrival of large numbers of people in specific locales creates both risks and opportunities. In most situations, it transforms the environment for designing and implementing poverty reduction programs. In some exceptional cases, it creates new dynamics for the entire country and national development strategies have to be adjusted accordingly. Development actors should help host communities manage these new circumstances so that they can continue to reduce poverty, while providing an accepting environment for the forcibly displaced.

A crisis that can be managed

About 65 million people live in forced displacement: almost 1 percent of the world's population.[1] The conflict in the Syrian Arab Republic and the ensuing flow of refugees toward the European Union have captured headlines across the world, but they are only part of a much broader story. For decades, large numbers of people have been forced to flee from their homes by conflict and violence, and most have been hosted in developing countries for prolonged periods. So the crisis of forced displacement is not new. What is new is the increasing scale and complexity of the crisis in a globalized world and the growing recognition that it is both a humanitarian and a development challenge.

The crisis entails a tremendous amount of suffering, yet it may still be within the range of what the international community can manage with adequate effort and effective collective action. It has two distinct components: refugees and asylum-seekers (about 24 million people)[2] who have crossed an international border; and internally displaced persons (IDPs, about 41 million people)[3] who have been displaced by conflict and violence in their own country (figure O.1 and map O.1). The differences between the two groups, especially their legal status, are significant. Yet, they often have endured similar hardships and they all need protection. Their experiences makes them distinct from economic migrants, who move in search of better opportunities, and from those displaced by natural disasters.

Adequate information is lacking to inform policy responses and programming decisions. Gaining an accurate picture of the forced displacement crisis is challenging due to political and technical issues that affect the availability and quality of data. Some of the numbers commonly used are no better than educated guesses, and there are major discrepancies across sources. For example, Eurostat estimated the number of refugees living in Norway in 2013 at 18,000 but the Norwegian Statistical Office had it at 132,000 due to differences in definitions.[4] And IDP numbers are far more often based on estimates than on vital registrations (and where births are recorded, deaths in many cases are not).

A very substantial effort can enhance the coverage, accuracy, reliability, and comparability of data across situations. But this requires strengthening data collection and dissemination mechanisms at all levels. It requires moving to an "open data" system with due regard to privacy and protection. It requires carrying out detailed assessments in each specific situation. And it requires developing a shared

platform to build evidence on what may be the most effective responses to the crisis.

Working together with humanitarian actors

Governments from both origin and host countries are at the center of the crisis. Their decisions affect the scale and destination of population movements—as well as the impacts and solutions in the short, medium, and long terms. External actors can support the adoption and implementation of sound responses, but the primary role rests with national and local authorities, private firms, and civil society.

Against this backdrop, humanitarian agencies have been calling for development institutions to support new approaches that can produce sustainable solutions. Development activities are part of a broader international effort that has many dimensions: political, security, humanitarian, and diplomatic. Each must be adequately resourced to deliver a comprehensive and effective response. Indeed, the engagement of development actors should be seen not as a substitute for other efforts but as an additional and complementary set of interventions.

The best results are likely to be achieved when humanitarian and development actors work together. The humanitarian-development nexus has long been seen as sequential, with an initial humanitarian response followed by a development effort when the situation becomes protracted. In fact, rather than replace or succeed each other, both sets of actors can engage in complementary efforts for greater impact throughout the entire period of forced displacement. Humanitarian and development agencies have different objectives, counterparts, and instruments: this can be a source of strength. They can both contribute to a comprehensive effort from the onset, learn from each other, and build synergies based on their respective comparative advantages.

The development approach is centered on such concepts as economic opportunity,

FIGURE O.1 An overview of the forced displacement crisis

a. The second largest refugee crisis since World War II...

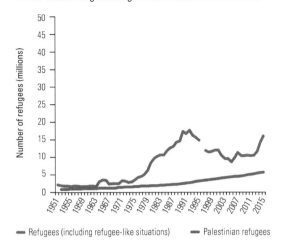

Refugees (including refugee-like situations) — Palestinian refugees

b. ...is paralleled by a rapid surge of internal displacement.

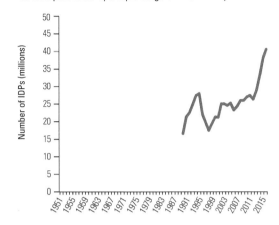

c. The crisis primarily affects the developing world...

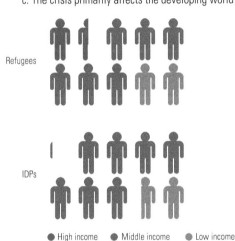

High income • Middle income • Low income

d. ...and has been mainly caused by the same 10 long-lasting conflicts.

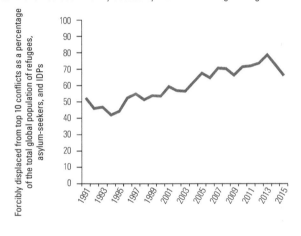

e. 94 percent of forcibly displaced live out of camps...

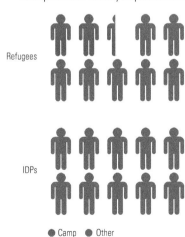

• Camp • Other

f. ...and half of the refugees have been in exile for less than 4 years.

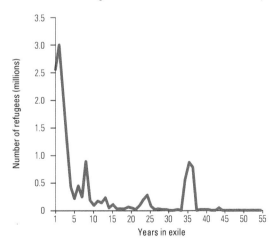

Sources: UNHCR 2016b; 2016c; UNRWA 2016; IDMC 2016, and Devictor and Do 2016.
Note: IDP = internally displaced person.

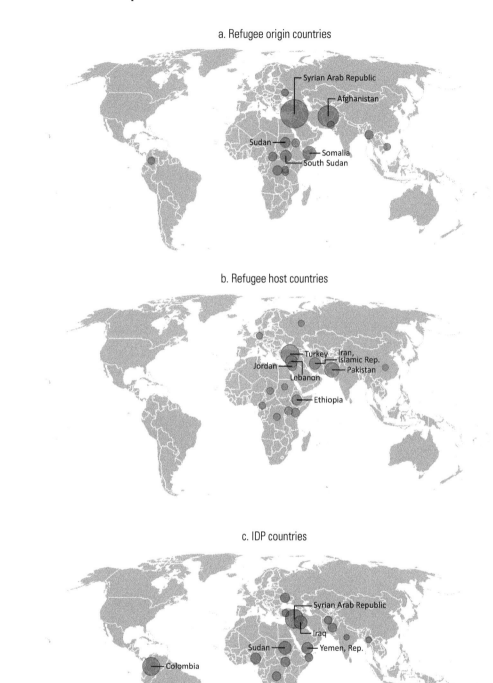

MAP 0.1 An uneven impact across the world

a. Refugee origin countries

Syrian Arab Republic
Afghanistan
Sudan
Somalia
South Sudan

b. Refugee host countries

Turkey
Iran, Islamic Rep.
Jordan
Pakistan
Lebanon
Ethiopia

c. IDP countries

Syrian Arab Republic
Iraq
Sudan
Yemen, Rep.
Colombia

5,000,000
1,000,000
100,000

Source: UNHCR 2016b.
Note: Includes refugee-like situations. Includes only internally displaced persons (IDPs) under United Nations High Commissioner for Refugees mandate.

medium-term sustainability, and cost-effectiveness. It sees the forcibly displaced and their hosts as economic agents who make choices and respond to incentives. It pays particular attention to institutions and policies. And it relies on partnerships with and between governments, the private sector, and civil society.

Development actors can provide financial resources with a medium-term perspective as well as a range of analytical and advisory services. They have access to economic policy makers, who are not traditional counterparts for humanitarian agencies. They can inform public debates and policy formulation, and help strengthen institutions. They can also develop innovative financing solutions to leverage a strong private sector response. But development actors may not be mandated or equipped to engage in some issues that are critical to the displacement agenda, especially in the political or legal arena. They also have limited capacity to deliver urgent assistance in environments with significant security risks.

To move forward, humanitarian and development actors should adopt a pragmatic approach and identify potential synergies in each situation—as part of a broader effort that also involves a wide range of government counterparts, the private sector, and civil society, as well as security and diplomatic actors.

The focus of engagement will necessarily change over time. At the onset of a crisis, before forced displacement has started in earnest, the question is whether there is scope for prevention and preparedness. During the crisis, support must be provided to those forcibly displaced as well as to their host communities. Over time external actors should help create conditions that enable the forcibly displaced to truly rebuild their lives.

At the onset—Taking a new look at prevention and preparedness

To mitigate the negative impact of forced displacement before it happens, efforts so

far have largely focused on conflict prevention. This is based on a simple truism: prevention is better than cure; since conflict causes forced displacement, preventing forced displacement calls for preventing or ending conflict. This is an important goal, but the track record of international interventions is mixed. In reality, many countries are at war—or at a high risk of war—with no clear political solution in sight. Can development actors do something to prevent some of the worst impacts of forced displacement even if there is no diplomatic or military settlement?

Forcibly displaced persons are not only victims, they are purposeful actors. They flee in response to threats, sometimes at gunpoint, often not. In the midst of conflict, they must choose whether to stay or to flee. These decisions are incredibly difficult, often made under duress and with imperfect information. With violence and poverty widespread, both staying and fleeing carry very high risks: people have to assess and compare the odds of survival under each scenario.

Understanding what makes some people stay and others go is critical to mitigating forced displacement. Security threats are the main reason to flee, outweighing all other factors: for example, 78 percent of Colombia's IDPs have been direct victims of violence.[5] Some people or groups of people are particularly at risk as violence is often targeted. Yet economic concerns and social networks can also determine who stays, who leaves, and where people go. Those who have opportunities away from home, because of their skills or their social networks, are more likely to flee than those who have strong ties to their land or cannot sell their assets. Government policies are not neutral in the process: punitive military tactics, discrimination against certain groups, or the withdrawal of resources and services from parts of the country can all accelerate forced displacement.

In many situations, forced displacement does not happen unexpectedly. In fact, refugees and IDP flows can often be forecast: this is because people try to stay home and to manage risks for as long as they can and embark on a perilous journey into exile only once other means of coping have been exhausted. On average, outflows of forcibly displaced persons peak 4.1 years after they start.[6] Today several countries are at war or on the brink but people have not yet fled their homes in large numbers: they are the likely hotspots for the coming years.

In any situation of forced displacement most people stay behind. At the end of 2015, more than 90 percent of the population was still in place in 80 percent of countries of origin. Only in Syria did the share of forcibly displaced exceed 25 percent of the population.[7] Although international attention is focused on those who flee—refugees and IDPs—those who stay behind, in an environment of violence and economic depression, also face formidable odds. They suffer greatly, often with limited external assistance. Eventually they may lose the ability to withstand even minor shocks and may be pushed into exile because their resilience has been dramatically eroded.

With violence being the main driver of forced displacement, development actors necessarily have a limited role. But they can contribute to making a difference:

- **Discourage government policies that induce forced displacement.** This is especially relevant when forced displacement is the result of decisions taken by the government of the country of origin. Development actors can engage in a dialogue with the authorities to highlight the high costs of forced displacement and to support better policy choices. They can also support regional initiatives to better manage cross-border movements.
- **Help host countries and host communities prepare.** When displacement can be forecast, there is time to prepare—for example with block grants that can be rapidly deployed to affected municipalities when the crisis hits. Authorities can be ready with a response that can be swiftly implemented when refugees or IDPs flow in. Development actors

should help develop advance warning systems—for example, by using big data technologies in partnership with the private sector—and support host governments in preparing contingency plans.
- **Strengthen the resilience of those who stay behind.** Development actors can finance projects to maintain livelihoods and to strengthen community-based institutions. They should focus on "stable parts of unstable countries" where they can complement humanitarian actions. They should also carefully manage the risks in such an approach, since those who are helped to stay could eventually become victims of violence. Interventions should not be seen as a substitute to providing asylum to those who flee.

During the crisis— Managing changes for host communities

Hosting large numbers of forcibly displaced persons creates new opportunities and new challenges, which affect the host communities' poverty reduction efforts, both positively and negatively. Support to host communities is often seen as an indirect way to assist refugees and IDPs, by helping to create an accepting or even a welcoming environment for forcibly displaced persons. But the development response should also aim to help reduce poverty among the hosts, as they adjust to a transformed context. This is an objective in its own right: host communities have development needs, and reducing their own poverty often remains among their foremost priorities.

For host communities, the influx of large numbers of forcibly displaced persons is essentially a demographic shock, which disrupts preexisting equilibria and creates mismatches in supply and demand in markets. With the passing of time, a new set of equilibria emerges. The question is whether this new environment is more or less conducive to poverty reduction among the hosts. The

FIGURE O.2 Shock and response for the host communities

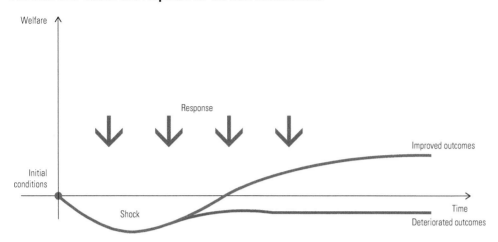

answer depends on the initial conditions, the size and nature of the shock, and the policy and investment response. Development actors should assist national and local authorities in articulating the most effective responses for a given set of initial conditions and shock (figure O.2).

In a number of areas, the challenges for host communities already existed before the influx of forcibly displaced persons. Refugees and IDPs may provide convenient scapegoats for deep-rooted issues, but they are often not the main cause of all the difficulties facing host countries. For example, over the last 25 years, hosting refugees may have contributed to causing conflict in only 8 out of 991 country-year episodes—and in each case, the country was already on the brink prior to their arrival.[8]

The same is true for economic growth. The impact of refugees, who typically represent less than 1 percent of the population, is limited compared to structural constraints or oil price fluctuations. It can be more substantial where the refugees account for a larger share of the population as in Jordan and Lebanon, although government policies still largely determine the eventual outcome. While private investment is needed to make up for the increase in labor supply (and to avoid a decline in wages), most affected countries have a very poor business environment. Of

the ten largest refugee-hosting countries in 2015, all but one are in the bottom half of the World Bank Group's Ease of Doing Business index.[9] And among the ten countries with the largest number of IDPs, the average ranking stood at 148 out of 189.[10]

Local impacts are unevenly distributed: some people gain, others lose out, particularly on jobs and prices. There can be a perception that forcibly displaced persons compete with the poorest hosts and push them deeper into poverty. Yet the reality is more nuanced. Overall, and assuming that the investment climate is sound, the presence of refugees and IDPs typically increases demand and creates jobs, but it also adds newcomers to the labor force. Employers and people whose skills complement those of the forcibly displaced tend to gain; but people who have skills similar to those of the forcibly displaced may lose their jobs. Who is affected and how is a function of government policies—and of whether refugees have the right to work (in which case they can compete for skilled positions in the formal sector) or not (in which case they are relegated to low-skill, informal jobs).

Similarly, the impact of prices is unevenly distributed: prices of land and housing typically go up, and owners benefit to the detriment of renters. Prices of food and other basic commodities may decline if aid is provided in-kind, and consumers gain while local producers lose. Understanding how the costs and benefits are distributed within these communities is crucial to mitigating the impacts of forced displacement.

The local impact on social, urban, and environmental services can also be significant. The inflow of forcibly displaced persons increases demand, while supply may take time to adjust. This is especially the case when refugees and IDPs are accommodated in lagging regions or in poorer parts of urban centers, where service availability was already spotty before their arrival. The impacts are closely associated with settlement patterns: the more concentrated the displaced, the greater the strain on a limited capacity. Both investments and policy reforms are needed to mitigate such effects.

The impact of forced displacement on host communities also depends on policies. The concentration of forcibly displaced persons in camps or in specific hosting areas may heighten challenges for host communities (for example in terms of jobs, prices, services, or social cohesion). When refugees have the right to work, they can fully use their skills and contribute more to the economy (including fiscal resources). Policies that are traditionally seen as more humane and beneficial for forcibly displaced persons also serve the host communities' own interests: they are not only right, they are also smart.

Mitigating the impact of forced displacement on host communities is not a strictly technical agenda. Political considerations often drive the host authorities' response, and "second-best" options may well be the best approaches in some situations. To help host communities make further progress in their own development and poverty reduction efforts in a transformed environment, support should aim to:

- **Address long-standing development issues, which the presence of forcibly displaced persons may exacerbate.** This largely consists of "traditional" development support to host countries and

communities, for example to improve the business environment or to reduce inequalities. It is particularly important for fragility, economic management, employment, and social cohesion.

- **Support those who have been hurt within host communities.** Some groups in host communities are disproportionately affected, especially through jobs and prices. Development actors should help these people stay in the labor market and maintain their livelihoods, or upgrade their skills. They should also help strengthen social protection systems to provide assistance to those who may not be able to do so.

- **Strengthen and expand service delivery** in the education and health sectors as well as for urban and environmental services. Accommodating forcibly displaced persons requires scaling up supply. Development actors should help build capacity and finance infrastructure and operations and maintenance expenditure in the short term. They should also help develop an adequate system that can be sustained in the medium term.

- **Encourage granting the forcibly displaced the freedom of movement and the right to work.** While often controversial, such policies are in the interest of host communities, regardless of their benefits for refugees and IDPs. Development actors should raise awareness of the positive impacts of these reforms and support their implementation. They should also help modernize the delivery of external assistance, so that it can better stimulate economic activity within host communities (for example, through cash rather than food aid) and increasingly rely on country systems.

During the crisis— Reducing vulnerabilities of the forcibly displaced

Development approaches are geared toward helping people escape poverty. The goal is no different for forcibly displaced persons. Whether they are fleeing conflict or are the targets of political violence, their lives are being turned upside down, and their hopes dashed. They are at risk of falling into a "poverty trap" with lasting impacts that can extend across several generations. Self-reliance is key to restoring their dignity, as well as their ability to earn a living.

Dedicated development interventions may be needed as forcibly displaced persons are often unable to take full advantage of existing opportunities for poverty reduction: the specific vulnerabilities they have acquired through their forced displacement experience make them less prone to socioeconomic inclusion and more exposed to risks (figure O.3). They need assistance to regain the capacity to improve their lives. The challenge is particularly acute when people are "in limbo," with uncertain prospects long into the future. In such cases, the development approach should aim to strengthen their capacity to seize opportunities not only in their current environment, but also under the likely scenarios for an eventual resolution of their situation.

Forcibly displaced persons—both refugees and IDPs—have typically suffered a major setback. They have lost many of their assets, sometimes everything. Their human and social capital depletes rapidly. They have often

experienced traumatic events, which can leave scars that are difficult to heal: in the Central African Republic, nearly half the displaced have had a direct experience of violence and more than a fourth have witnessed killings.[11] When the forcibly displaced do not have access to economic opportunities, they may have to adopt short-term coping strategies to survive—putting children to work, having daughters marry early, disposing of any remaining assets at fire-sale prices. The experience of loss and trauma distinguishes them from other poor people and from economic migrants in their host communities.

Women and girls face particular challenges—and opportunities. In some situations, displacement can provide space for "positive" change and empowerment, as when gender norms are more progressive than in the place of origin, or when traditional divisions of labor are disrupted. But women and girls also risk rape, sexual abuse, and other gender-based violence—before and during flight as well as in exile. Recent reports about the sexual exploitation of Syrian refugee women during their passage to Europe provide a powerful reminder of what is common across many situations.[12]

The initial setbacks can be compounded in the host environment. Forcibly displaced persons need economic opportunities to avoid falling into poverty or dependency. But

FIGURE O.3 **The multiple dimensions of vulnerability**

they can face severe legal restrictions on their right to work or to move freely. Both refugees and IDPs may also end up in areas where there simply are no jobs or opportunities for them, as in a lagging region or a place where there is no demand for their skills. Eighty-eight percent of refugees and 94 percent of IDPs live in economies performing below the global average, and in these countries, 72 percent live in regions where incomes are below the national average.[13] In addition, because of the uncertainty surrounding them, forcibly displaced persons have short planning horizons that can lead to less than optimal decisions. All these factors severely constrain their prospects: they find themselves with limited options, even more limited than other poor people and economic migrants in the same communities.

To help forcibly displaced persons overcome their distinct vulnerabilities, development actors should help them access jobs and economic opportunities:

- **Support policies that enhance freedom of movement and the right to work.** This is especially important where refugees and IDPs are in unsustainable and undesirable situations. Development partners can document the potential benefits of such measures—for both forcibly displaced persons and for their host communities—and support their adoption.
- **Help create economic opportunities where there are large numbers of forcibly displaced persons.** This requires a strong engagement by the private sector, possibly supported by external actors. It should also benefit host communities, with a focus on places where activities are likely to be sustainable once support programs are completed.
- **Invest in skills and education that are in demand in the labor market.** This can help adults adjust to their new environment and prevent children from becoming part of a "lost generation." Increasing access, relevance, and qual-

ity may require substantial external support.
- **Provide continuing support to those who may not be able to seize opportunities in the short term, both in camps and in urban settings.** This could build on lessons learned from development experience in reforming and modernizing social protection systems and on innovative schemes such as the "graduation approach."

Toward a longer-term solution—Helping to rebuild lives

Return is often regarded as the most obvious solution to forced displacement, but is it? In every situation some people return, others do not, and the proportions vary. Yet over the last six years, return accounted for only 27 percent of those who exited refugee status globally.[14] Large majorities of forcibly displaced persons are reluctant to return to a place associated with war and trauma and where economic opportunities are lacking. In many situations, they develop more complex strategies, with family members moving to different places through an iterative process of staggered or even cyclical movements.

For development actors, the "end point" of engagement is not about where people live—it is about whether they still need dedicated development support. The rationale for providing such assistance dissipates when the forcibly displaced have overcome their vulnerabilities and can take full advantage of broader poverty reduction programs. This socioeconomic approach complements the traditional framework of rights and legal protection. It also acknowledges the importance of both economic rights and effective access to opportunities. And it recognizes that in some cases there may be tension between the two: people can have rights in a place where there is no opportunity for them, or they may have opportunities in a place where they have no rights. The challenge is to find a solution where they can enjoy both.

Against this backdrop, return is a complex process of reestablishing bonds in a transformed environment, rather than going back to a status quo ante. Large numbers of returnees do not go back to their place of origin but settle instead in other areas in their home country, especially in urban areas, due to a mix of security and economic concerns: this caused significant growth in cities such as Kabul in Afghanistan, Juba in South Sudan, Luanda in Angola, and Monrovia in Liberia.[15] And not all returns have a happy ending: some returnees have to flee again, while others become IDPs in their own country. Of the 15 largest episodes of return, about one-third were followed by a new round of fighting within a couple of years: either the returns were premature, or the inflow of returnees derailed a fragile recovery.[16]

The challenge is thus to ensure that return is successful. Security, social acceptance, and access to economic opportunities are key. Refugees who can recover their land and property are often among the first to return, especially for rural households. The difficult process of socioeconomic reintegration is much easier for those who come back with resources, skills, and networks: for instance, among Liberian refugees in Ghana, those who were better off were keener to return—and more successful when doing so.[17] Policies that enable refugees and IDPs to earn an income and to maintain or further develop their skills while in displacement contribute to an eventual successful and sustainable return.

Integration in the place of displacement is another option, but it is also complex. For IDPs, it is about settling into their new environment sustainably. For refugees, it requires securing a legal status that can provide predictable and reliable terms of stay, such as renewable residence and work permits. But this can be difficult: most host countries and communities are unwilling to accept, at least explicitly, the continuing presence of large numbers of refugees other than as "temporary" (even when in long-lasting situations).

As a result, social and economic integration often proceeds "de facto," without a formal status. People may have access to economic opportunities, but they remain shrouded in uncertainty, with no legal protection and a risk of institutionalized discrimination. The extent to which this actually hampers socioeconomic progress varies across countries, but in the long term it is critical. Some innovative legal solutions have been developed, as in West Africa, which provide adequate economic rights short of naturalization.[18]

An equitable sharing of responsibilities is essential to resolve the current crisis, and high-income countries should do more in providing solutions. Their economies have greater capacity to absorb newcomers than those of developing host countries, and the potential benefits for economic growth are much larger. A few Organisation for Economic Co-operation and Development (OECD) countries have opened their doors, but most remain reluctant to assume their international responsibilities on a relevant scale. New approaches are also needed to help refugees integrate into society, as the effectiveness of existing programs is mixed. For example, it takes less than 10 years in the United States and more than 15 years in the European Union for refugees to reach the labor force participation of economic migrants.[19] Successful economic integration hinges on human capital (including skills and language), security of legal status, and availability of opportunities, and the first few years in country have an outsized effect on later employment prospects.

To help the forcibly displaced rebuild their lives in a durable manner, development actors should:

• **Support returnees and the communities that receive them.** The impact of return on receiving communities is in many respects similar to the impact of forced displacement on host communities: it is a shock that has to be managed. Receiving communities are likely to face considerable economic and social difficulties, which typically affect both the returnees and those who stayed throughout the conflict. Development actors should support the countries of return in their recovery efforts. They should also help create socioeconomic opportunities for the returnees and their communities, to the extent that these are economically viable and can be sustained.

- **Help people who are "de facto" integrated acquire a satisfactory legal status.** For example, providing formal legal migrant status to de facto integrated refugees may be a way to recognize the reality of their situation and the normality of human mobility. Such an approach distinguishes between citizenship (formal political membership and associated rights) and residency (economic and social integration). And it makes economic security a priority over political membership. Development actors should support countries willing to explore such solutions, including with financing.

- **Work to end situations of "continuing limbo" where people remain dependent in camps for extended periods.** Development actors should support efforts to transform camps into settlements. They should also work with other partners to enhance the way assistance is provided so as to gradually reduce dependency—for example, by strengthening targeting, supporting people in rejoining the labor force, and building capacity to allow for a gradual shift to country systems.

- **Remain engaged over the medium term to help overcome lasting vulnerabilities.** Forced displacement can leave scars that take decades, sometimes generations, to heal. Development support may be needed for very long periods. This would typically include assistance to overcome trauma or destitution, building on programs that have been developed for marginalized or excluded groups.

Making the most of development finance

Significant financing is necessary to respond to forced displacement crises. The international community provides generous support mainly through humanitarian programs: about US$22 billion in 2015, or several hundreds of US$ per displaced person per year. But there is a critical flaw in this model: forcibly displaced persons have to be sustained by the international community at such a high cost in large part because they are prevented from working. In a global context of slow economic growth and fiscal pressure, grants and highly concessional resources are limited in relation to increasing needs. Development actors should help work toward solutions that can be more cost-effective and sustainable.

There is scope for development actors to broaden the range of financing approaches to engage in forced displacement. This requires greater resource mobilization, better resource allocation (both volume and terms), and more innovative financing instruments. For middle-income host countries, access to concessional financing is critical, and loans need to be blended with grants to lower interest rates or extend repayment periods. Low-income countries need to have access to additional financing, over and above what they would be eligible to receive for their own population, to fund refugee-focused activities.

The challenge is not only mobilizing resources, but also deploying them most effectively. For example, financing should focus not only on investment but also on supporting the adoption of sound policies, as a complement to humanitarian aid, through policy or results-based financing. Public resources could also stimulate stronger private sector engagement—for example by reducing investment risks. This is critical to create economic opportunities for both the forcibly displaced and host communities.

The global costs of the forced displacement crisis are significant. Left without adequate socioeconomic support, the forcibly displaced face a future of hardship and marginalization, as do those who are negatively affected in host communities. This can fuel political and social instability in entire regions and affect the underpinnings of globalization. The engagement of development actors can help reduce the costs of the crisis, by advancing an agenda of prevention and preparedness; by helping host communities address long-standing development issues, scale up service delivery, and strengthen social protection; by supporting the forcibly displaced in their efforts to access jobs; and by contributing to durable solutions, where refugees and IDPs can enjoy both legal rights and economic opportunities.

The forced displacement crisis calls for a global response. Events in origin and host countries are intrinsically linked, and they may affect all parts of the world. A partial response limited to some issues or some countries will remain less than optimal. Nor is a series of individual initiatives or bilateral agreements likely to provide anything more than temporary relief or address the underlying issue of collective action. What is needed is a comprehensive response, driven by affected governments and stakeholders, and supported by the international community in line with the spirit and principles of international cooperation. Development actors have a significant role to play in this most humane of endeavors.

The World Bank Group is committed to such global response. It can contribute a range of services, from analytics to convening to financing. It is determined to work with governments, the private sector, and civil society, at local, national, and regional levels. It is an integral part of a broader partnership, which includes political, diplomatic, security, and humanitarian actors.

Notes

1. UNHCR 2015i.
2. Calculations based on UNHCR 2016b, and UNRWA 2016.
3. IDMC 2016.
4. ECOSOC 2015.
5. Ibáñez and Moya 2016.
6. Authors' calculation based on UNHCR refugee data (end-2014). Outflow is calculated as the yearly change in stock of refugees from each origin country with more than 25,000 refugees during the time period of 1990–2014 (62 countries). The peak is calculated as the maximum outflow, the reference year as the first year when the outflow exceeds 25,000 people.
7. UNHCR 2016b.
8. Authors' calculations. These cases were the destabilization of host countries (Côte d'Ivoire, Guinea, Sierra Leone) by Liberian refugees in the mid-1990s / early 2000s; the destabilization of Eastern Zaire in 1994, and the subsequent civil war in what became the Democratic Republic of Congo; the inflow of refugees from Darfur and the subsequent 2005 war in Chad; population movements between Burundi and Rwanda which preceded the 1993 and 1994 genocides; and the increase in civil strife in Northwest Pakistan which is hosting large numbers of Afghan refugees.
9. World Bank 2016b.
10. World Bank 2016b.
11. JIPS 2012b.
12. *New York Times* 2016.
13. Authors' calculations based on UNHCR refugee data (end-2014), IDMC IDP data (end-2014), and World Bank Group economic indicators.
14. UNHCR 2015a.
15. Harild, Christensen, and Zetter 2015; Omata 2013.
16. Authors' calculation based on UNHCR refugee data (end-2014). Cases of return followed by renewed bout of conflict include Afghanistan (returns in 2001 to 2005); Iraq (returns in 2003 to 2005), Burundi (returns in 1996 to 1997); the Democratic Republic of Congo (returns in 1997 to 1998); Somalia (returns in 1993 to 1995).
17. Omata 2012b.
18. Boulton 2009.
19. Eurostat 2008; Cortes 2004.

How Severe Is the Crisis?

How many people are affected by forced displacement and what do we know about their situation? In the absence of adequate data, this seemingly simple question has no straightforward answer.

Over the last few years, alarmist messages have often prevailed in public debates and media reports. This has conveyed a sense of a crisis spinning out of control. Forced displacement is causing much misery across large parts of Sub-Saharan Africa and of the Middle East, and all regions are affected to some degree. Yet the world has been through crises of similar magnitude in the past and a number of forced displacement situations have been successfully resolved. While the current crisis is severe, it may still be within the range of what the international community can manage with enough effort and concerted action.

The forced displacement crisis is largely rooted in a relatively small number of conflicts, which have been going on for years or even decades. It primarily affects developing countries: about ten countries in protracted conflict and about 15 of their neighbors. The "global" forced displacement crisis is in fact a juxtaposition of local and regional crises, each with its distinct features, and each calling for a distinct response.

The understanding of each forced displacement crisis is often incomplete. For example, the average duration of exile is *shorter* than that is commonly reported; there is *no* evidence that internally

displaced persons (IDPs)[1] eventually become refugees; and the overwhelming majority of forcibly displaced persons live *outside* camps, often in urban settings.

The information on which policy makers can draw to make the decisions affecting both the forcibly displaced and their hosts remains insufficient, due to a range of political and technical issues. A large effort is needed to enhance the coverage, accuracy, reliability, and comparability of data across forced displacement situations. This includes strengthening data collection and dissemination mechanisms; moving toward an "open data" system (with due regard to protection concerns); carrying out detailed situation-specific assessments of the challenges faced by the forcibly displaced and their hosts; and developing a shared platform for building evidence on what may constitute the best responses to crisis.

The crisis in perspective

One percent of humankind

About 65 million people were living in forced displacement at the end of 2015, or almost 1 percent of the world's population.[2] If all forcibly displaced persons formed a single country, it would be the 21st largest in the world, on a par with Thailand or the United Kingdom.

Three distinct groups of people are included in this total (legal definitions are in

FIGURE 1.1 A threefold crisis: The global forcibly displaced population

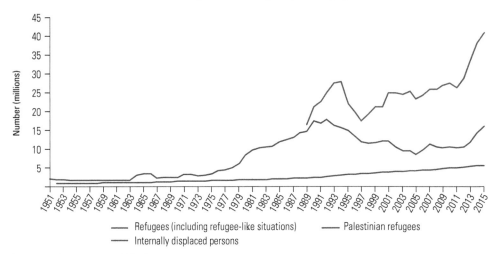

Sources: UNHCR 2016b, 2016c; UNRWA 2016.
Note: UNHCR numbers include refugees and refugee-like situations.

annex 1A and detailed numbers in annex 1B): about 16 million refugees (and an additional 3 million asylum-seekers); about 5 million Palestinian refugees;[3] and about 41 million IDPs.[4] The number of refugees is currently at its second-highest level since 1951: it peaked at the end of the Cold War, at about 10 percent above current levels. The number of Palestinian refugees is steadily increasing, as a result of demographic growth. The number of IDPs has increased very rapidly over the last few years, in part due to the war in the Syrian Arab Republic (figure 1.1).

Historical comparisons should be drawn very carefully, since reliable long-term time series do not exist. Refugee numbers were focused on people of European descent and Palestinians until the late 1970s. IDP statistics have only been available since 1979, and significant methodological changes were introduced in 1993. In absolute terms, today's total of forcibly displaced exceeds population movements in the aftermath of World War II (30 million people) or of the 1947 Partition in South Asia (14 million people). It may be comparable to that in 1971, when the war of independence for Bangladesh generated an estimated 10 million refugees and 30 million IDPs,[5] while the Vietnam War and other conflicts were also raging on.

A small part of the broader trend of human mobility

Forced displacement is part of a wider trend. Mobility has been a characteristic of human societies since the dawn of history. It has yielded countless benefits across the globe and has shaped the world in which we live. Today is no different: mobility is a critical feature of our globalized world and it contributes significantly to global welfare.

The overwhelming majority of migrants leave their places of origin voluntarily in search of economic opportunities, and they move to places where they expect to find demand for their skills (figure 1.2 and box 1.1). Such movements dwarf the numbers of forcibly displaced persons:[6] as of end-2015, there were an estimated 250 million international migrants, about 3.5 percent of the global population, against about 24 million refugees and asylum-seekers;[7] there were also an estimated 740 million internal migrants (when people move within their own country), about 11 percent of the global population, against some 41 million IDPs.

Conflating conflict-induced forced displacement with economic migration and other forms of human mobility is generating some confusion, which can make it difficult to design adequate development responses. That people move for different reasons and

FIGURE 1.2 Refugees are only a small share of people on the move

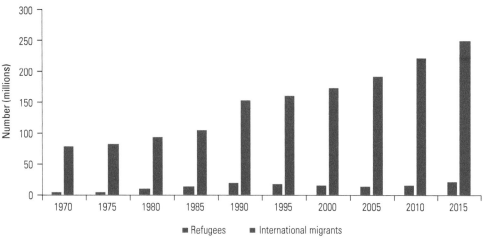

Source: Ratha et al. 2016.

BOX 1.1 Lessons from economic migration

The benefits of economic migration may not materialize after forced displacement, at least in the short term. Economic migrants choose to move to areas where their skills can be used more productively than at home. This typically yields significant benefits for migrants, host communities, and origin countries.[a] By contrast, those who are forcibly displaced seek safety first, and may end up in areas with no accessible job opportunity.[b] If they are not allowed to work or if they are unable to move on, which is the case for many refugees, their living standards and their potential contribution to society are hurt, leaving them little option but continued dependency on humanitarian aid.[c]

The passage of time may partly blur the distinction between forcibly displaced persons and economic migrants. The main asset of the forcibly displaced is often their capacity to work, and like economic migrants they need to find ways to generate income. Over time, the economic impact of forcibly displaced persons who are either allowed to work or to move to find work may come to partly resemble that of economic migrants.

Economic theory suggests that the benefits of migration depend heavily on the productivity differentials between origin and host countries. Usually, the larger the difference, the higher the benefits, for both the host country and the migrants: in a higher-productivity environment, lower-skilled economic migrants will better complement local workers, and earn far more.[d] This is why migration from low- to high-income countries has an overall positive impact in destination countries, in terms of economic growth, local wages and employment, and public finance, and a positive impact on migrants' real incomes (and on their ability to send remittances).[e]

By contrast, migration between low-income countries (and low-productivity environments) generates far smaller gains because there is less complementarity of skills with local workers.[f] Where the inflow of migrants is small relative to the size of the population and where the investment climate is favorable, a developing country might still derive benefits in terms of increased output and investment, even if there are short-term difficulties. But where the inflow is very large and the investment climate is poor, the outcome is likely to be less positive.[g] Movements of refugees from such countries to high-income environments may have a positive effect for all.

a. Papademetriou, Sumption, and Somerville 2009; Ratha et al. 2016.
b. Dadush and Niebuhr 2016.
c. Dadush and Niebuhr 2016.
d. Dadush and Niebuhr 2016.
e. World Bank 2006.
f. Maystadt and Verwimp 2009.
g. Dadush and Niebuhr 2016.

BOX 1.2 People move for different reasons

Economic migration is integral to economic development and poverty reduction. As industrial and services sectors emerge and grow, workers move to places where they can find work, which is an ongoing trend in low- and middle-income countries. The vast majority of economic migration is taking place within national borders, although some people choose to work and live in foreign countries. The forcibly displaced have a different legal status and distinct protection needs. And unlike economic migrants, they often end up in places where they have no opportunity to use their skills.[a]

Displacement induced by natural disaster differs from that caused by violence and conflict, even if its impact is catastrophic. For example, the political dimension of the crisis and its resolution is often less pronounced, and the social fabric is not affected in the same way. Protection issues are also different and may be less critical. These factors may allow for a somewhat simpler recovery process after a natural disaster, especially when most of those displaced by disaster seek refuge in their own country, often quite near to their former homes.

Population movements prompted by climate change include a mix of disaster displacement and economic migration. With extreme and sudden climate events, people may have to leave because of natural disasters. With slow-onset changes, people may need to move as their incomes shrink (as, for example, through lower agricultural yields) in a process that may not be substantively different from economic migration (as when people are affected by a decline in commodity prices or lose their jobs due to mechanization).[b] change is likely to increase the number of people who are facing such dire choices, and hence the scale of such movements (including "desperate" economic migration).

a. Some economic migrants, however, are also in dire need of enhanced protection. This includes people who are moving because of economic considerations, but whose despair and lack of alternative options are evident in the high risks they are taking. Such people are currently not effectively supported by the international legal architecture. Their experience and their needs are distinct from those of refugees and IDPs, but they are yet to be effectively addressed. See Betts (2010).
b. The ongoing migration crisis across the Mediterranean Sea has shed some light on an additional group—that of "survival migrants,"
c. who are moving to seek better opportunities but are doing so under desperate conditions (as demonstrated by the risks they are willing to take). The international legal framework for dealing with this group is both insufficient and ineffective.

under different circumstances (box 1.2) has consequences for their ability to engage in economic activity, escape poverty, build independent futures, and contribute to the communities they live in. It also implies that they have distinct needs for support, including legal protection and development assistance.

Most observers expect population movements to intensify over the coming decades, driven by continued demographic growth in countries of origin, environmental pressures, large and growing inequalities across regions and countries, and new communications technologies.[8]

A crisis in the developing world

Forced displacement is predominantly a developing world issue (figure 1.3).[9] The large majority of people displaced by conflict do not have the resources or opportunities to flee beyond neighboring areas. They have to remain internally displaced or cross borders in the region. At the end of 2015, developing countries hosted 99 percent of all IDPs

and 89 percent of all refugees (including Palestinian refugees). Of these, almost 58 percent of IDPs and 34 percent of refugees (including Palestinian refugees) were then in fragile states. Contrary to some common perceptions, the number of refugees in European Union (EU) countries, including the large flows of asylum-seekers in 2015, is not only small in relative terms, but also below the peak of the early 1990s (figure 1.4).

Considerable regional variations

Global trends mask considerable variations across developing regions, in aggregate numbers and relative shares of refugees and IDPs (figure 1.5).[10] By end-2015, Africa and the Middle East accounted for almost 60 percent of all forcibly displaced persons.

In Sub-Saharan Africa, there have been several times more IDPs than refugees every year since 2001. For most of the period, the number of refugees was relatively stable between 2 million and 3 million before a sharp increase since 2011 to over 4 million.

FIGURE 1.3 Refugees and IDPs are mainly in low- and middle-income countries

a. Refugees

b. IDPs

● High Income ● Middle Income ● Low Income

● High Income ● Middle Income ● Low Income

Sources: UNHCR 2016b and IDMC 2016.
Notes: Calculated based on World Bank country income classifications and UNHCR end-2015 data on refugees and people in refugee-like situations. And calculated based on World Bank country income classifications and IDMC end-2015 data on internally displaced persons (IDPs).

The number of IDPs, in contrast, fluctuated widely, between 6 million and 12 million people, reflecting in particular the ebbs and flows of conflicts in the Central African Republic, eastern Democratic Republic of Congo, Somalia, South Sudan, Sudan, and more recently, northern Nigeria.

In the Middle East and North Africa (excluding Turkey), the number of Palestinian refugees has continued to grow. Their living conditions have also deteriorated in some host countries, especially Syria. The number of other refugees has fluctuated between 2 million and 4 million, reflecting successive conflicts, first in Iraq and later in Syria. In parallel, the number of IDPs has surged from about 1 million in 2001 to over 13 million in 2015. The acceleration has been particularly rapid since 2011, in large part due to the war in Syria, but also to continued insecurity in Iraq and to the conflicts in Libya and the Republic of Yemen.

In South Asia, since 2001, the number of refugees has varied between 1.5 million and 2.5 million, largely reflecting the evolution of

FIGURE 1.4 The European Union now has fewer refugees than in the early 1990s

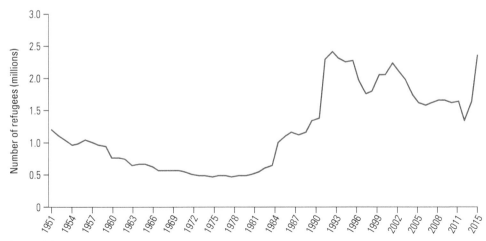

Sources: UNHCR 2016b, 2016c.
Note: Includes refugee-like situations and asylum-seekers in the EU 28.

FIGURE 1.5 Refugees and IDPs in the world's developing regions

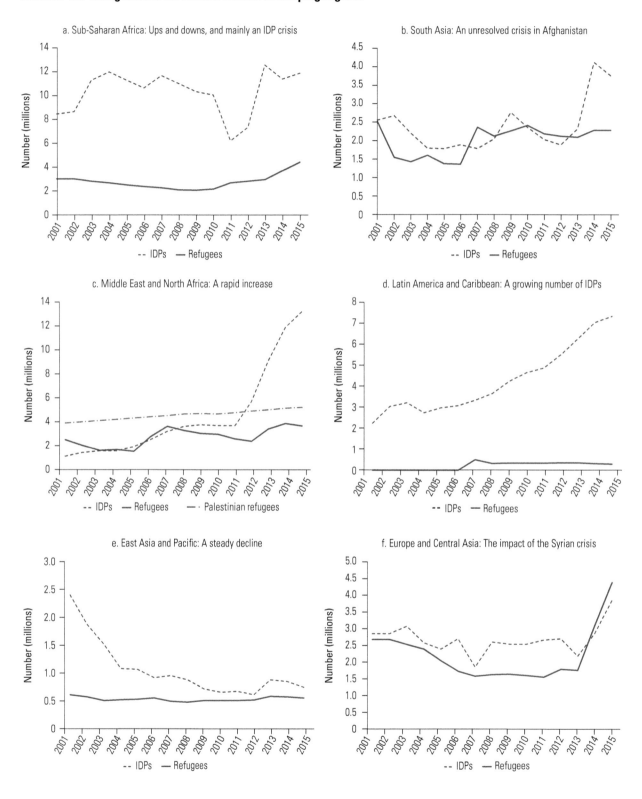

a. Sub-Saharan Africa: Ups and downs, and mainly an IDP crisis

b. South Asia: An unresolved crisis in Afghanistan

c. Middle East and North Africa: A rapid increase

d. Latin America and Caribbean: A growing number of IDPs

e. East Asia and Pacific: A steady decline

f. Europe and Central Asia: The impact of the Syrian crisis

Sources: UNHCR 2016b, 2016c, and UNRWA 2016.
Note: Based on UNHCR and UNRWA data and World Bank definition of regions. IDP = internally displaced person.

the conflict in Afghanistan. The number of IDPs, which had fluctuated between 1.5 million and 3 million from 2001 to 2012, almost doubled in 2013 and 2014 before decreasing in 2015 to a level still well above the average for the past 15 years. The spike was mainly caused by new movements from northwest Pakistan.

In East Asia and the Pacific, the number of refugees has remained stable at around 500,000 people since 2001. The number of IDPs has decreased sharply from about 2.5 million to less than 1 million, as some of the forced displacement situations were resolved in countries such as Indonesia and the Philippines (though Myanmar remains a notable exception).

In Latin America and the Caribbean, the number of refugees remains below 400,000. But the number of IDPs has nearly quadrupled since 2001, reflecting a continuing increase in Colombia, and additional movements in Central America as a result of criminal violence.

In Europe and Central Asia (including EU member countries), the number of refugees fluctuated between 1.5 million and 3 million until 2013, but it climbed sharply with the arrival of Syrian refugees in Turkey. IDP

numbers have fluctuated between around 2 million and, more recently, 4 million. They reflect the legacy of past conflicts, including those in the Caucasus, Cyprus, eastern Turkey, former Yugoslavia, and a more recent influx in Ukraine.

Ten conflicts at the root of the crisis

The story of global displacement can be traced to just a few conflicts. The same ten have accounted for the majority of the forcibly displaced under the United Nations High Commissioner for Refugees' (UNHCR's) mandate, both refugees and IDPs, every year since 1991 (figure 1.6).[11] In South Asia and the Middle East, these include prolonged conflicts in Afghanistan and Iraq and the more recent Syrian crisis; in Africa, persistent conflict and instability in Burundi, the Democratic Republic of Congo, Somalia, and Sudan; in Latin America, four decades of internal armed conflict in Colombia; and in Europe and Central Asia, wars in the Caucasus and the former Yugoslavia (figure 1.7). Protracted forced displacement situations are but a symptom of protracted conflicts.

FIGURE 1.6 The same 10 conflicts have caused the majority of forced displacement every year since 1991

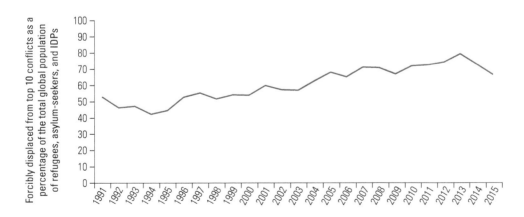

Sources: UNHCR 2016b, 2016c.
Note: The top conflicts are in the following countries: Afghanistan, Azerbaijan, Burundi, Colombia, Democratic Republic of Congo, Iraq, Somalia, Sudan, and former Yugoslavia (Bosnia and Herzegovina, Croatia, Kosovo, the former Yugoslav Republic of Macedonia, Montenegro, Serbia, and Slovenia). The total includes internally displaced persons (IDPs) protected or assisted by UNHCR, asylum-seekers, and refugees; and excludes IDPs not protected or assisted by UNHCR and Palestinian refugees under UNRWA's mandate.

FIGURE 1.7 Top 15 countries and territories of origin for forced displacement

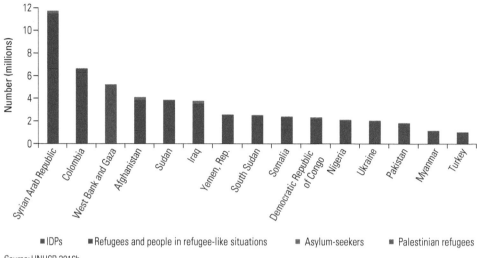

Source: UNHCR 2016b.

The persistent refugee crisis[12]

As of end-2015, the three largest countries of origin for refugees—Syria (4.8 million), Afghanistan (2.7 million), and Somalia (1.1 million)—accounted for half of all refugees under UNHCR mandate. Other large countries of origin included South Sudan, Sudan, the Democratic Republic of Congo, the Central African Republic, Myanmar, Eritrea, and Colombia (map 1.1). These countries have consistently accounted for more than 60 percent of the total since 2006. In total, at the end of 2015, 32 countries were the source of large numbers of refugees (over 25,000)—about one country out of six worldwide. The Middle East was the origin of 34 percent of refugees, Sub-Saharan Africa 33 percent, and South Asia 19 percent (excluding Palestinian refugees).

In most countries of origin, refugees account for less than 5 percent of the population, but in six, they account for more: Syria, 26 percent; Somalia, 10 percent; the

MAP 1.1 Main refugee origin countries

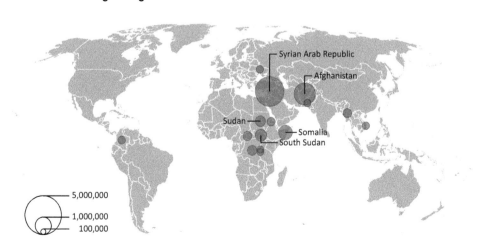

Source: UNHCR 2016b.
Note: Includes refugee-like situations.

MAP 1.2 **Main refugee host countries**

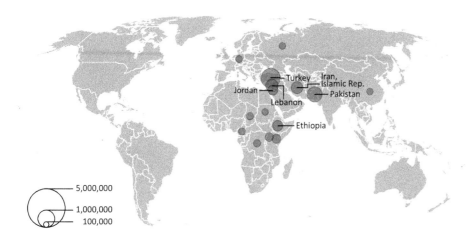

Source: UNHCR 2016b.
Note: Includes refugee-like situations.

Central African Republic, 10 percent; Afghanistan, 8 percent; Eritrea, 8 percent; and South Sudan, 6 percent.

An uneven sharing of hosting responsibilities

Refugee-hosting countries are typically the neighbors of countries of origin. Although almost all countries host some refugees, responsibilities are unevenly shared (map 1.2). As of end-2015, three of Syria's neighbors (Turkey, Lebanon, and Jordan) hosted 27 percent of all refugees worldwide; two of Afghanistan's neighbors (Pakistan and the Islamic Republic of Iran) 16 percent; and two of Somalia's and South Sudan's neighbors (Ethiopia and Kenya) 7 percent. In addition, some countries are accommodating large numbers of asylum-seekers for whom the determination of refugee status is ongoing. This includes South Africa (1.1 million), Germany (421,000), the United States (286,000), Turkey (212,000), and Sweden (157,000).

The stability in the list of countries of origin almost automatically translates into a similar degree of stability among key host countries. Since 1991, about 15 countries, overwhelmingly in the developing world, have consistently hosted the bulk of refugees (figure 1.8).[13]

In most host countries, refugees account for less than 1 percent of the population, which is relatively modest (box 1.3). In a few (namely Turkey, Chad, Djibouti, and South Sudan), refugees account for 2 to 3.5 percent of the population. Only in Lebanon and Jordan, which besides accommodating large numbers of Palestinian refugees have also received successive waves of Iraqi and Syrian refugees does the ratio exceed 4 percent (figure 1.9).

An accelerating IDP crisis

Most IDPs live in relatively few countries (map 1.3). In 2015, the ten largest IDP countries (Syria, Colombia, Iraq, Sudan, the Republic of Yemen, Nigeria, South Sudan, Ukraine, the Democratic Republic of Congo, and Pakistan) accounted for about three-quarters of the global total. Moreover, these same countries have accounted for over half the world's IDPs every year since disaggregated data became available in 2001. Of all countries where IDPs were reported (53 in total), about 32 percent had more than 500,000 IDPs, 28 percent between 100,000 and 500,000 IDPs, 23 percent between 25,000 and 100,000 IDPs, and 17 percent less than 25,000 IDPs.

IDPs account for more than 5 percent of the population in 12 countries: Azerbaijan, the Central African Republic, Colombia,

FIGURE 1.8 The same 15 countries have been hosting a majority of refugees every year since 1991

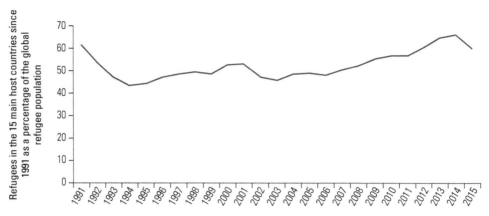

Sources: UNHCR 2016b, 2016c.

BOX 1.3 Comparing shares—refugees and economic migrants

The typical share of economic migrants in a host population is much larger than that of refugees: over 50 percent in most Gulf countries—for example, the United Arab Emirates (88 percent), Qatar (91 percent), Kuwait (72 percent), and Bahrain (54 percent); above 20 percent in countries like Australia and Canada; and typically 10 to 15 percent in the United States and in the main EU destination countries.[a] The EU has about 33 million people born outside the bloc: by contrast, it received about 1.3 million refugees by 2015. Among developing countries, those hosting refugees often also welcome economic migrants, sometimes in far larger numbers. There were an estimated 94 million migrants in the global "South" in 2015, against 13 million refugees.

a. IOM 2014.

FIGURE 1.9 Refugees typically account for a small share of the host country's population

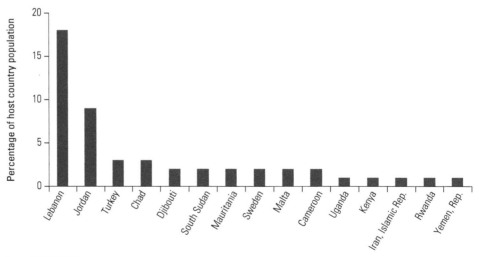

Source: UNHCR 2016b.
Note: Includes only refugees under United Nations High Commissioner for Refugees (UNHCR) mandate; does not include Palestinian refugees under the United Nations Relief and Works Agency for Palestine Refugees in the Near East (UNRWA) mandate. Excludes Nauru.

MAP 1.3 Main IDP countries

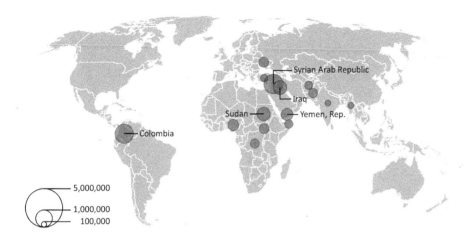

Source: UNHCR 2016b.
Note: This includes only UNHCR-monitored internally displaced persons (IDPs).

Cyprus, the Democratic Republic of Congo, Iraq, Libya, El Salvador, Somalia, South Sudan, Sudan, and Syria.

The stability of IDP countries varies significantly. About 27 percent of IDPs (11 million people) live in countries where development actors cannot engage at scale because of the intensity of conflict, for example Syria, Libya, or the Republic of Yemen. Another 37 percent (15 million) live in environments that are still largely in flux, such as in eastern Democratic Republic of Congo, Iraq, northern Nigeria, Somalia, or South Sudan. The last group (15 million people) are people who have been IDPs for a long time, and may have achieved a degree of socio-economic inclusion in stable hosting areas, for example in countries such as Colombia, India, and Bosnia and Herzegovina.

Some unexpected characteristics of the crisis

Less than four years in exile for half of refugees

The duration of forced displacement varies: the exile of Kosovars in 1999 lasted for several weeks, while it has reached close to 70 years for Palestinians. From a development perspective, the duration of displacement increases the impact on the displaced: everything else equal, the longer the forcibly displaced spend "in limbo," the more difficult their recovery. The average duration of forced displacement also influences public perceptions in host countries.[14]

For people who are currently refugees, the average duration of exile stands at 10.3 years, and the median duration at four years—that is half of them have spent four years or more in exile, half less.[15] Since 1991, the average duration has fluctuated between about eight years in 1991 and a peak of fifteen years in 2006.[16] The number of refugees in protracted situations (five years of exile or more) has been fairly stable since 1991, at 5 to 7 million: it stood at 6.6 million at the end of 2015. For this group, the average duration of exile reached 21.2 years (and the median 19 years), though this is largely influenced by the situation of Afghan refugees.[17]

If all situations are aggregated (figure 1.13), there are about 8.9 million people who have been displaced over the last four years. This includes about 4.8 million Syrians, as well as people fleeing from South Sudan (0.7 million), Afghanistan (0.3 million), Ukraine (0.3 million), the Central African Republic (0.3 million), and Pakistan (0.2 million). Another large cohort, of about 2.2 million people, has spent between

FIGURE 1.10 How many years have refugees spent in exile?

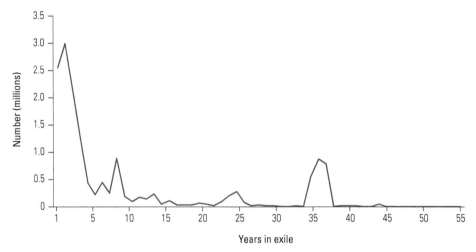

Source: Devictor and Do 2016.

5 and 9 years in exile. It includes refugees from Afghanistan (0.5 million), the bulk of the current Somali refugees (0.4 million), and people fleeing from Colombia (0.3 million) and Myanmar (0.2 million). About 2 million people have been in exile between 10 and 34 years. This includes three relatively large groups, about 0.2 million Sudanese, who left their country around 14 years ago, and 0.1 million Somalis and 0.1 million Eritreans who left their country between 23 and 26 years ago. Finally, about 2.2 million people have been in exile for 35 to 37 years, including 1.9 million Afghans and 0.3 million ethnic Chinese who fled into China during the 1979 war with Vietnam. There are a few situations that are even more protracted, for example up to 55 years for Western Sahara Territory.

Comparable data are not available for IDPs. The definition of a "protracted situation" for IDPs is complex, considering that there is no clear definition of what would constitute a measurable end-point for their ordeal. By 2014, there were 53 countries in which people had been living in internal displacement for more than 10 years.[18] However this includes a large number of people who may have decided to permanently resettle in their host areas. Case studies might well provide more useful insights than these aggregate global figures.

Are IDPs refugees in waiting?

Most refugees have been IDPs prior to crossing a border. This is because fleeing and moving to a foreign country is often a long and complex journey: while on the move, and as long as they have not successfully exited their own country, future refugees are IDPs.

Once people settle, however, there is no evidence of significant shifts from IDP to refugee situations. In fact, in most situations, the number of IDPs and the number of refugees increase or decline in tandem. When internal displacement is protracted (for example in Colombia), this often does not result in large refugee outflows. Refugees and IDPs are fleeing the same risks by going to different destinations: past the initial time of confusion the composition of both groups can be fairly stable.

Most forcibly displaced out of camps, often in urban centers

About 24 percent of refugees live in managed camps or in collective centers. They are largely concentrated in Sub-Saharan Africa and South Asia.[19] Most refugees in other regions live in individual accommodation (figure 1.11). The largest refugee camps are in Africa, especially around Somalia and South Sudan. As of end-2015,

FIGURE 1.11 Most refugees live out of camps, and camps are concentrated in Africa and South Asia

a. Refugees by accommodation type

■ Camp ■ Other

b. Refugees by accommodation type, by region

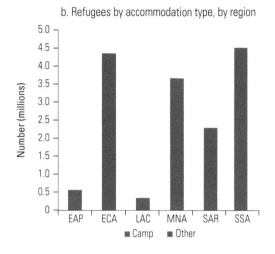

■ Camp ■ Other

Source: UNHCR 2016b.
Note: Based on UNHCR end-2015 data including refugees and refugee-like situations. '"Camp" refers to UNHCR categories of "planned/managed camp," "collective center," and "reception/transit camp." "Other" includes "individual accommodation," "self-settled camp," and "undefined/unknown." Regions are based on World Bank definitions. EAP = East Asia and Pacific; ECA = Europe and Central Asia; LAC = Latin America and the Caribbean; MNA = Middle East and North Africa; SAR = South Asia; SSA = Sub-Saharan Africa.

these included Dadaab, in Kenya (with about 300,000 to 400,000 refugees, mainly from Somalia); Dollo Ado, in Ethiopia (with about 200,000 refugees, largely from Somalia); and Kakuma, in Kenya (with about 160,000 refugees, primarily from Somalia and South Sudan). There were also large camps in Jordan, such as Zaatari (with about 80,000 refugees, mainly from Syria). Smaller (managed) refugee camps account for about 3.4 million people.

IDPs also overwhelmingly live in individual accommodations (figure 1.12). Less than 1 percent of them live in managed camps and another 11 percent in self-settled camps, mainly in Sub-Saharan Africa.[20] In contrast, most IDPs in other regions live in individual accommodation.

Forced displacement is also largely and increasingly an urban phenomenon (figure 1.13). About 50 percent of refugees and IDPs live in cities and towns where they seek security, anonymity, better access to services, and job opportunities. This is especially the case in middle-income environments in the Middle East, Europe, and the Americas. It is less so in Africa and South Asia, but given the projected rapid urbanization of these regions, there too displaced persons are

increasingly likely to seek refuge in cities and towns. When forced displacement leads to urbanization (albeit under duress), it may be difficult to reverse the flows on a large scale. Indeed, urbanization is a long-term trend and is overwhelmingly a one-way process: returns from cities to rural settings are rare, especially in developing countries.

Insufficient data

Enhancing the comprehensiveness, quality, and reliability of available data is a critical part of the development agenda on forced displacement. Data provide the basis on which support programs and policy advice can be developed. They also shape public opinion and underpin the political discourse on forced displacement. Yet, figures that are currently available have significant limitations.

How reliable are available data?

Methods and definitions for collecting and aggregating data vary widely across countries. Some data may provide acceptable insights into the crisis, but in many cases they provide only an incomplete picture and they are often not comparable across

FIGURE 1.12 The vast majority of IDPs live in individual accommodations

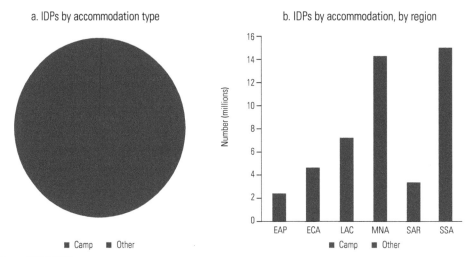

a. IDPs by accommodation type

b. IDPs by accommodation, by region

■ Camp   ■ Other

■ Camp   ■ Other

Source: UNHCR 2016b.
Note: Based on UNHCR end-2015 data including only internally displaced persons (IDPs) protected or assisted by UNHCR. "Camp" refers to UNHCR categories of "planned/managed camp," "collective center," and "reception/transit camp." "Other" includes "individual accommodation," "self-settled camp," and "undefined/unknown." The number of IDPs is derived by the difference between the population of concern to the refugee population. Regions are based on World Bank definitions. EAP = East Asia and Pacific; ECA = Europe and Central Asia; LAC = Latin America and the Caribbean; MNA = Middle East and North Africa; SAR = South Asia; SSA = Sub-Saharan Africa.

different situations. An assessment of the methodology used to derive estimates (table 1.1) suggests that existing figures ought to be taken with a degree of caution, and that data users should be aware of their limitations and of the corresponding error margins. This is especially the case for IDP numbers, which are the least robust—even though this group represents the bulk of the forcibly displaced. At this stage, it is not possible to assess how close some estimates may be to the actual situation on the ground, nor whether they provide an over- or an underevaluation.

To gain a full understanding of a forced displacement situation, aggregate data often

FIGURE 1.13 Forced displacement is more urban in middle-income countries, and more rural in low-income countries

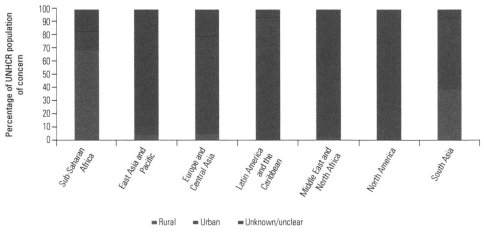

■ Rural   ■ Urban   ■ Unknown/unclear

Source: UNHCR 2016b.
Note: UNHCR = United Nations High Commissioner for Refugees.

TABLE 1.1 Rating of methodologies

Robustness of methodologies used to estimate populations[a]	Refugee situations (%)	IDP situations (%)	Refugees and IDPs (%)
A (highest)	88		22
B	12	2	5
C		46	34
D (lowest)		52	39

Note: IDP = internally displaced person.

a. The robustness of data collection methodology is assessed as follows: A = figures are established based on an actual counting of persons (registration) by a national or international institution; B = figures are established based on an actual counting of persons (registration) by a national or international institution for a portion of the population and on an estimate for the other part, or data originate from different sources including statistical ones and a review process is in place; C = there is no information on parts of the country; D = there is no single institution in charge of monitoring and different undocumented methodologies are used for available data, or there is no information on large parts of the country, or only outdated data are available.

need to be complemented by microlevel studies, for example to determine the factors that may cause people to move, to assess their socioeconomic situation, or to evaluate their economic impact on host communities. This area of study has been largely neglected by economists,[21] and there are only few quantitative studies, which are often limited in scope,[22] and focused on short-term impacts in camps or rural settings (even as forcibly displaced persons are increasingly urbanized).[23] Research is constrained not only by the lack of data, but also by econometric and methodological challenges—sampling, counterfactual scenarios, and so on.[24] Qualitative case studies may provide additional information, but the degree of methodological rigor is highly variable, ranging from anecdotal reports to operational analyses by humanitarian and aid agencies, and from advocacy pieces to anthropological studies.

Refugees: Compilation complications

Collecting accurate statistical data on refugees is complex. At the global level, UNHCR is leading this effort, relying on direct registration or on data provided by host governments.[25] International organizations such as Eurostat for the EU, national institutions, and nongovernmental organizations also compile information, with varying degrees of completeness, quality and timeliness.[26] Where appropriate, UNHCR and its partners can provide resources and technical assistance for data collection.[27]

Statistics on Palestinian refugees are based on registration. Such registration is voluntary, although it is required to access services provided by the United Nations Relief and Works Agency for Palestine Refugees in the Near East (UNRWA). Deregistration in the case of death of a family member is also voluntary, and there may be few incentives to deregister. Palestinian refugees living outside UNRWA's five areas of operation (Jordan, Lebanon, Syria, Gaza, and the West Bank) fall under the responsibility of UNHCR and are included in UNHCR statistics.

Yet, detailed definitions and data collection methodologies vary across countries and agencies, which can lead to substantial variations in aggregate numbers (box 1.4).[28] For example, some countries consider the children of refugees as refugees themselves, while other countries give them a different status. Refugees may not present themselves for registration when they perceive the risks of registration as outweighing its benefits (as for large numbers of Libyans who have fled to Tunisia). Conversely, there may be weak incentives for deregistration (as in the event of death) when it is linked to the provision of services or other entitlements. In mass refugee situations and when populations are highly mobile, maintaining a refugee register can be problematic. Refugee data may also be politically sensitive: data privacy is critical where protection trumps many other considerations, yet it may also enable political manipulation—as, for example, to demonstrate that a situation has been resolved or that it still requires resolution.

IDPs: A blurred picture

Gathering data on IDPs is even more complex than for refugees. Statistics are collected by a number of actors, including governments; international actors such as UNHCR, the International Committee of the Red Cross, the World Food Programme, and the International Organization for Migration (IOM); nongovernmental organizations; and the media.[29] The Office for the Coordination of Humanitarian Affairs of the United Nations Secretariat (OCHA) also compiles and disseminates statistical information gathered by operational agencies at the field level. Aggregate estimates are rarely consistent across sources and disaggregated breakdowns by age and sex are available for only a few countries.[30]

Data published by the Internal Displacement Monitoring Centre (IDMC) are often used as references. These estimates are based on a wide range of secondary sources, including national governments, the United Nations (UN) and other international organizations, national and international nongovernmental organizations, human rights organizations, and the media. IDMC publishes estimates of internal displacement caused by conflict, generalized violence, and human rights violations for over 50 countries.[31]

IDMC acknowledges the challenges tied to such an exercise and the corresponding limitations in terms of data quality, reliability, and comparability (box 1.5).[32] For example, it reported sweeping revisions of 2014 figures due to methodological changes in the way sources collect and analyze data, multiplying by four the estimated number of IDPs in Côte d'Ivoire and dividing the equivalent figure by three in Nigeria.

Host communities: No numbers

There is no global estimate for the number of people living in host communities "affected" by forced displacement (box 1.6). A few anecdotal reports on specific situations aside, systematic collection of data and an agreed definition of what constitutes an "affected community" are lacking. Yet, the number of people living in host communities and affected by forced displacement (positively or negatively) is likely to be large, and the welfare of these communities is critical for the political economy of asylum and integration.

Data on returnees are also in short supply. UNHCR publishes data on refugees who have returned to their host countries, and IDMC collects information on IDP returnees. In practice, the quality of data is more solid for those who have returned with assistance from UNHCR or other international agencies, than for unassisted returns. An additional group of concern is composed of stateless people (box 1.7).

An agenda for better data

A substantial effort is needed to enhance the availability, quality, reliability, and comparability of data on forced displacement. This will require concerted action by all concerned, affected governments, international organizations, bilateral donors, and nongovernmental organizations. While data collection and analysis can be expensive, they often lead to far lower costs or much higher effectiveness in the planning and implementation of relief and development activities. As such it is a critical investment and requires an upfront commitment of resources.

BOX 1.5 The challenges of data collection for IDPs

Statistical definitions. Although IDMC's definitions are based on the UN Guiding Principles, there are variations across sources with regard to definitions and methods. For example, nomadic populations account for relatively large numbers of IDPs in the Horn of Africa and increasingly so in the Sahel: defining what constitutes internal displacement for such groups is difficult.[a] Some countries register children born in displacement as IDPs (as in Azerbaijan, Cyprus, and Georgia), others do not; some countries systematically adjust register numbers for death, others do not (as in Colombia). Comparing or adding data across situations hence becomes difficult.

Lack of a clearly measurable "end-event." Large numbers of IDPs have moved from rural to urban settings. Their displacement is part of an urbanization process (albeit under terrible circumstances) which is unlikely to be reversed. In

countries such as Colombia, IDP status is not attached to an individual but to a family, and is transmitted down the generations (as a claim for potential compensation). In others, deregistration signifies not the achievement of a durable solution but rather the end of state or international support. The absence of a clear and operational approach to defining the "end" of internal displacement may be one of the factors behind the continued rise in global IDP numbers.

Political considerations. The registration of IDPs can be greatly undermined by the unwillingness of a government to acknowledge their situation and enable humanitarian agencies to respond. Some countries are reluctant to acknowledge the existence of IDPs or are inclined to manipulate numbers to demonstrate progress in military operations (or to suggest a deterioration of the situation). Other countries may find it politically expedient to artificially prolong IDP status.

Practical challenges. The fluidity of population movements and security concerns combine to make primary data collection almost impossible in many areas. Those collecting data often focus on IDPs in relatively stable and accessible locations, such as camps, collective centers, and residential areas with high concentrations of IDPs. In the areas most difficult to access, they rely on "local informers" who may not be in a position to provide numbers. It is also often hard to differentiate IDPs from other persons who have moved within a country (often for reasons of work, family, housing, or education) or to adjust for the fact that IDPs may have been displaced several times. In some countries, data collectors use different coefficients to convert households into individuals. And there is a substantial risk of over- or undercounting when aggregating data collected from different sources.

a. This is typically defined as nomads not having access to their traditional routes, but such routes vary.

Strengthen the collection and dissemination of basic data

Basic forced displacement data includes numbers of displaced persons, demographic characteristics (such as age and gender), location, accommodation, and so on. To strengthen their quality, complementary efforts are needed along three directions: first, to develop a single methodology (including a common set of definitions) that can be used by all those involved, so as to allow for comparability; second, to enhance collection capacity on the ground, including by increasingly relying on country systems where it is appropriate; and third, to enhance transparency on the limitations and error margins associated with specific data (box 1.8).

Move toward an "open data" system

Forced displacement data are currently available in aggregate form only. Yet, experience in other areas has shown that the publication of raw data by governments and international organizations often triggers a strong response by the research community (box 1.9). It also enables strong quality control by the users themselves, which in turn provides an impetus to upgrading data systems. It can yield unexpected results, in the form of new findings and analysis to enhance the global understanding of an issue and the design of responses.

There are, of course, important protection concerns over forced displacement data: by definition, refugees and IDPs are fleeing a threat, and the information they provide

BOX 1.6 Estimating the number of affected "hosts"

Being "affected" is a difficult concept, which may vary over time or even within a community. For a rural refugee camp, the impact might be significant (positive or negative) but it is geographically limited to the immediate vicinity, while for refugees dispersed in an urban environment, it may be more diffuse. Short of household-level longitudinal surveys, it is difficult to go beyond calculating the number of people who live in an area where forcibly displaced persons are hosted. Yet no simple methodology exists to make such a calculation or to establish a "threshold" above which a flow is considered large enough to have a socioeconomic impact on host communities.

Is it possible at least to establish some orders of magnitude?[a] A rough calculation suggests that the number of people living in communities hosting refugees can be estimated at four times the number of refugees if a 5 percent threshold is selected (that is, if refugees account for 5 percent or more of the total population) and at ten times the number of refugees if a 1 percent threshold is selected. There are of course huge variations across situations. Yet they suggest that the number of people living in host communities is sizable.

IDPs have additional complexities. The mere definition of "hosts" is problematic, as IDPs are nationals and there is hence no "host country," even though there may be "host communities" in areas receiving large numbers of displaced persons. When a conflict is ongoing (typically in many IDP countries), the entire population may be affected by violence, and the relative impact of IDPs may not be determinant. Further, when people have been settled in an urban environment for a long time, the impact on the original city dwellers may not be much different from that of other rural migrants. The ambiguities and limitations of IDP definitions also complicate the issue. A case-by-case analysis, based on household-level data, would be needed to determine who is affected and to what extent.

a. The following two-step approach was followed. The first step consists in calculating the density of refugees within a particular area. UNHCR is publishing data on the physical location of refugees, at a disaggregated level (equivalent to a county in most countries). By overlaying these estimates with local population census data, it is possible to calculate refugee densities (there are some methodological difficulties in doing this, since some data sets are incomplete or not available at equivalent levels of disaggregation). The second step consists in defining a "threshold density" above which a community is considered affected. Past the threshold, all people living in the area are considered affected; under the threshold nobody is.

BOX 1.7 Another group of concern: Stateless people

Statelessness—not being considered nationals by any state—affects at least ten milli.on people in the world according to UNHCR. Given that the World Bank estimates that some 1.5 billion people have no documents to prove their identity, the number of people at risk of statelessness may be far higher.[a] The largest stateless populations are in Asia, Africa, and the Middle East, but there is no continent or state that does not have some stateless people.[b] The major causes of statelessness are discrimination in law or practice (typically based on ethnicity, race, gender, religion, or linguistic minority status); state succession; and conflicts between nationality laws.

Stateless persons often live in precarious and vulnerable situations in their countries of habitual residence. Many are denied the right to education, health care, and formal employment; many face restrictions to their freedom of movement and may be at risk of arbitrary and prolonged detention. Such deprivations may be so severe as to force them to flee their homeland or place of residence.

a. See World Bank ID4D web page (http://blogs.worldbank.org/category/tags/id4d).
b. See UNHCR's Statistical Yearbook and Global Trends reports for country reporting on stateless persons (http://www.unhcr.org/figures-at-a-glance.html).

The presentation by Norway and UNHCR of a "Report on Statistics on Refugees and IDPs" at the 46th session of the UN Statistical Commission in March 2015 initiated an inter-governmental process to harmonize methodologies and prepare for a greater reliance on national statistical systems.[a] Under this process, national statistical offices will work together and develop a set of recommendations for use by countries and international organizations to improve data collection methods, reporting, data disaggregation, and overall quality. Agencies such as UNHCR and IDMC can play a complementary role in ensuring quality, providing technical assistance, and aggregating data for global analyses.

a. ECOSOC 2015.

under the seal of confidentiality needs to be safeguarded. Various methods have been used to anonymize raw data across a broad range of other areas, like medical records, and are commonly used by governments across the world.

Carry out country-level analyses of the challenges faced by the forcibly displaced and their hosts

A detailed understanding of the challenges and opportunities is needed to design effective development interventions that can yield sustainable results over the medium term. For example, detailed information is needed on the socioeconomic characteristics of refugees and IDPs, their skills, the ordeals they have gone through, their locations, the jobs and services that are available in the areas where they are accommodated, and so on. For example, such work has been piloted in Jordan and Lebanon to assess the poverty and vulnerability of Syrian refugees, and this should be extended to other settings. Strengthening the capacity of national research centers to take part in or to lead such work will be critical for sustainability.

Develop a shared platform to build evidence on responses to the crisis

Evidence that is critical to designing sound development interventions, such as information on what may work, and in which context, is lacking. Collating lessons of experience and carrying out rigorous impact evaluations is essential to inform the design of future operations. Given scarce resources and multiple actors involved, it may be important to develop a platform where information can be exchanged, where governments and donors can learn from each other, and where further investigations can be planned in a coordinated manner. The government of the United Kingdom, UNHCR, and the World Bank Group are in the process of developing such a platform, which could be joined and used by others.

In 2004, a British heart surgeon Sir Bruce Keogh, persuaded his colleagues to publish comparable data on their individual clinical outcomes. This prompted surgeons to reflect on their practices. As a result, seven years later, dramatic improvements in survival rates were reported: in some procedures more than a third of patients survived when they might previously have died.[a]

This effort was symptomatic of a broader approach to unleash the potential of data sharing. Some governments and international institutions have now published data on a broad range of issues, which has proven instrumental in reinforcing users' feedback and stimulating research. For example, the World Bank Group launched its Open Data Initiative in 2010. Under this initiative, visitors to the open data website can easily find, download, manipulate, use, and reuse the data compiled by the World Bank, without restriction. This has allowed individuals, groups, and organizations to create applications, programs, visualizations, and other tools that innovate and help monitor and measure progress of various development initiatives and projects.

a. Kelsey 2011.

Annex 1A

Legal definitions

The 1951 Convention Relating to the Status of Refugees (1951 Convention), later amended by the 1967 Protocol,[33] defines refugees in terms of their vulnerability due to the denial or loss of state protection.[34] A refugee is "a person who is outside his or her country of nationality or habitual residence; has a well-founded fear of being persecuted because of his or her race, religion, nationality, membership of a particular social group, or political opinion; and is unable or unwilling to avail him or herself of the protection of that country, or to return there, for fear of persecution."[35] Refugee status is not accorded to those who flee intolerable economic conditions, poverty, famine or environmental catastrophes (unless these are consequences of or related to persecution).

In Africa, the 1969 Convention Governing the Specific Aspects of Refugee Problems in Africa (Organization of African Unity [OAU] Convention) adds to the 1951 Convention definition by recognizing as refugees people who are forced to flee due to "external aggression, occupation, foreign domination or events seriously disturbing public order in either part or the whole of his country of origin or nationality." In Latin America, the 1984 Cartagena Declaration on Refugees (Cartagena Declaration), which was heavily influenced by the OAU Convention, similarly expands the definition of refugees to include "persons who have fled their country because their lives, safety or freedom have been threatened by generalized violence, foreign aggression, internal conflicts, massive violations of human rights or other circumstances which have seriously disturbed public order."

The legal definition of Palestinian refugees is unique and distinct from the 1951 Convention.[36] These refugees fall within the mandate of the United Nations Relief and Works Agency for Palestine Refugees in the Near East (UNRWA).[37] UNRWA defines Palestinian refugees as persons, and their patrilineal descendants, whose normal place of residence was the British Mandate for Palestine during the period 1 June 1946 to 15 May 1948, and who lost their homes and livelihoods as a result of the 1948 conflict. People displaced by the 1967 and 1982 Arab-Israeli conflicts are also entitled to receive UNRWA services. The status of Palestinian refugees is linked to their political aspirations for recognition of their "right of return," and it is maintained even in the event of naturalization (such as acquisition of Jordanian citizenship) or resettlement in a third country (as in Europe). Palestinian refugees receiving protection or assistance from UNRWA are excluded from the 1951 Convention and its 1967 Protocol, unless such protection or assistance has ceased.[38]

Asylum-seekers are individuals who have sought international protection but whose claims for protection have not yet been determined. The right to seek and enjoy asylum is implemented in part by the 1951 Convention and its 1967 Protocol. Central to the right to asylum is the principle of non-refoulement, which prohibits states from expelling or returning a refugee to a territory where she or he would be at risk of threats to life or freedom. States are required to make independent inquiries as to the need for international protection of persons seeking asylum and allow such persons access to fair and efficient procedures for determining their international protection needs and recognize their refugee status. While their claims for protection are being determined, asylum-seekers may not be returned to their country of origin. The status of "refugee" is recognized by states or, in some instances, by UNHCR under its mandate, based on a determination of whether or not a person fulfills the criteria contained in the 1951 Convention or other applicable legal instruments.[39] Refugee determination processes vary according to the national law and policy in which they are embedded. Most national procedures require those seeking asylum to make a claim, which is examined by competent authorities to lead to a decision. Refugee status can also be recognized on a prima facie basis. In this situation, groups of persons are acknowledged as refugees on a group basis because of the "readily apparent and objective reasons for flight and circumstances in the country of origin."[40] Although a prima facie approach may be applied within individual refugee status determination procedures, it is more often used in group situations, for example where individual status determination is impractical, impossible or unnecessary in large-scale situations.[41]

There is no international legal framework for protection, assistance, or solutions for internally displaced persons (IDPs): these people remain a state responsibility. Many national laws and regulations on internal displacement do not include a definition of internal displacement, but those that do often reflect the description of IDPs contained in the Guiding Principles on internal displacement, established by the United Nations in 2004.[42] Under these principles, IDPs are "persons or groups of persons who have been forced or obliged to flee or to leave their homes or places of habitual residence, in particular as a result of or in order to avoid the effects of armed conflict, situations of generalized violence, violations of human rights or natural or human-made disasters, and who have not crossed an internationally recognized State border."[43] The African Union Convention for the Protection and Assistance of Internally Displaced Persons in Africa, (the Kampala Convention) which came into force in 2012, uses the same definition.[44] The United Nations (UN) Guiding Principles, the Kampala Convention and the Inter-Agency Standing Committee (IASC) Framework on Durable Solutions for IDPs identify three ways in which internal displacement can end: voluntary and sustainable reintegration at the place of origin (return); sustainable local integration in areas where IDPs take refuge (local integration); and voluntary and sustainable integration in another part of the country (settlement elsewhere in the country).[45]

Finally, host communities are not defined in legal conventions and international and regional agreements on forced displacement, and the people whose welfare is impacted by the presence of displaced populations are typically not included in statistics of people affected by forced displacement.

Annex 1B

TABLE 1B.1 Forced displacement situations as of end-2015

a. All situations with more than 25,000 refugees, including people in refugee-like situations

Country of asylum	Country of origin	Refugees
Turkey	Syrian Arab Republic	2,503,549
Pakistan	Afghanistan	1,560,592
Lebanon	Syrian Arab Republic	1,062,690
Iran, Islamic Rep.	Afghanistan	951,142
Jordan	Syrian Arab Republic	628,223
Kenya	Somalia	417,920
Russian Federation	Ukraine	311,407
China	Vietnam	300,896
Chad	Sudan	299,750
Ethiopia	South Sudan	281,508
Cameroon	Central African Republic	267,463
Afghanistan	Pakistan	257,523
Ethiopia	Somalia	256,669
Yemen, Rep.	Somalia	253,215
Congo, Dem. Rep.	Rwanda	245,052
Iraq	Syrian Arab Republic	244,642
South Sudan	Sudan	241,002
Bangladesh	Myanmar	231,948
Uganda	Congo, Dem. Rep.	201,782
Uganda	South Sudan	199,359
Sudan	South Sudan	194,404
Venezuela, R.B.	Colombia	173,673
Tanzania	Burundi	155,755
Ethiopia	Eritrea	155,231
Ecuador	Colombia	120,685
Egypt, Arab Rep.	Syrian Arab Republic	117,635
Germany	Syrian Arab Republic	115,604
India	China	110,098
Congo, Dem. Rep.	Central African Republic	107,929
Thailand	Myanmar	106,349
Sudan	Eritrea	98,676
Kenya	South Sudan	95,671

Country of asylum	Country of origin	Refugees
Algeria	Western Sahara Territory	90,000
Malaysia	Myanmar	88,637
United States	China	74,020
Rwanda	Congo, Dem. Rep.	73,864
Cameroon	Nigeria	71,840
Rwanda	Burundi	70,848
Egypt, Arab Rep.	Palestinian	70,021
France	Various	68,443
Niger	Nigeria	68,321
India	Sri Lanka	64,208
Chad	Central African Republic	63,397
Niger	Mali	56,012
Tanzania	Congo, Dem. Rep.	55,803
Burundi	Congo, Dem. Rep.	53,029
Sweden	Syrian Arab Republic	52,707
Germany	Iraq	51,396
Mauritania	Mali	50,233
South Africa	Somalia	41,458
Ethiopia	Sudan	37,785
Liberia	Côte d'Ivoire	36,041
Burkina Faso	Mali	33,574
Jordan	Iraq	33,256
South Africa	Congo, Dem. Rep.	32,582
Israel	Eritrea	31,708
Germany	Afghanistan	30,026
Iran, Islamic Rep.	Iraq	28,268
Uganda	Somalia	27,720
Uganda	Burundi	26,256
Mauritania	Western Sahara Territory	26,007
Serbia and Kosovo	Croatia	25,962

(Table continues next page)

TABLE 1B.1 **Forced displacement situations as of end-2015** *(continued)*

b. All situations with more than 25,000 asylum-seekers

Country of asylum	Asylum-seekers	Country of asylum	Asylum-seekers
South Africa	1,096,063	Egypt, Arab Rep.	38,171
Germany	420,625	Hungary	36,693
United States	286,168	Belgium	36,009
Turkey	212,408	Uganda	35,779
Sweden	157,046	Switzerland	32,701
Austria	80,075	Angola	30,143
France	63,057	Netherlands	28,051
Malaysia	60,415	Libya	27,479
Italy	60,156	Greece	26,141
United Kingdom	45,870	Norway	25,316

c. All situations with more than 25,000 IDPs

Country / territory	2015	Country / territory	2015
Syrian Arab Republic	6,600,000	El Salvador	289,000
Colombia	6,270,000	Mexico	287,000
Iraq	3,290,000	Cyprus	272,000
Sudan	3,182,000	Guatemala	251,000
Yemen, Rep.	2,509,000	Georgia	239,000
Nigeria	2,096,000	Palestine	221,000
South Sudan	1,697,000	Honduras	174,000
Ukraine	1,679,000	Niger	153,000
Congo, Dem. Rep.	1,500,000	Cameroon	124,000
Pakistan	1,459,000	Chad	107,000
Somalia	1,223,000	Burundi	99,000
Afghanistan	1,174,000	Bosnia and Herzegovina	98,000
Turkey	954,000	Abyei Area	82,000
Myanmar	644,000	Egypt, Arab Rep.	78,000
India	612,000	Philippines	62,000
Azerbaijan	564,000	Peru	60,000
Libya	500,000	Mali	50,000
Central African Republic	452,000	Nepal	50,000
Ethiopia	450,000	Sri Lanka	44,000
Bangladesh	426,000	Thailand	35,000
Kenya	309,000	Uganda	30,000
Côte d'Ivoire	303,000	Russian Federation	27,000

Sources: Refugee and asylum-seeker data from UNHCR 2016b; internally displaced person (IDP) data from IDMC 2015.

Notes

1. See annex 1A for definition.
2. UNHCR 2015i.
3. The legal definition of Palestinian refugees is specific to this situation, and differs in important ways from the definition of refugees under the 1951 Convention. In particular, Palestinians may still be considered refugees even if they acquire a new citizenship. The definition used by the United Nations Relief and Works Agency for Palestine Refugees in the Near East (UNRWA) is "persons whose normal place of residence was Palestine during the period 1 June 1946 to 15 May 1948, and who lost both home and means of livelihood as a result of the 1948 conflict." https://www.unrwa.org/palestine-refugees.
4. UNHCR 2016b; UNRWA 2016; IDMC 2016.
5. UNHCR 2000.
6. IOM 2014.
7. Ratha et al. 2016.
8. World Bank 2016c.
9. This section draws largely on a forthcoming report from the World Bank, "Stocktaking of Global Forced Displacement Data."
10. Based on UNHCR and UNRWA data and World Bank definition of regions. "Sub-Saharan Africa" includes Angola, Benin, Botswana, Burkina Faso, Burundi, Cameroon, the Central African Republic, Chad, Comoros, the Democratic Republic of Congo, the Republic of Congo, Côte d'Ivoire, Eritrea, Ethiopia, Gabon, The Gambia, Ghana, Guinea, Guinea-Bissau, Kenya, Lesotho, Liberia, Madagascar, Malawi, Mali, Mauritania, Mauritius, Mozambique, Namibia, Niger, Nigeria, Rwanda, Senegal, Seychelles, Sierra Leone, Somalia, South Africa, South Sudan, Sudan, Swaziland, Tanzania, Togo, Uganda, Zambia, Zimbabwe. "South Asia" includes Afghanistan, Bangladesh, Bhutan, India, Maldives, Nepal, Pakistan, and Sri Lanka. "Middle East and North Africa" includes Algeria, Bahrain, Djibouti, the Arab Republic of Egypt, the Islamic Republic of Iran, Iraq, Israel, Jordan, Kuwait, Leba-non, Libya, Malta, Morocco, Oman, Qatar, Saudi Arabia, the Syrian Arab Republic, Tunisia, the United Arab Emirates, West Bank and Gaza, the Republic of Yemen. "Latin America and Caribbean" includes Antigua and Barbuda, Argentina, Aruba, The Bahamas, Barbados, Belize, Bolivia, Brazil, British Virgin Islands, Chile, Colombia, Costa Rica, Cuba, Curaçao, Dominica, the Dominican Republic, Ecuador, El Salvador, Grenada, Guatemala, Guyana, Haiti, Honduras, Jamaica, Mexico, Nicaragua, Panama, Paraguay, Peru, Puerto Rico, Sint Maarten, St. Kitts and Nevis, St. Lucia, St. Vincent and the Grenadines, Suriname, Trinidad and Tobago, Turks and Caicos Islands, Uruguay, República Bolivariana de Venezuela, Virgin Islands (U.S.). "East Asia and Pacific" includes American Samoa; Australia; Brunei Darussalam; Cambodia; China; Fiji; French Polynesia; Guam; Hong Kong SAR, China; Indonesia; Japan; Kiribati; the Democratic People's Republic of Korea; the Republic of Korea; the Lao People's Democratic Republic; Macao SAR, China; Malaysia; the Marshall Islands; the Federated States of Micronesia; Mongolia; Myanmar; Nauru; New Caledonia; New Zealand; Northern Mariana Islands; Palau; Papua New Guinea; the Philippines; Samoa; Singapore; the Solomon Islands; Taiwan, China; Thailand; Timor-Leste; Tonga; Tuvalu; Vanuatu; Vietnam. "Europe and Central Asia" and EU member countries include Albania, Andorra, Armenia, Austria, Azerbaijan, Belarus, Belgium, Bosnia and Herzegovina, Bulgaria, Channel Islands, Croatia, Cyprus, Czech Republic, Denmark, Estonia, Faeroe Islands, Finland, France, Georgia, Germany, Gibraltar, Greece, Greenland, Hungary, Iceland, Ireland, Isle of Man, Italy, Kazakhstan, Kosovo, the Kyrgyz Republic, Latvia, Liechtenstein, Lithuania, Luxembourg, the former Yugoslav Republic of Macedonia, Moldovia, Monaco, Montenegro, the Netherlands, Norway, Poland, Portugal, Romania, the Russian Federation, San Marino, Serbia, the Slovak Republic, Slovenia, Spain, Sweden, Switzerland, Tajikistan, Ukraine, the United Kingdom, Uzbekistan.

11. Major displacement crises are identified based on their cumulative displacement figure over the period 1991–2015.
12. Unless specified otherwise, all numbers quoted in the text include only refugees under UNHCR mandate, that is, not Palestinian refugees.
13. These are: Bangladesh, Chad, China, Ethiopia, Germany, the Islamic Republic of Iran, Iraq, Jordan, Kenya, Lebanon, Pakistan, Sudan, Turkey, Uganda, and the Republic of Yemen.
14. Calculations are not based on individual data, which would provide a more accurate estimate of how long on average a person is in displacement, but on 'situations' (that is, refugee populations in host countries grouped by country of origin—for example, Ethiopia currently hosts refugees from Eritrea, Somalia, South Sudan and Sudan and so has four refugee situations). Calculations do not take into account fluctuations in refugee numbers if the size of the situation remains over 25,000 people. Additional methodological issues further distort estimates of average duration, for example South Sudanese displacement is not considered to be protracted because disaggregated data on South Sudan, is only available from the country's independence in 2011. The choice of "five years" and 25,000 persons are arbitrary and significantly influence results: a 2015 study (Crawford et al. 2015) using three years as a threshold found the number of people in protracted situations almost double.
15. Devictor and Do 2016.
16. This average is very sensitive to specific situations. For example, if Afghan refugees and a smaller contingent of ethnic Chinese who fled Vietnam to China during the 1979 war are excluded from the calculation, the average duration of exile for current refugees drops to 5.3 years. If Syrian refugees are excluded, it goes up to 14.5 years. Yet, if both Afghanistan and Syria (the large numbers on both ends of the spectrum) are taken out, the average goes back to about 11.3 years, and the median to about 4 years. See Devictor and Do (2016).
17. This is the case if both Afghan refugees and a smaller contingent of ethnic Chinese who fled Vietnam to China during the 1979 war are excluded.
18. IDMC 2015.
19. Based on World Bank Group definitions of regions, note 10.
20. Based on World Bank Group definitions of regions, note 10.
21. Ruiz and Vargas-Silva 2013.
22. Ruiz and Vargas-Silva 2013.
23. Ruiz and Vargas-Silva 2013; Kriebaum 2016.
24. Ruiz and Vargas-Silva 2013; Zetter and Vargas-Silva 2011.
25. The Office of the High Commissioner maintains a statistical online database with data on country of residence and origin, including demographics and locations of these populations. Further, UNHCR has annual data on refugee flows and stocks dating back to 1951, the year the Office of the High Commissioner was created, and is currently working on making these historical data available online. The UN data portal (http://data.un.org), maintained by the Statistics Division of the Department of Economic and Social Affairs of the United Nations contains refugee data starting from 1975. UNHCR regularly publishes statistical reports, particularly Global Trends, Mid-year trends, Asylum trends, and the Statistical Yearbook.
26. In the absence of host government figures, UNHCR estimates refugee population in many industrialized countries based on ten years of individual asylum-seeker recognition.
27. In 2015, data on refugees were provided for 184 countries. Data were collected by UNHCR, by governments, or by other organizations. By the end of 2014, individual refugee registration was the source of about 77 percent of the data on refugees under the UNHCR mandate; estimation accounted for 13 percent of data; combined estimation and registration for 5 percent; and other sources for 5 percent. UNHCR also provides statistics on asylum-seekers "persons whose application for asylum or refugee status is pending at any stage in the asylum procedure," although these reflect differences across countries in the administrative rules governing the asylum process, in particular the criteria for individuals to access

the asylum procedure. While refugee status is often determined on an individual basis, in the case of mass influxes of people fleeing war, group determination of refugee status may be made on a prima facie basis to enable the urgent provision of protection and assistance. The category of asylum-seekers excludes anyone immediately granted refugee status on a prima facie basis, including Syrian refugees granted Temporary Protection visas in Turkey.

28. In addition to persons recognized as refugees under the 1951 Convention, 1967 Protocol and OAU Convention, UNHCR data also includes persons recognized as refugees in accordance with the UNHCR Statute. UNHCR published statistics also include people in refugee-like situations, that is, individuals outside their country or territory of origin who face protection risks similar to those of refugees, but for whom refugee status has, for practical or other reasons, not been ascertained, for example 200,000 undocumented Rohingya in Bangladeshis originating from Myanmar who are considered to be living in a refugee-like situation and the UNHCR has highlighted concerns for their protection.

29. UNHCR statistics on internally displaced persons are limited to countries (numbering 24 in 2013) where the organization is engaged with such populations.

30. The Joint IDP Profiling Service (JIPS) is an inter-agency service that supports international and national actors in collecting data on displacement situations through collaborative data-collection exercises. In particular, the Service aims at addressing gaps in disaggregated data (by location, sex, age, and diversity) and promoting evidence-based responses to displacement in the context of the search for durable solutions.

31. IDMC also produces estimates of people internally displaced by natural disasters.

32. Time-series of country data include a number of data preceded by the mention "up to" and others preceded by "at least," making it impossible to add across countries in a meaningful manner.

33. The 1967 Protocol expanded the application of the 1951 Convention beyond the protection of European refugees following World War II.

34. Reid 2005.

35. Individuals who fulfill the definition of refugees are entitled to the rights and are bound by the duties set out in the 1951 Convention, most significantly the rights to nondiscrimination, nonpenalization and non-refoulement (which prohibits the return of a refugee to a territory where their life or freedom is threatened).

36. Palestinian refugees are specifically excluded from the 1951 Convention, 1967 Protocol, and UNHCR Statute.

37. UNRWA was established by the General Assembly resolution 302 (IV) of 8 December 1949 and began operation on May 1, 1950. It succeeded the United Nations Relief for Palestine Refugees (UNRPR), established in 1948. The UN General Assembly has repeatedly renewed UNRWA's mandate, most recently extending it to June 30, 2017.

38. Article 1D of the 1951 Convention.

39. The recognition of refugee status is a declaratory act. As the UNHCR Handbook on Procedures and Criteria for Determining Refugee Status points out, "[Fulfilling the criteria contained in the 1951 Convention] would necessarily occur prior to the time at which his refugee status is formally determined. Recognition of his refugee status does not therefore make him a refugee but declares him to be one. He does not become a refugee because of recognition, but is recognized because he is a refugee." 2011 UNHCR Handbook on Procedures and Criteria for Determining Refugee Status under the 1951 Convention, Chapter I, General Principles on the Criteria for the Determination of Refugee Status, Article 28.

40. UNHCR 2015g.

41. UNHCR 2015g.

42. The UN Guiding Principles are not a binding instrument but establish principles that are consistent with international human rights and humanitarian law and analogous refugee law.

43. The UN Guiding Principles acknowledge large-scale development projects as a cause of displacement. The 2006 Great

Lakes Protocol on the Protection and Assistance of Internally Displaced Persons (Great Lakes Protocol) and the 2009 African Union Convention for the Protection and Assistance of Internally Displaced Persons in Africa (Kampala Convention) explicitly extend the definition of IDPs to include those displaced by development projects.

44. African Union 2012.

45. IASC 2010.

Taking a New Look at Prevention and Preparedness

2

Prevention is better than cure. Considering the immense suffering at stake, this simple truism applies in the case of forced displacement. To avoid the crisis altogether, efforts to prevent and end conflict and to lessen human rights violations are critical: all 71 conflicts that have taken place since 1991 have caused forced displacement.[1] Success requires a combination of diplomacy, peace-keeping, and peace-building as well as a complementary engagement by development and humanitarian actors. In reality, however, the track record of such international interventions is mixed, with both successes and failures.

When there is no diplomatic or military settlement, can some of the worst impacts of forced displacement be prevented? This is an important question in today's world: several countries are at war, or at a high risk of war, with no clear political solution in sight. In such contexts, is there scope for prevention and preparedness activities that may be less ambitious than the full achievement of peace but that can still make a difference on the ground?

Such a notion of prevention is relatively restrictive (box 2.1): it is not about preventing conflict in general, but about preventing the negative development impacts of forced displacement while taking the geopolitical context as a given. It is also not about trying to prevent people from escaping violence and seeking asylum, which is a fundamental and essential human right. Nor is it about stymieing other forms of population movements, including economic migration (or secondary movements by the forcibly displaced from a country of first asylum to another country), since from an economic perspective, such movements can have significant positive effects.

The forcibly displaced are not only victims, they are purposeful actors. Some people flee at gunpoint, but others have to make incredibly difficult decisions, and in particular to choose whether to flee or to stay in a context of violence. In an environment of conflict and poverty, both options entail very high risks. The decisions are made under duress, with imperfect information, based on an assessment of the odds of survival under each scenario.

Against this backdrop, the determinants of forced displacement include a mix of security, economic, and social considerations. Evidence suggests that security plays the main role, whether in deciding to flee or in choosing a destination. Economic concerns and social networks can also be important factors in determining who decides to stay, who decides to leave, and where to go. Government policies, whether in terms of security or socioeconomic development, can hence influence the scope and nature of forced displacement, positively or negatively.

Forced displacement is a process with its own dynamics. Most people try to manage the risks of violence before fleeing, and in most situations it takes some time before displacement starts in earnest and eventually reaches a peak—often several years.

BOX 2.1 A brief overview of the forced displacement prevention agenda

In the face of colossal human suffering and formidable costs from forced displacement crises, scholars, humanitarian actors, and diplomats began to investigate prevention as early as the 1930s. They gave it a renewed impetus in the 1990s, when the United Nations High Commissioner for Refugees (UNHCR) piloted a framework of "preventive protection" defined as "the elimination of causes of departures, rather than the erection of barriers that leave causes intact but make departure impossible."[a] Preventive protection included the reinforcement of national protection capabilities, advocacy, early warning systems, human rights monitoring, and conflict mediation.[b] Yet, success has remained elusive.

The prevention literature has traditionally focused on "root causes" of forced displacement. It distinguishes between structural or underlying causes (such as weak governance, poverty, low level of institutional development, inequality, human rights abuses, political exclusion, environmental degradation, and social fragmentation), proximate factors (escalation of violence, persecution, threats and perceived threats, collapse of livelihoods, and new opportunities in other areas), and enabling conditions (availability of transport, financial resources, level of education, networks, legislative frameworks, and border control). With this framework, the key objective for development actors is to help prevent conflict, violence, and persecution through a broad-based agenda of poverty reduction, shared prosperity, and good governance.

The prevention agenda has been roundly criticized as drawing attention from the need for robust asylum systems;[c] as being reductionist and failing to recognize the importance of context;[d] and as being too broad and unfocused to be of operational value. There is also a recognition that neither humanitarian nor development actors are equipped to prevent deliberate actions by armed groups and state actors,[e] as in 1995, when thousands of civilians were massacred in a so-called "UN safe area" of Srebrenica (Bosnia and Herzegovina).

By its nature, prevention yields results that are hard to observe—when it is successful, nothing happens—and even more difficult to attribute.[f] Yet, it must remain a central element of international efforts to alleviate the suffering caused by conflicts and displacement.

a. Zapater 2010; Ramcharan 1989; Goodwill-Gill 1996, p. 286; Fawcett and Tanner 1999; UNHCR 1991, para. 4; UNHCR 1996; Phuong 2005, p. 122–125.
b. Mangala 2001, pp. 1067–1095; UNHCR 2015h. UNGA 1993 also sets out these three pillars (in point 15) of "addressing prevention, protection and solutions on a comprehensive regional basis"
c. Goodwin-Gill 1996, p. 289.
d. Zapater 2010; Harild, Christensen, and Zetter 2015.
e. See Zapater 2010, p.10; UNCEB 2015, p.3.
f. Zapatar 2010; Talviste, Williamson, and Zeidan 2012; Frelick 1992; OCHA 1999.

This implies that flows of refugees and internally displaced persons (IDPs) can be forecast to some extent, and that there may be some space for a preparedness agenda.

Most of the population, however, stays behind. These people typically face formidable odds. In a deteriorated economic environment they suffer greatly, often with little external assistance. The gradual erosion of their living conditions may reduce their resilience, and relatively minor external shocks may then suffice to push them into displacement.

To stay or not to stay? Weighing the risks

Forced displacement is about survival. Those living amid violence often have to choose between the risk of becoming victims and the risk of leaving what they have for an uncertain future. For people already living in extreme poverty or severely impoverished by conflict, the loss of assets can be life threatening; for others it could mark the beginning of a hard-to-escape cycle of impoverishment and economic hardship.[2] Both staying and leaving carry high risks, and either may threaten the survival of the person.

While often regarded as passive victims who have no choice but to leave from an area engulfed in violence, people living in the midst of conflict are in fact trying to manage a situation of high risk and high uncertainty, and to stay alive.[3] They are making decisions based on what they perceive to be the optimal coping strategy at a given time. Those choices are typically made under duress, in situations of high stress, and without any good alternative, but often there is still some space for decision making.[4]

Forced displacement is one of several possible coping strategies in the midst of conflict.[5] Other options may include remaining in place or even joining an armed group.[6] People who stay, have to adjust their daily lives to the rules imposed by the controlling group:[7] some may form alliances, others may retreat into their private lives to decrease the chances of victimization.[8] Other people may join armed groups to secure protection for themselves and their families and increase their chances of survival, to seize assets and accumulate wealth, or to settle old scores:[9] those who were originally targeted may end up becoming perpetrators of violence themselves.[10]

Such coping strategies are forged over time and may change as the situation develops. Once conflict has begun and people have come into contact with warring parties, they assess and reassess the threats they are exposed to and the resources they have at their disposal to mitigate such threats, the strength of their social networks, and their investments in the community.[11] They leave when the risks of holding out or the costs of complying with demands by armed groups exceed the risks of leaving and their attachment to home. Information is critical in making such decisions, but it is often imperfect.

In all situations of forced displacement, some people stay while others flee. Understanding what makes some people decide to leave at a given moment, and how they choose their destination, is critical to developing an effective prevention and preparedness agenda.

What makes people go?[12]

Deciding to flee

Security risks are the main drivers
Evidence from a range of microlevel studies shows that security-related risks are the main trigger of forced displacement and that they outweigh all other considerations. Case studies from locations as varied as El Salvador,[13] Nepal,[14] prerevolutionary China,[15] Colombia,[16] civil war Spain,[17] and Indonesia[18] have found violence to be the strongest correlate with the decision to flee. Qualitative studies undertaken across a range of countries in Africa and the Middle East further confirm that this pattern is general.

The scale of forced displacement is greatest where violence is generalized.[19] Genocide is associated with the largest displacement (relative to population). Civil wars come second: they are often driven by identity politics and are played out within communities as much as on the frontlines;[20] foreign involvement can exacerbate violence and escalate forced displacement. By contrast, wars between states produce relatively fewer refugees and IDPs. And so do ethnic rebellions (when they do not turn into full-blown civil wars), as violence usually remains contained and people may decide to engage in the fighting rather than flee. In extreme cases, as in Central America, widespread violent crime has triggered large-scale displacement even without conflict.

This explains why the changing nature of a conflict—from contests for territory between state actors and regional rebellions to a proliferation of situations of generalized violence—contributes to a surge in forced displacement. Still, it is the geographic spread of a conflict, rather than the intensity of violence, that is a predictor of forced displacement:[21] the number of refugees and IDPs is largely a function of the number of people who are exposed to violence. But people are less likely to move when violence prevails along exit routes.

In the midst of conflict, not everybody is exposed to the same risks. The forcibly displaced are rarely fleeing chaos but instead they are escaping a situation of (often imperfectly) targeted violence (box 2.2). Any analysis of the dynamics of forced displacement needs to incorporate the strategic calculations and behaviors of the parties to the conflict. In some cases, the displacement of a population may be part of a deliberate effort by armed groups to assert control over a territory or to take assets. In other cases, it may be a military tactic to eliminate potential supporters of an enemy group. In many situations, people who live in extremely violent environments, such as Somalia, can also know from experience where and when violence is likely and this can enable them to navigate through conflict.[22]

Are most people fleeing an actual danger or are they prudently leaving before risks materialize? The response varies across situations and individuals: risk tolerance is highly subjective. In Colombia, 78 percent of IDPs moved after having been direct victims of violence.[23] In Nepal, the probability of leaving was 30 times higher among those who had been victimized than among those who feared violence but had not directly experienced it. People who move before having experienced violence typically have more time to plan and suffer lower losses: In Colombia, these amounted to 20 percent of assets compared with 33 percent for other IDPs.[24]

Economic considerations play a secondary role

Cross-country quantitative studies and empirical analyses show that economic factors play only a secondary role in forced displacement.[25] Economic factors such as poverty, inequality, and low institutional development increase the odds of conflict, but among conflict-affected countries, there is no clear and strong correlation between forced displacement and economic development, as measured by GDP.

Yet individuals still consider economic factors when weighing their chances under different scenarios: their situation in the place of origin, their prospects in the place of destination, the nature of their assets, and the affordability of the journey.

Individuals are more likely to leave when physical danger is compounded by economic

BOX 2.2 The (imperfect) targeting of violence

Violence against civilians during conflict is seldom indiscriminate. Armed groups are strategic actors who attack people based on their objectives and the constraints they face. They often use violence selectively and target specific population groups.[a]

For example, during the civil war in Algeria, enfeebled Islamist groups relied on massacres to deter defections.[b] In the 1980s, armed groups in El Salvador, including the army, employed violence to control civilians, and in neighboring Guatemala they attacked rural populations for economic gain.[c] Armed groups in Nepal and Aceh, Indonesia, triggered displacement to reshape the political landscape and drive rebel groups from their civilian base.[d] In Mindanao, the

Philippines, violence is considered a way of controlling the loyalties of the local population.[e] In Colombia, it was used as a strategy to hinder collective action, damage social networks, and intimidate and control civilian populations.[f] In the extreme case of genocide, the killing of selected groups of civilians is the central goal of the conflict, as was the case in Bosnia and Herzegovina, Rwanda, and Darfur.

Widespread aggression against civilians is therefore rarely an accidental byproduct of conflict, but rather the result of strategic calculations, in some cases by the government. If armed actors during a civil war are hegemonic in a territory, violence against civilians tends to be limited and targeted only at particular individuals. Conversely, in contested

territories, attacks intensify and are directed at selected groups of people, to undermine support to rival groups, force collaboration, seize valuable assets, or control territories.[g]

The probability of becoming a victim of violence is thus not evenly distributed across society. The characteristics of those who fall prey are highly contextual: they vary across conflicts and may change over time. In Nepal for example, violence was often aimed at people with certain political affiliations.[h] In Colombia, small landowners, families with young household heads, and female-headed households were most likely to be the target of direct threats.[i] Often, men and women face different forms of violence and risks.

a. Ibáñez and Moya 2016; Kalyvas 1999.
b. Kalyvas 1996.
c. Stanley 1987; Morrison and May 1994.
d. Williams 2008; Czaika and Kis-Katos 2009.
e. Coletta 2011.
f. Ibáñez and Moya 2016.
g. Kalyvas 1999, 2006; Azam and Hoeffler 2002; Wood 2010.
h. Adhikari 2013.
i. Engel and Ibáñez 2007.

hardship, or when economic opportunities are scarce. Since fleeing involves tremendous uncertainty, people can be willing to take greater security risks if they believe that their economic condition is acceptable.[26] But when their economic opportunities are destroyed they may be less willing to take those risks.[27] The loss of livelihoods and the collapse of institutions and services trigger forced displacement at lower levels of personal risk and are associated with large-scale forced displacement.[28]

People who have better prospects in a place of asylum are more likely to leave. For example, in Bosnia and Herzegovina and Colombia people who were better able to compete in labor markets were more willing to move.[29] In northern Mali, educated people and urban trading elites are overrepresented among the forcibly displaced. Ukraine has a disproportionate share of the elderly among IDPs, a rare feature, in part explained by the country's aging demographics, but also by the decision of the government to withhold pension payments in rebel-held parts of the country.[30]

Households for whom forced displacement has a higher opportunity cost may be willing to accept higher risks to protect their income and wealth, as documented in Colombia and Nepal. People whose livelihoods are tied to a certain location, or who have assets that they cannot easily sell, such as farmland, are more likely to stay longer: those who can easily dispose of their assets, like livestock, are more likely to leave.[31]

The cost of forced displacement can also be an obstacle. Fleeing entails paying for transportation and incurring a loss of income during the journey. Wealthier households may sell assets to support themselves during their displacement, but the poorest cannot.[32] Those without the means to leave may thus be overrepresented among the people who stay behind and who attempt to mitigate the effects of violence through other strategies.

Social networks may encourage staying or going

Forced displacement decisions are made against a social and cultural backdrop. Social scientists and anthropologists have long documented that social networks and community ties, embedded in the culture of a society, exert a strong influence over individuals' decision making.[33] This is also true when people face the biggest choice—to stay or to leave when violence seems imminent. The strength of social networks, participation in community organizations, and peer decisions are all important in individuals' choices, but depending on context, they may either enable people to stay or drive displacement.

Social networks can help people stay, as they have done in countries such as Colombia and Nepal.[34] Those involved in community organizations or who have lived in the same place for many years tend to stay longer, even in the midst of conflict. Informal networks often gain in significance when the state and its institutions have broken down or turned against citizens.[35] Communities with larger membership in social organizations can better defend themselves against physical threat.[36] Such organizations may also be instrumental in helping people cope with conflict and stay.[37]

Social networks can also facilitate displacement. People are more likely to move if they have prior migratory experience or if they have networks that can tell them how to relocate successfully.[38] Such networks reduce the costs and the uncertainty involved in a move, by transmitting information about the journey and place of destination. Individuals can then better compare and assess the relative costs and risks of staying or leaving. The importance of such information has been illustrated by the widespread use of social media among refugees who have recently entered the European Union (EU).

The influence of peers on the decisions of individuals has not yet been systematically documented. However, as peer pressure and mimetic behaviors are significant factors in other decisions, it is likely that they are also at play in the decision to flee. Anecdotal reports from situations as diverse as France in 1940 and post-genocide Rwanda suggest that "herd behavior" and generalized panic movements can drive large-scale displacement. Better understanding these processes may be helpful in identifying ways in which to reduce forced displacement flows.

Choosing where to go

The forcibly displaced often face a choice, to remain in their country as IDPs or to flee abroad and become refugees. Unsurprisingly, when they have a choice, most people prefer to stay in a relatively familiar environment. In most conflicts IDPs represent a large majority of the forcibly displaced, often 65 to 85 percent. Exceptions mainly include situations of political persecution or repression (where internal exile is not an option), conflicts when the state targets civilians, and instances where specific groups have stronger ethnic bonds across borders than in their own country.[39]

The primacy of security considerations is evident in the choice of destination, as the forcibly displaced consistently seek safer locations than the place of origin. Violence deters movement to certain areas in countries as varied as Colombia, Indonesia, and Guatemala,[40] even when the forcibly displaced were sympathetic to the groups perpetrating it.[41] Areas of potential instability are also unlikely to receive many displaced. In many cases, the forcibly displaced flee to areas where they may find people with similar political identities as themselves. In northern Mali for example, strategies largely reflected ethnicity: Songhai fled toward Bamako and became IDPs, while Kel Tamasheq and Arabs left the country and became refugees.[42] In Colombia, most people who were collectively targeted tried to move to a rival stronghold, to cluster with others who were similarly targeted, or to seek anonymity in a city.[43] In both Nicaragua (during the Contra

war) and Nepal those who fled violence (the forcibly displaced) and those who sought economic opportunities (economic migrants) moved to different destinations.[44]

Economic considerations are usually important, too (box 2.3). Among potential safe destinations, and to the extent they can do so, the forcibly displaced are likely to move to places that are more developed, and where they might have better chances of avoiding impoverishment.[45] Areas with higher wages and better social services are more attractive as they potentially offer more opportunities.[46] In some contexts, such as in South Sudan and parts of the Democratic Republic of Congo, people try to remain close to their place of origin in order to maintain access to their fields.[47] The cost of the journey also influences the choice of destination.[48] The availability of social assistance (including humanitarian aid) may draw the forcibly displaced, but empirical studies in Colombia and Sudan show that potential support by family and friends can play a larger role in determining a destination.[49]

There is often time to prepare before the crisis

The predictability of forced displacement

Forced displacement is rarely a one-off event that coincides with the onset of conflict: rather it is a process that occurs over an extended period of time. In most situations, people flee in successive waves, and the numbers of forcibly displaced vary with the ebb and flow of the conflict. Such dynamics largely depend on context: the nature, spread, and intensity of the conflict, as well as country factors. Yet, for each episode, there is often an onset phase, during which the number of forcibly displaced only gradually accelerates towards a peak. In fact, for all episodes of major forced displacement since 1991, the "peak" outflow was reached on average 4.1 years after the first large outflow.

This is because most people first try to manage the situation, and resort to fleeing only when all other means to cope have been exhausted.[50] At relatively low levels of intensity violence does not trigger much

---

BOX 2.3 **Socioeconomic status and displacement strategies**

For Somali refugees some strategies and destinations are more accessible and therefore relevant for certain groups of refugees. Asylum-seeking in the West is often a more viable strategy for those who can mobilize significant resources, while labor migration to the Middle East is more accessible for poorer

households as it requires fewer resources.[a] In Kenya, those with economic capital tend to reside in upscale areas of Nairobi, those with clan or lineage connection to Kenyan Somalis can live in the Eastleigh area of Nairobi while those with both poor social and economic capital often remain in camps at the border.[b]

a. Sturridge 2011.
b. Sturridge 2011.

displacement: it may even deter it if people prefer the safety of their own homes to the uncertainty of an environment where travel is unsafe and public order is collapsing. But beyond a certain threshold, displacement accelerates: the risks of remaining in place outweigh the costs and the dangers of leaving.

Threat levels and the cost of compliance with the warring parties significantly determine the length of time an individual is able to remain in place. Those who are willing and able to bear the costs and to meet the demands of the fighting parties are likely to stay longer. They will likely leave when the costs of compliance exceed the value of staying.[51]

The probability of forced displacement also appears to diminish over time, as those who decide to stay during the initial period are increasingly reluctant to move in subsequent years.[52] The probability that they leave declines with time, at least until a new shock happens.[53] This suggests a complex process where individuals try to cope with violence before leaving their home, and where those who decide to stay during the initial spell of shock adapt to living within a war.

The pattern of displacement

Once the journey begins, it can take many forms. Route making depends on a number of factors ranging from the location of relatives and friends to the accessibility of safe areas. There are numerous reports of people engaging in multiple displacements, and moving several times before settling in a place of asylum.[54] In some cases, forced displacement becomes circular, with people fleeing back and forth between several locations, as they track the ebb and flow of hostilities.[55] In the absence of systematic microlevel studies, it is difficult to assess the extent to which these patterns are generalized, rather than relatively rare events. Regardless, there is a consensus that forced displacement is often a complex journey. For those engaged in multiple displacements, each new round of movement results in further depletion of assets and impoverishment, and as such, in new vulnerabilities.

Displacement strategies vary. In some situations, such as with the recent flow of Syrian refugees to the EU, many households send out an advance-party, usually consisting of able-bodied men. In others, such as in Darfur, people are likely to flee in entire families.[56] There are also situations where households split between those who stay and those who go, for example with IDPs in northern Mali.[57] In some contexts, forced displacement is a massive undertaking, involving entire communities (e.g., Kosovo), while in other contexts, people move individually (e.g., in Colombia for 76 percent of displacement).[58] Such patterns play an essential role in exacerbating or on the contrary in mitigating forcibly displaced persons' vulnerabilities.

What happens to those who stay behind?

For every individual who flees from conflict, there are others who opt to stay—in most cases, the overwhelming majority of the population. At the end of 2014, out of 49 countries experiencing large outflows of refugees and IDPs, over 90 percent of the population was still in place in 42 countries; over 95 percent in 37 countries; and over 99 percent in 22 countries. The share of forcibly displaced exceeded 10 percent of the population in only seven countries, and only in the Syrian Arab Republic did it exceed 20 percent.[59] Although large-scale movement is an inevitable by-product of conflict, many people opt to manage the fallout from conflict and violence at home, rather than undertake a risky and hazardous move. Indeed countries that have spent decades ravaged by war are not depopulated, which suggests a formidable degree of resilience by those who stay behind.

Relatively little is known about the economic conditions of the people who stay in war-torn areas, in large part due to the challenges of gathering data in insecure areas. Yet, it can be assumed that most of those who stay behind live in acute poverty as the devastating effect of conflict wreaks havoc on economic activity and service delivery. The impacts of conflict can include a collapse of trade and investment, the destruction of infrastructure, large losses of assets, and a weakening of institutional capacity.[60] In the face of violence, households often modify their economic behavior by cutting visible investment, increasing the share of land left idle, and retreating from markets.[61] Anecdotal reports suggest that many people who stay behind resort to selling assets to subsist, and that they become increasingly impoverished and vulnerable with each passing year of conflict.

Given their diminished resilience, those who stay behind are increasingly unable to cope with exogenous shocks, so that events unrelated to conflict may trigger waves of displacement (box 2.4). For example, during the 2008 drought in Somalia, large numbers of people who had endured the conflict for almost two decades finally fled to neighboring countries when they lost their cattle and their livelihoods: for them, the risk of living amidst violence was no longer worth taking.[62] Policy makers and external stakeholders often direct their attention to the displaced, but those who stay behind also experience considerable suffering and hardship.

An agenda for development actors

Because violence is the main driver of forced displacement, the role of development actors is limited, especially in conflict areas where they are often absent. Yet in some areas their early engagement could help prevent some of the negative development impacts on the forcibly displaced and their host communities: by engaging in a dialogue on policies that may induce displacement, by helping host countries prepare for the shock, and by supporting those who stay behind.

BOX 2.4 Mixed migration

The concept of mixed migration gained traction in the mid-2000s to describe situations where people flee both security risks and economic despair.[a] This resonated particularly in the Horn of Africa, for drought-triggered movements out of Somalia and migrations out of Eritrea, and more recently in the Sahel. It has led to an argument that the line between forced displacement and economic migration is often blurred.

It would seem, however, that forced displacement situations where economic motivations play a large role are limited to two groups. The first is where people who initially stayed in a war zone see their economic situation gradually deteriorate until an exogenous shock tips the balance and forces them out: although the economic shock is the proximate trigger, the conflict remains the underlying driver. The second is where people flee a combination of political oppression and the absence of prospects in their country of origin. These people share some characteristics with economic migrants, but they represent only a small fraction of the forcibly displaced worldwide.

Mixed migration can also refer to the same routes and the same smuggling networks being used by economic migrants and forcibly displaced. From a host country's perspective, the inflow is indeed a mixed inflow, even though each individual has distinct reasons to move.

Mixed migration can easily become a catch-all definition. Except in the most extreme cases, forced displacement entails an element of economic calculation, as people weigh security risks against the risk of impoverishment. It is a complex decision-making process informed by a broad range of considerations. In this sense, most episodes of forced displacement may be characterized as "mixed migration," even where violence is the ultimate driver.

In spite of a small zone of overlap, there remains a fundamental difference between forced displacement and economic migration. The forcibly displaced overwhelmingly flee conflict (or its consequences), while economic migrants predominantly seek economic opportunities outside their country. Given differences in the international legal framework between the two groups (including legal protections), the risk is that the hasty generalization of this concept undermines the fundamental right to seek asylum.

A more useful concept may be that of "survival migration."[b] It may be appropriate to adjust the current binary characterization of human mobility into economic migrants and refugees to make room for a third category, that of "survival migrants." This category would include people who are not fleeing violence or persecution and thus do not qualify as refugees. But the type of risks they are willing to take and the sort of ordeals they are willing to undergo suggest that they have little choice but to move. Poverty and the lack of economic opportunities are the main drivers of such movements, made increasingly possible by global interconnectedness. A framework for addressing this issue may be needed as traditional mechanisms for managing economic migrations prove increasingly ineffective, and refugee law does not apply.

a. Van Hear 2009.
b. Betts 2010, 2013.

Discourage policies that induce displacement

Violence and forced displacement can be the result of actions taken by the country of origin's government. This includes political exclusion or persecution, targeted killings and expulsions, and economic and social policies that discriminate or make it difficult for people to subsist in violent areas.

Where it is appropriate, development actors should engage in a dialogue with the government to highlight the costs associated with forced displacement (box 2.5) and advocate for different policy choices. This is an integral part of their mandate: forced displacement has a substantial poverty impact on those affected, and the ramifications can extend well beyond the borders of the origin country—ignoring it is likely to jeopardize poverty reduction efforts.

This dialogue is likely to be difficult as policies that induce displacement are typically decided (or at least tolerated) at the highest echelons of government and driven by uncompromising political calculations. Development actors will need to use their judgment in deciding whether and how to manage such engagement. But they are already used to engaging in thorny policy dialogues with governments on a range of controversial topics. They often rely on analytical work and evidence to assess the costs of varying policy options, advisory services to help define technical solutions, and lending—including budget support—to support policy reforms. Such instruments could be used to advance a dialogue on forced displacement.

The focus of such efforts shall vary by country. Where government actions (or inactions) are the main drivers of forced displacement—actively by pushing people into displacement or passively by failing to protect those at risk—development actors should engage in a dialogue with the authorities to highlight the development impact of such actions. When forced displacement is generated by nongovernment actors with whom development actors have little contact, or where the relations with the authorities are not robust enough for them to exert any influence, they can help document the

development costs of forced displacement as part of a broader diplomatic engagement. Where persecution is pushing certain groups into forced displacement, they can quantify the costs of such exclusionary policies and advocate for their removal.

Development actors can also help to raise awareness and propose remedies when forced displacement is the unintended result of misguided policy. For example, the decision by

---

BOX 2.5 Socioeconomic impact of forced displacement on countries of origin: How to quantify it?

Quantifying the socioeconomic impact of forced displacement on countries of origin is complex. There has been no systematic research on this issue, and the methodological difficulties are considerable. For example, it is often hard to disentangle the socioeconomic impact of forced displacement from that of conflict. There is also typically no "control group" or counterfactual to compare the situation with: any workable model to find the causal impact of forced displacement on countries of origin would require a comparison between two geographic areas that have suffered similar levels of violence, but with only one experiencing displacement.

Such an analysis thus needs to be carried out case by case. It should typically look at two types of development impacts of forced displacement on the origin country.

The impact on fragility: Forced displacement is a result of fragility, but it can also be a factor of fragility. Because it affects some groups disproportionately, it can alter the social makeup of a community or leave significant voids in its leadership. There have been instances where the forcibly displaced have used exile as a sanctuary and remained engaged in the

conflict, through political support or by providing remittances. Large-scale departures can also cause demographic shifts, and—especially for internal displacement—lead to new regional imbalances. Forced displacement and fragility can be mutually reinforcing, leading to a potential vicious circle that is difficult to escape.

The impact on socioeconomic conditions: The economic and social costs of forced displacement, including direct and opportunity costs, can be heavy for the origin country, especially through the loss of capital and human resources. They largely depend on who leaves and who stays and whether the forcibly displaced move to other parts of the country or go into exile. Institutional capacity and service delivery can be affected when the forcibly displaced include large numbers of state employees. In the Central African Republic, Muslim retailers who handled much of the trade and transport activities became forcibly displaced: imports from neighboring countries dropped, and necessities became more scarce and expensive.[a] By contrast, remittances can help build the resilience of the remaining population.

a. FAO/WFP 2014.

---

a government to forfeit social protection benefits to those living in some parts of the country may force people to move: the government of Nepal decided to do the opposite and continued to provide social support in rebel-held areas, thus avoiding costs it would have had to bear otherwise.[63]

Help host countries and communities prepare

Since episodes of forced displacement can often be predicted, there is an opportunity for potential host countries and host communities to prepare, so as to better mitigate the short-term impact of an inflow of refugees or IDPs.

Early warning systems

In order to prepare, a mechanism is needed to forecast forced displacement episodes (events and non-events) with a reasonable degree of accuracy as to the likely orders of flow magnitudes and potential destinations. Over the last two decades, scholars and humanitarian actors have attempted to identify parameters to predict forced displacement. But the results often fell short, and most humanitarian agencies instead rely on judgment and experience, at the risk of being accused of subjectivity in politically charged environments.

The emergence of big data makes it possible to engage in a new approach: big data has proven effective at predicting the timing and volume of economic migration to specific areas with an impressive degree of accuracy (box 2.6).[64] The challenge is to adapt and extend the corresponding methodologies to forecasting forced displacement flows, including by defining the data to be collected and analyzed, and by compensating for the fact that access to the internet and modern communications technologies in some conflict-affected areas may be patchy.

Big data is a fast-moving industry, with constant technological advances. Nimbleness is therefore key. Private sector actors may be ideally positioned to develop and enhance the instruments that are needed to forecast forced displacement. Development actors can support this agenda by establishing robust partnerships with the private sector, and by providing seed resources to finance such efforts.

Preparedness

Potential host countries can take several steps before large numbers of refugees arrive, to better absorb the shock. This includes: contingency planning and institutional readiness (plans to locate the forcibly displaced, setting up or strengthening of institutions to deal with the inflow, and so on); the development of instruments to transfer resources rapidly to the communities as they start receiving people (for example, block grants); a strengthening of social protection systems to be able to rapidly support those who will be affected within host communities; and the establishment of a "surge capacity" for service delivery.

This agenda is largely unexplored. Experience with other shock management (for example, natural disasters) suggests that impacts can be greatly reduced through prevention and rapid response. This can be significantly more cost-effective than the closing of borders to mitigate the socioeconomic impact of forced displacement on host communities. It is an area where development actors can bring significant experience, including in terms of financial engineering (box 2.7).

Strengthen the resilience of those who stay behind

Development actors can help strengthen the resilience of those who stay behind by financing investment projects in stable parts of unstable countries to maintain livelihoods and strengthen community-based institutions. To do so, development actors need to extend the

---

BOX 2.6 **Using big data to predict economic migration to Australia**

A study conducted by the United Nations Population Fund and Global Pulse found that internet queries related to job opportunities in specific locations, such as "jobs in Melbourne" or "work in Australia," had a high correlation with official migration statistics.[a] This suggests that people conduct online searches to explore employment opportunities just prior to migrating. Search data can hence be used as a proxy for the intent to migrate and to predict flows, just as mining of search volumes can help predict flu and Dengue fever outbreaks, or unemployment trends.

a. UN Global Pulse 2014.

BOX 2.7 Learning from disaster preparedness

Development actors' experience with disaster management can provide important lessons to inform the elaboration of a preparedness agenda for potential host counties. In the past decade or so, many countries have recognized the importance of mainstreaming preparedness into key investments and broader development planning: for example, the Philippines is integrating disaster risk management into multiple levels of government planning. The process of strengthening risk management, through better information, timely financing, contingency funds, and enabling policies and planning, has proven to be sometimes more important than the actual achievement of discrete activities.

Planning is critical to preparedness, and so is capacity building. For example, the World Bank Group is supporting the Senegalese Civil Protection Agency to strengthen its risk management capacity by setting up coordination mechanisms for early warning, preparedness and response. Contingency funds can help accelerate resource mobilization in an emergency or pre-emergency situation. Support to those directly affected can also be prepared, for instance by building flexible and scalable social protection programs to respond to larger-scale disasters; adapting beneficiary targeting mechanisms to disaster response; integrating disaster-sensitive monitoring and evaluation into social protection programming; and adapting benefit transfer mechanisms to strengthen disaster resilience.[a]

a. World Bank 2013c.

frontier of their interventions. There is limited use in implementing development projects in violent and unstable environments, but islands of stability and relative normalcy exist even in the midst of conflict (for example, in parts of Somalia or Afghanistan where development interventions can have an impact). Developing adequate approaches and instruments to engage in such areas, so as to reinforce the resilience of those who stay behind, could make a significant contribution to reducing forced displacement (box 2.8).

BOX 2.8 Migration and development

Would support to those who stay behind increase or reduce forced displacement? Research shows that some countries display a clear and pronounced inverted U-shape relationship—known as the mobility transition—between overall economic development and out-migration.[a] Starting from low levels of development, rising incomes are accompanied by rising rates of emigration, until a turning point, when further increases in income are accompanied by falling rates of out-migration. The turning point depends on country contexts (and probably cultural factors), but is typically at a level of prosperity that corresponds to middle-income status. In other words, in most low-income countries, development is an accelerator rather than an inhibitor of out-migration.

But this does not apply in most conflict situations. It is another instance where distinguishing between economic migration and forced displacement is critical. The mechanisms that prompt an increase in voluntary emigration when GDP rises in the country of origin all reflect medium-term economic and social changes that are induced by development—and that do not play out in war-torn areas: demographic transition (where rising incomes can be associated with demographic changes that favor emigration);[b] credit constraints (where rising incomes help potential migrants finance the cost of international mobility);[c] information asymmetry (the transfer of information to potential migrants by migrants who have left can accelerate migration even as origin-country incomes rise);[d] structural change and worker dislocation (where economic development is associated with structural change that alters the costs and benefits of emigration);[e] inequality (where economic development is associated with changes in the distribution of income that affect the demand for migration);[f] and immigration barriers abroad (where a mobility transition is shaped by changes in the supply of legal migration opportunities).[g]

a. Clemens 2014; Zelinsky 1971; Akerman 1976; Gould 1979; Martin 1993; Hatton and Williamson 1994.
b. Easterlin 1961; Tomaske 1971; Zelinsky 1971; Hatton and Williamson 1994; Lucas 2005.
c. Vanderkamp 1971; Faini and Venturini 1993; Hatton and Williamson 1994; Ghatak and Levine 1994; Gould 1980; Lucas 2005.
d. Greenwood 1969; Massey 1988; Gould 1980; Baines 1994.
e. Zelinsky 1971; Massey 1988.
f. Gould 1980; Martin and Taylor 1996; Stark 1984; Stark, Taylor, and Yitzhaki 1986, 1988a, 1988b; Stark and Taylor 1991; Stark 2006.
g. Hatton and Williamson 2005a, 2005b, and 2011.

BOX 2.9 Strengthening resilience in Ethiopia

In 2005, the government of Ethiopia launched the Productive Safety Nets Program with support from development partners. This program is now implemented in 411 districts in Ethiopia, reaching up to 10 million food-insecure people a year and has a budget of around $3.6 billion from the government and 11 development partners. It has made notable contributions to reduce household vulnerability and food insecurity, improve resilience to shocks, and promote sustainable community development in rural areas of Ethiopia. It has focused on public works to improve rural infrastructure and enhanced access to education and health services.

The needs of those who stay behind in relatively stable areas are often similar to those of other highly vulnerable populations in lagging regions, where economic activity is slow and effective institutions are lacking. The agenda is essentially twofold: to maintain livelihoods, including trade, and to support community organizations, which are an important part of the resilience agenda.

Development actors have extensive experience in helping strengthen community-level resilience in difficult contexts, as through Afghanistan's National Solidary Program, or in supporting poor areas, as through Ethiopia's Productive Safety Nets Program (box 2.9). Such experience may of course need to be adjusted to contexts which are less stable, in particular to intervene in areas which are not under the control of an internationally-recognized government.

For the international community as a whole, such engagement in "frontier" areas is likely to be a sound investment. The costs of such programs are likely to be far lower than the costs of dealing with forced displacement, even from a strictly financial perspective. Even if people eventually flee, efforts to strengthen their resilience can have a positive impact, as they may enter the ordeal of forced displacement better prepared, by having lost fewer assets and maintained stronger social bonds up to that point.

Needless to say, risks are substantial, as additional support may convince people to continue to live in the midst of conflict, making them potential victims of violence. Such risks must be well analyzed and effectively mitigated for development actors to engage.

Notes

1. List of conflicts from UCDP/PRIO 2015. Large-scale displacement was reflected in UNHCR statistics for 57 of the 71 conflicts. The 14 episodes of conflicts from the UCD/PRIO dataset which did not produce large forced displacement as registered by UNHCR are as follows: Algeria (1994–1999), Colombia (1994, 1996), the Republic of Congo (1997–1998), India (1990–1994, 1999–2010), Israel (2006, 2014), Nepal (2002–2005), Peru (1990–1991), the Philippines (1990–1991, 2003), Turkey (1992–1993), the Republic of Yemen (1994). In all these cases, people were displaced, although those who were affected were not always recognized as such, often for political reasons.
2. Adhikari 2013.
3. Kalyvas 1999; Wood 2010.
4. See Davenport, Moore, and Poe 2003; Moore and Shellman 2004, 2006; Melander and Öberg 2006, 2007; Ibáñez and Moya 2016; Adhikari 2011.
5. Bennett et al. 2016.
6. Korf 2004; Kalyvas and Kocher 2007; Steele 2009; Justino 2011.
7. Korf 2004; Lindley 2010a; Zetter, Purdekova, and Ibáñez 2013.
8. Korf 2004; Lindley 2010a.
9. Kalyvas and Kocher 2007; Verwimp 2005.
10. Davenport, Moore, and Poe 2003.
11. Adhikari 2013.
12. Unless otherwise specified, forced displacement numbers used in this section are based on UNHCR data for 1991–2014; large displacement is defined as those involving at least 25,000 persons; conflict data are from the UCD/PRIO database; major conflicts are those causing more than 1,000 battle deaths in a given year. "Democracy" is measured from the Polity 2 dataset. Data on ethno-linguistic fractionalization, religious fractionalization, non-contiguity, and mountainous terrain are based on Fearon and Laitin 2003. Economic data are from the World Development Indicators (WDI) dataset.
13. Stanley 1987.

14. Williams 2008; Bohra-Mishra and Massey 2011; Adhikari 2013.
15. Gottschang 1987.
16. Lozano-Gracia et al. 2010; Engel and Ibáñez 2007.
17. Balcells 2012.
18. Czaika and Kis-Katos 2009.
19. See Schmeidl 1997; Melander and Öberg 2006.
20. Bennett et al. 2016.
21. See Melander and Öberg 2006.
22. Lindley 2010a.
23. Ibáñez and Moya 2016.
24. Ibáñez and Vélez 2008.
25. See Hakovirta 1986; Zolberg, Suhrke, and Aguayo 1989; Clark 1989; Schmeidl 1995, 1997, 1998; Gibney, Apodaca, and Mc-Cann 1996; Cohen and Deng 1998; Weiner 1996; Apodaca 1998; Davenport, Moore, and Poe 2003; Ibáñez 2014; Engel and Ibáñez 2007; Ibáñez and Vélez 2008; Williams 2008, 2013; Kondylis 2010; Bohra-Mishra and Massey 2011; Adhikari 2013; Stanley 1987.
26. Adhikari 2013.
27. Adhikari 2013.
28. Adhikari 2013; Williams 2008, 2013; Czaika and Kis-Katos 2009; Lozano-Gracia et al. 2010.
29. Ibáñez 2014; Kondylis 2010.
30. Ferris et al. 2015.
31. Engel and Ibáñez 2007; Ibáñez and Vélez 2008; Adhikari 2013.
32. Ibáñez and Moya 2016; Lozano-Gracia et al. 2010
33. Uhlenberg 1973; Kasarda and Janowitz 1974; Irwin and Lyson 1999.
34. Adhikari 2013; Ibáñez and Vélez 2008.
35. Harpviken 2009; Wood 2010; Coletta and Cullen 2000.
36. Adhikari 2013.
37. In northern Darfur, such organizations have not only helped address food security and livelihood concerns but also negotiated with warring parties. See Jaspars and O'Callaghan 2010.
38. Mishra 2012; Davenport, Moore, and Poe 2003; Lozano-Gracia et al. 2010; Schmeidl 1997; Zetter, Purdekova, and Ibáñez 2013.
39. Moore and Shellman 2004, 2006.
40. Ibáñez and Moya 2016; Morrison and May 1994; Czaika and Kis-Katos 2009.
41. Balcells 2012.
42. Etang-Ndip, Hoogeveen and Lendorfer 2015.
43. Steele 2009.
44. Lundquist and Massey 2005; Bohra-Mishra and Massey 2011.
45. Balcells 2012; Ibáñez and Moya 2016.
46. Lozano-Gracia et al. 2010; Czaika and Kis-Katos 2009; Moore and Shellman 2006.
47. FOA and Tanner 2007.
48. Morrison and May 1994; Lozano-Gracia et al. 2010.
49. Ibáñez and Moya 2016; FOA and Tanner 2007.
50. Adhikari 2011.
51. Adhikari 2011.
52. Melander and Öberg 2006.
53. Adhikari 2011.
54. Lindley 2009.
55. Raeymaekers 2011.
56. FOA and Tanner 2007.
57. Etang-Ndip, Hoogeveen and Lendorfer 2015.
58. Ibáñez and Moya 2016.
59. Calculations based on UNHCR data for refugees, IDMC data for IDPs, and World Bank Group data for populations. The proportion of forcibly displaced may be higher if it is calculated for only those regions engulfed by violence, but there is often no reliable population estimate for the corresponding areas.
60. See World Bank 2011a.
61. Deininger 2003; Grun 2008; Bozzoli and Brück 2009.
62. Hammond 2014b.
63. Adhikari 2013.
64. The term "big data" refers to extremely large sets of data that can be computationally analyzed to understand underlying patterns and trends.

Managing Changes for Host Communities

3

How can host countries and communities be best supported in their own development efforts, when their circumstances are transformed by an influx of forcibly displaced?

Host communities often have development needs. Hosting large numbers of forcibly displaced transforms the environment in which development strategies are designed and implemented. It creates new opportunities and challenges, and it affects poverty reduction efforts, positively and negatively. Supporting host communities is often seen as an indirect way to assist refugees and internally displaced persons (IDPs), by helping create or sustain an accepting—even welcoming—environment for the forcibly displaced.[1] In fact, the development response should aim to help reduce poverty among the hosts themselves as an objective in its own right.

For host communities, the influx of large numbers of forcibly displaced is a demographic shock that disrupts existing equilibria and creates mismatches in demand and supply in multiple markets. With the passage of time, a new set of equilibria emerges: the question is whether this new environment is more, or less, conducive to poverty reduction among the hosts. This in turn depends on three sets of factors: the initial conditions; the magnitude and nature of the shock; and the policy and investment response.

The impact of forced displacement is generally local and limited, although there are exceptions. In most refugee-hosting countries, refugees account for less than 1 percent of the total population. The national impact is modest, even though some parts of the country or certain communities may be disproportionately affected. Similarly in most IDP countries, the impact is mainly felt at local level, as population groups are rebalanced across regions.

In a number of areas, the challenges faced by host communities existed before the influx of forcibly displaced and they are mainly exacerbated by the presence of newcomers. While refugees and IDPs can provide convenient scapegoats for deep-rooted issues, they are often not the main cause of many of the difficulties that host countries and communities face. For example, in the case of fragility and security, social cohesion, and economic growth, the impact is typically fairly limited and largely reflects issues that predate the arrival of the forcibly displaced.

In other areas, the impact is unevenly distributed within host communities: some people gain, others lose out. This is particularly true for jobs and prices. There is a common assumption that forcibly displaced persons often compete with the poorest hosts for jobs, goods, and services. Yet the presence of large numbers of forcibly displaced persons also creates new markets and new opportunities for growth and poverty reduction. Hence, the net impact has both positive and negative elements. Understanding how the costs and benefits are distributed is crucial to determine whether compensatory measures are needed.

The impact on social, urban, and environmental services can be significant. The inflow of forcibly displaced persons increases demand, while supply may take time to adjust. This is especially the case when refugees and IDPs are accommodated in lagging regions or in relatively poorer parts of urban centers, where service availability was already spotty before their arrival. The impact also depends on whether refugees and IDPs are concentrated in a small geographic area, or widely distributed across the entire country. It needs to be mitigated with adequate investments and policy reforms.

Overall, medium-term impacts largely depend on host country's policies. In particular, concentrating the forcibly displaced in camps or in specific hosting areas may heighten challenges while reducing opportunities for the host community to benefit from their presence. Allowing them to contribute to the local economy may generate larger benefits for the hosts. Policies traditionally seen as more humane and more beneficial for the forcibly displaced may also serve the host communities' interests.

Still, mitigating the impact of forced displacement on host communities is not merely a technical agenda: the policy response is largely determined by political considerations. A thorough understanding of the political and social dynamics at play in the host environment is critical (box 3.1). Development actors can help shape the policy-making environment through analytics and contributions to the public debate.

BOX 3.1 A host country perspective

How do host countries perceive the challenges they are facing? A December 2015 opinion research study discussed this question with key opinion leaders in six countries hosting large numbers of refugees and IDPs: Ethiopia, Jordan, Kenya, Lebanon, Turkey, and Uganda.[a] The study provides a sense of the political context in which development responses can be designed and implemented.

Overall perspective
Respondents from all countries emphatically stated their conviction that the crisis is both unacceptable and unsustainable. They described potential catastrophic implications—regional and global—if the crisis is not addressed by the international community.

They shared a consensus that the national interests of host countries and the welfare of refugees and IDPs are inextricably linked. They found it virtually impossible to discuss the impact of the forced displacement situation or to make recommendations for improving socioeconomic welfare in their own country without addressing the experience and needs of displaced persons.

Still, they underlined the reluctance of host countries to acknowledge and manage the long-term nature of the crisis. For example, many of them in Lebanon and Turkey were reluctant to talk about "opportunities" associated with the influx of refugees, and a few rejected the notion of integration outright. "No one in the political class wants to keep Syrians here forever. Nobody is ready to accept them for staying forever. We need improved resilience of Syrians without integrating. Very important not to use the integration word" (Lebanon). They often made a distinction, however, between refugees (a "tragedy") and IDPs (a "problem"). They noted in some cases that the political interests of host governments often prevailed over the needs of the forcibly displaced.

Impacts and priorities
The impact of the crisis has been so pervasive and the resulting social, economic, and environmental problems are perceived as being so intertwined that many respondents were reluctant to identify areas of greatest impact or to prioritize their concerns. "It's not one thing or another; it's everything. The refugee problem is a problem for all of society. The drain on the national economy, the violence and crime, the competition for services, the increase in social tensions and public resentment. It's something that affects us all at all levels."[b]

Most respondents pointed to the pressing need for host countries to address the matters of refugee

(Box continues next page)

BOX 3.1 A host country perspective *(continued)*

status, identity, and rights. They warned of a potential lost generation if adequate education systems for displaced children are not in place. They reported strain on the host countries' social fabric, with resentment toward displaced persons commonplace, as hosts feel that they have to compete with the newcomers for services. Some respondents suspected refugee camps of being breeding grounds for radicalization and arms transfer, while viewing successful assimilation of refugees into urban areas as a potential breach of public security.

From the respondents' perspective, the most troubling problem involved those people who have spent their entire lives within the refugee camps, with no remaining legal or cultural ties to their countries of origin and no rights or official identity in the host country. While virtually all respondents described full assimilation as the only logical and humane solution, few of them viewed it as a realistic option for many refugees in

the foreseeable future. "Every child that has been born in the camp since 1992 should be given Kenyan citizenship. They don't even speak Somali. If they're not Kenyan, then I ask you, who are they and where do they belong? They can't be expected to spend the rest of their lives in the camps, with no jobs, no culture, and no identity, completely dependent on handouts from people they don't even know. This is simply not acceptable."[c]

All respondents reported that the presence of refugees in their countries challenged concepts of national and cultural identity, for both local citizens and refugees. They felt that the relationship of refugees to the culture and national identity of the host country was dependent on many factors, including the intensity of ethnic and factional divisions within the country; economic class and educational level; village vs. urban setting; encamped vs. assimilated; and the level of competition for public resources and opportunities. Respondents from all countries

noted that the prolonged presence of refugees in their countries posed a challenge that would ultimately redefine the identity of both the host country and the refugees themselves.

External support
Respondents typically expressed skepticism about aid effectiveness. Despite large amounts of aid that have flowed to host countries, they perceived the funds to have been deployed without an overarching long-term strategy and without coordination. But the majority of respondents did not believe that the problems caused by displacement at current levels could be mitigated over time, even if financial resources were increased, redundancies eliminated, new partnerships formed, and programs implemented. In the words of a typical respondent, "if some type of solution isn't found for the root causes of this situation, then none of these things we are discussing will matter."[c]

a. This qualitative study was carried out by a team of consultants working for the World Bank Group through interviews with preidentified opinion leaders. The study was designed to examine respondents' attitudes toward a variety of issues related to the forced displacement situation. The 41 opinion leaders who participated in these confidential discussions with research consultants represented a mix of academics, think tank researchers, nongovernmental organization (NGO) executives, and a small number of media professionals.
b. Kenyan respondent.
c. Kenyan respondent.
d. Kenyan respondent.

Initial conditions, shock, and response

Since time immemorial, the arrival of outsiders in a community has stirred a range of reactions. This also happens when large numbers of forcibly displaced flow in. Their movement inevitably has consequences for the host countries and communities, at

national and local levels.[2] The nature of this impact, however, has long been contentious and continues to be hotly debated.[3] For some, the arrival of forcibly displaced places a heavy burden on their hosts: "they steal jobs," "they freeload on aid and public benefits," "they destroy cultural structures."[4] For others, they provide opportunities by bringing in labor, skills, and resources. Such binary discourse is increasingly recognized as overly reductive: in reality, the experience is more nuanced.

For host countries and communities, the sudden influx of large numbers of forcibly displaced persons is a demographic shock. There is a relatively rapid (and sometimes abrupt) increase in population, which disrupts preexisting equilibria. It causes some temporary disorganization at least at local level, which often negatively affects the host community. It creates mismatches in demand and supply in a number of markets, such as for services and jobs. It alters balances across ethnic or social groups within host communities, which may help appease or exacerbate social tensions. With the passage of time, the shock is absorbed, some positive outcomes emerge, and new equilibria set in (figure 3.1).

The challenge for development actors is to help offset the impact of the shock: to minimize the period of disruption and to reach a set of equilibria that are superior to the preexisting ones. Whether the new environment is more, or less, conducive to poverty reduction within host communities depends on three sets of factors: the initial conditions; the magnitude and nature of the shock; and the policy and investment response. Initial conditions often play an important role, and so does the nature of the shock, including the composition of the flow (e.g., demographics, ethnicity) and its destination. What constitutes an optimal approach in one case may

hence not be so in another: responses have to be tailored to each context.

The eventual socioeconomic outcomes are often complex and nuanced. They may vary across "markets" and other social aspects of public life: for example, the presence of forcibly displaced persons may result in an increase in housing prices, while at the same time dampen food prices. They may also be different in the case of refugees and IDPs: IDPs share citizenship and they typically have economic rights which can make their integration easier; on the other hand, they live in a country which, almost by definition, is beset by fragility and conflict.

The shock often has significant distributional effects. Host countries and host communities are not homogenous. In any process of socioeconomic change, some groups may gain while others can be hurt. Forced displacement is unlikely to present an exception to this rule. The inflow of refugees can alter the distribution of socioeconomic outcomes among the host population.[5] This both transforms the political economy and modifies relationships within host communities. It is also an important consideration for the authorities as they define their response.

Objective impacts also depend on subjective perceptions: these can turn into self-fulfilling prophecies when they affect behaviors and policy outcomes.[6] For instance, a long-term empirical study found some disconnect between reality and perceptions in some

FIGURE 3.1 **Shock and response for the host communities**

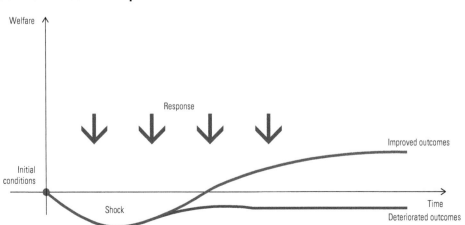

Ugandan host communities living close to Congolese refugee settlements: their welfare had improved, but they felt it had deteriorated, which in turn affected their relationship with the refugees.[7]

Exacerbating existing challenges: The country-level impact on fragility, social cohesion, and the economy

Fragility and national security— Anxieties can be exaggerated

Preserving national security is the primary duty of political leaders in host countries. It is paramount in defining policies vis-à-vis the forcibly displaced, which is why the interior ministry, defense forces, and local police are usually key actors in managing forced displacement.[8] Refugees are often perceived as potentially dangerous aliens, while IDPs can be viewed as deepening instability in an already fraught situation (or as reminders that the causes of conflict and displacement are not yet resolved).

So, do the forcibly displaced spread conflict to host countries and communities?[9] Only in exceptional circumstances. The presence of refugees mainly exacerbates preexisting factors of fragility. Critical factors are the initial conditions (high fragility, ethnic fragmentation, political exclusion, weak legitimacy of the government, and so on), and the size and composition of the flow (and whether it can aggravate social or ethnic unbalances in the host society).

A case-by-case review of 82 countries that received more than 25,000 refugees for at least one year over 1991–2014 shows that 68 percent of host countries did not experience any conflict during the entire period. Of the remaining 32 percent, forced displacement was mostly not concomitant with, or subsequent to the onset of, the conflict (that is, it was a consequence rather than a cause). Overall, out of 991 country-year episodes, hosting refugees may have contributed to causing conflict in only 8 cases.[10] In all of these cases, there were multiple preexisting factors of fragility, refugee flows were large compared with the host population (typically above 3 percent),

they were mixed with militarized elements, and there were strong ethnic affiliations with parts of the host countries.

Host countries' policies and capacity also play a role. Refugee movements seem to be more likely to produce conflict when the government lacks political legitimacy, when ethnic difference is politicized, and when host country leaders use the presence of refugees for political purposes. They are most dangerous when the host state lacks the willingness and ability to address difficult political and social issues or to contain militancy.[11] For example the presence of post-1994 Rwandese refugees sparked a conflict in Zaire, while it did not in Tanzania.[12]

Restricting the refugees' freedom of movement, and hosting them in camps, does not provide for an adequate (or at least for a sufficient) response to mitigate underlying weaknesses in the host society.[13] In all cases where their presence contributed to igniting a conflict, a large majority of refugees were accommodated in camps.[14] In fact areas hosting large numbers of refugees are comparatively more secure than the rest of the country.[15] The focus should rather be on tackling preexisting challenges by, for example, strengthening legitimate institutions and governance structures, building localized conflict-resolution mechanisms, and providing citizens with security and access to justice.[16]

The case of IDPs—whose arrival is preceded by conflict—is more complex, and the question of whether their movements help spread violence is hard to resolve empirically as there are many channels through which violence spreads during a war.[17] Anecdotally, however, in many countries hosting large numbers of IDPs over a protracted period, conflict has not spread to the key hosting areas (as in Colombia, Georgia, Turkey, and Ukraine). In situations of conflict and violence, the presence of large flows of IDPs is only one among many threats to national security, and often not the main one.

There are concerns, including in high-income countries, that hosting forcibly displaced may increase the risk of terrorist attacks.[18] The global public discourse is increasingly permeated by the notion that the displaced may be prone to committing acts of terror in host countries. This is fueling security concerns and exclusionary sentiment,[19] but there is limited evidence to justify such anxieties (box 3.2).

Social cohesion—Little is known

Two dimensions of impact

The impact of forced displacement on the cultural identity and social cohesion of host communities is often the subject of acrimonious debate (box 3.3). This debate is not new: it largely builds on fears over the impact of economic migration, in an increasingly globalized world where traditional norms and values are challenged and often upended. Yet, it provides the backdrop against which policies towards refugees and IDPs are designed and adopted.

In the context of forced displacement, social cohesion issues can be articulated along two dimensions: within host communities, and between host communities and the forcibly displaced.

The inflow of forcibly displaced often transforms dynamics within host communities. It alters the social makeup of the community by affecting various groups in different ways. Those who gain and those who lose from the presence of refugees and IDPs see their personal trajectories diverge. This can shift the composition and the relative social status of various groups, and change their relationships. It can also give rise to resentment and social tensions.

An inflow of forcibly displaced may also create tensions between hosts and the newly arrived who often bring their own norms, values, and behaviors. Such inflows have

---

BOX 3.2 Terrorism and the displaced—Myths and reality

There is only one area where there is robust evidence of a clear link between forced displacement and terrorism: the displaced are frequently among the main victims of terrorist groups. Out of about 40,000 terrorist attacks in which at least one person was killed between 1970 and 2013, approximately 70 per cent happened in countries already experiencing conflict, and those who became displaced were often among the targets.[a] In fact, displacement is at times a deliberate objective of extremist groups, for example in Northern Nigeria with Boko Haram, or in Northern Uganda with the Lord's Resistance Army.

There are suspicions that terrorist groups may infiltrate asylum flows but evidence is largely anecdotal. For example, it was widely reported that two of the attackers in the November 2015 carnage in Paris had been registered as refugees, but they were part of a larger group mainly composed of French and Belgian nationals. The April 2015 Garissa massacre in Kenya was initially blamed on Somali refugees, but it appears to have been orchestrated by Kenyan and Tanzanian nationals. Among 784,000 refugees resettled in the United States since September 11, 2001, only 3 have been arrested on terrorism charges (2 of whom were not planning an attack on the United States):[b] what is unclear is whether these individuals were deliberately sent by terrorist groups, whether they were already radicalized when they arrived, or whether they became radicalized subsequently.[c] There is no evidence to date that would justify concerns that refugees may be particularly vulnerable to radicalization.

In some cases, while in exile people may continue to have allegiances or linkages (historical, ethnic, religious, etc.) to groups or communities that are associated with conflicts or violence in their country of origin and some may become involved in supporting or committing terrorist acts. Yet, the attacks typically do not affect the host country, but the country of origin, and in fact host countries have at times supported or condoned such activities.

In fact the drivers of terrorist activity are often complex and multi-layered, and initial conditions in the host country may play an important role. Countries with greater social hostilities between different ethnic, religious and linguistic groups, lack of intergroup cohesion and high levels of group grievances have been found to be more prone to terrorism: out of about 6,100 major terrorist acts since 1996, over 90 per cent happened in countries with the lowest quartile of social cohesion.[d] In order to reduce the likelihood of terrorism, authorities and their partners should focus on addressing such tensions.

a. This study covered 178 countries.
b. Newland 2015.
c. Koser and Cunningham 2015.
d. Global Development Index 2014.

---

sometimes ignited competition and tensions over land and resources, leading to violent confrontations, as with Mozambican refugees in Malawi, Eritrean refugees in Eastern Sudan, and displaced Ugandans in Northern Uganda.[20] The impact depends in part on the host community's overall readiness to accept outsiders, but also on the magnitude of the inflow and on the preexisting relationship between the displaced and their hosts (box 3.4).

These two dimensions of social cohesion are intimately linked. A more resilient community may be more self-confident in accepting others. In contrast, a xenophobic public discourse can rapidly lead to prejudice and hostility directed at minority groups in the broader society.[21] For example, during episodes of xenophobic violence in South Africa in 2008 and 2015, the victims were not only Mozambican and Somali refugees, but also South Africans who fit the stereotype of "looking foreign."[22] Similarly, xenophobic rhetoric directed at refugees in some Organisation for Economic Co-operation and Development (OECD) countries often affects nationals with a foreign background.

Factors affecting impact

Host communities are not static. The assumption that they constitute stable entities disrupted by the arrival of outsiders is often problematic. In fact, they are usually in a state of flux, even before the arrival of forcibly displaced. As in many low- and middle-income countries, they are subject to formidable pressures, including the structural and social transformations induced by development. Refugees and IDPs are sometimes perceived as the cause of changes they have little to do with.

Does the impact on social cohesion depend on the cultural and linguistic proximity of the displaced and their hosts?[23] The evidence is mixed. Proximity can be positive (Pashtun Afghans hosted in Pakistan) or negative (Rwandese in eastern Zaire).[24] Lack of proximity can also generate resentment and social tensions, for example in Guinea where hosts found themselves compelled to learn the refugees' languages as their numbers grew rapidly.[25] Rather than

BOX 3.3 What is "social cohesion"?

Despite its frequent use in academic literature and political discourse, social cohesion remains a vaguely defined concept.[a] It is sometimes described as a "state of affairs concerning both the vertical and the horizontal inter-actions among members of society, as characterized by a set of attitudes and norms that include trust, a sense of belonging, and the willingness to participate and help, as well as their behavioral manifestations."[b] This encompasses both the relationship between state and society at large (vertical) and the interactions among groups within society (horizontal), including gender, class, ethnicity, and religion. The concept can also be articulated in economic language (equality of chances and equality in conditions); in political terms (involvement in managing public affairs); and in sociocultural terms (common values, feelings of belonging).[c]

Social cohesion is largely a social construct. Subjective perceptions may be as important as objective facts. Political discourse can affect outcomes by influencing attitudes, behaviors, and actions of individuals and groups. Concepts such as national identity can easily be misconstrued or manipulated, especially in countries where identity is based primarily on ethnic or religious affiliation. Discussions about social cohesion contain an important subjective element, peppered with occasional references to a mythicized and possibly embellished "before," and shot through with strong feelings over the impact of "others" on the social fabric, even in regions where there are no such aliens.

From a development perspective social cohesion, while largely intangible, is essential. It is, for example, associated with positive development outcomes, such as safe and productive communities, while social fragmentation is associated with negative outcomes, such as spatial segregation and crime.[d] It remains, however, a neglected area of research, particularly for forced displacement.[e]

a. Jenson 1998; Acket et al. 2011.
b. Chan et al 2006.
c. Acket et al. 2011.
d. Foa 2011; Putnam, Leonardi, and Nanetti 1993; Knack 2002; Coffé and Geys 2005.
e. Chan et al. 2006; Acket et al. 2011.

proximity itself, it is the preexisting relationship between the forcibly displaced and their hosts that seems to be important, as well as the availability of resources both groups are competing for.[26] The political narrative weaved around these interactions can also mitigate or amplify the impact.

Social cohesion outcomes are affected by perceptions of injustice in aid programs, even when these are not rooted in objective facts.[27] The welfare of forcibly displaced who receive assistance is in large part set by the humanitarian norms applied by aid

In Lebanon, tensions with Syrian refugees reportedly go beyond economic concerns.[a] They reflect a long history of interactions, including through Syrian political and military interventions in Lebanon over the last three decades and the presence of seasonal Syrian workers and other economic migrants in Lebanon. Stereotypes of Syrians are either military officers or menial workers with low social standing,[b] and they provide the backdrop against which Lebanese hosts accept Syrian refugees. Negative perceptions are largely based on media reports rather than on personal experience: those who have more social interactions with Syrian refugees tend to be less hostile.[c]

In Colombia, tensions between IDPs and hosts often exacerbate racial and regional prejudices. For example, some hosts refused to house Afro-Colombians and indigenous IDPs. Signs such as "apartment for rent, but not for blacks" appeared in some host communities. Some hosts felt coexistence with Afro-Colombians to be difficult claiming that they played "very loud music" and "when you rent to one then ten arrive."[d]

In Azerbaijan, IDPs are housed in designated IDP settlements apart from the nondisplaced, and their children are segregated in IDP schools. This has narrowed their opportunities to connect with the nondisplaced, and is leading to marginalization and stigmatization. In spite of strong ideological support for IDPs, there are reportedly widespread perceptions among host communities that in some way IDPs are responsible for the loss of their lands because they had not put up greater resistance to protect them.[e]

In Ukraine, the presence of IDPs is placing great strain on basic service delivery infrastructure in host communities.[f] Host communities have grown resentful and distrustful of authorities whom they blame for failing to compensate for the inflow and to protect local residents from economic shocks. This has further reduced the already low level of trust in local authorities and national institutions that predated the conflict.

a. UNHCR 2014d.
b. UNHCR 2014d.
c. UNHCR 2014d; Harb and Saab 2014.
d. Lopez, Arredondo, and Salcedo 2011.
e. World Bank 2011b.
f. World Bank 2015h.

agencies while that of the host community depends on the local socioeconomic environment. In other words, in areas where welfare levels come below humanitarian norms, hosts may fare worse than the forcibly displaced; in wealthier locations where welfare levels are above humanitarian norms, hosts tend to fare better. Still, many hosts regard the displaced as benefiting from "privileged" access to resources that are denied to them. For example, around the Buduburam refugee camp in Ghana, perceived discrimination over the distribution of land and water created tensions between hosts and refugees.[28] In Colombia, hostility toward displaced persons was exacerbated by the aid offered by the state: host communities resented the "special treatment" provided to IDPs vis-à-vis the non-IDP poor,[29] resulting in accusations that the displaced persons were "not truly displaced," "bad workers," or "people who do not work at all."

Social cohesion concerns evolve over time. With the passing of time, new symbiotic relationships gradually emerge between the displaced and their hosts. With IDPs, this often paves the way for their gradual inclusion into a transformed community. For refugees (and those IDPs subject to institutionalized segregation), the absence of legal solutions may prolong exclusion, which can weaken social cohesion, including among the hosts (box 3.5).[30] Longer-term concerns, such as insecurities over the ethnic or religious makeup of society, can also emerge, for example in some countries with many refugees, and where demographic growth is faster among the displaced than the hosts.

Economic growth and the budget—Medium-term impacts depend on whether refugees and IDPs can work

For most host countries, refugees account for less than 1 percent of the population. As such, their impact can only be relatively limited, especially compared to other factors that affect economic aggregates, such as global growth trends and commodity price fluctuations. For countries that host large numbers of refugees relative to their population the impact can be significant but it is often difficult to disentangle it from other economic spillovers of neighboring conflicts. Countries with large numbers of IDPs are almost by definition subject to high levels of violence, at least in some regions: the redistribution of the population can have large macroeconomic impacts, but they are difficult to separate from the other effects of the conflict.

The effect of hosting refugees on economic growth evolves over time, and largely depends on whether and how refugees are integrated into the labor market. In the short term, a refugee surge often translates into a modest increase in GDP growth, reflecting the support provided to refugees and the entry of newcomers into the labor force.[31] Lessons from economic migration suggest that the medium- and long-term impact is more complex and depends on whether refugees are allowed to join the labor market, and under what conditions. Legal rights, transferable job qualifications, and labor market flexibility largely determine the impact.[32]

The fiscal impact of hosting refugees also depends on their integration in the labor market. In the short term, it can be sizable, especially in the absence of substantial external assistance. For example, additional fiscal expenditure was estimated at 1 to 1.5 percent of GDP in Malawi in 1988–89,[33] and at 2 to 7 percent of GDP in Albania in the aftermath of the Kosovo crisis.[34] Such spending can soar when refugee flows are large: Turkey has reported spending more than US$6 billion to accommodate Syrian refugees over the last four years.[35] And it can be exacerbated by government policies: for example, where there are large consumption subsidies, a large inflow of people automatically triggers increased expenditure, thus increasing the pressure on fiscal accounts. In the medium term, the fiscal impact critically depends on whether refugees can engage in the formal economic sector and so contribute to tax revenues: if

> ## BOX 3.5 Forced displacement and crime
>
> Idleness and lack of hope can be factors of crime. Forcibly displaced persons are often perceived as potential criminals, as any outsider in close-knit communities. Evidence is limited and can be biased, for instance if asylum-seekers are disproportionately profiled by police forces. Yet, evidence points to a different conclusion. In the United Kingdom, asylum-seekers tend to be disproportionately represented in crime statistics, but once they are granted a formal refugee status and are allowed to engage in economic activity, they are no more likely to commit crime than other people in the same socioeconomic groups.[a] Similarly, in Switzerland, asylum-seekers who have been exposed to conflict and violence during childhood are more prone to violent crimes, but once they can access the labor market, the difference disappears.[b]
>
> a. Bell, Fasani, and Machin 2013.
> b. Couttenier et al. 2016.

they do, experience with economic migration suggests that it is eventually largely neutral.

In countries where the bulk of basic commodities are imported, the arrival of forcibly displaced persons may contribute to a trade deficit, at least in the short term, as the increase in demand translates into additional imports. Eventually, if the forcibly displaced are allowed to work, exports may also grow, which attenuates the earlier impact. The exchange rate may also appreciate in the short term, reflecting injections of foreign exchange into the economy—aid and refugee assets—along with an increase in demand for nontradable assets. However, such movements are often only temporary.

The macroeconomic impact can be far greater in countries that accommodate very large numbers of refugees relative to their population. This is the case for example in Jordan and Lebanon. In both countries, the presence of refugees has radically changed the environment in which the authorities were implementing poverty reduction and development programs for their own populations. The impact is substantial, and has many consequences, on growth, fiscal accounts, social services delivery, and poverty. Large amounts of external assistance are needed to support these countries in facing such challenges.[36]

Some gain, others lose: Local impacts on jobs and prices

Jobs

A local impact that can be significant
The impact of the displaced on the labor market is mostly local, but it can be significant. An inflow of forcibly displaced persons (whether refugees or IDPs) increases both the aggregate demand for goods and services and the labor supply in some segments of the job market. The increase in demand is typically driven by the consumption patterns of the forcibly displaced, humanitarian aid, and remittances. Depending on the structure of the economy, it may also create new jobs (box 3.6). The increase in labor supply may create competition with workers from host communities, and increase unemployment or depress wages. This can in principle be corrected either by a fall in wages or by an increase in investment: in the absence of either, it will lead to unemployment and dependency.

Initial conditions in the host economy largely determine the eventual impact of forced displacement on host communities. For instance, most large host countries are low- or middle-income, with high rates of unemployment that predate the influx of forcibly displaced. Such challenges tend to be particularly pressing in the regions of first arrival, which are often borderlands or lagging regions. Job creation is often hindered by a poor investment climate, which further complicates the investment response to a shock of this nature. Among the twelve largest host countries in 2014, all but two are in the bottom half of the World Bank Group's Ease of Doing Business index,[37] and their average ranking is 142 out of 189 countries.[38] Similarly, of the ten countries with the largest number of IDPs in 2014, six feature among the 30 worst destinations worldwide for business, with an average ranking of 121 out of 189.

The impact of aid workers on the local job market has been discussed in several studies. Evidence suggests that the direct impact is often minimal and transitory, and is focused on selected high-skilled individuals, in particular in the service sector.[39] For such people, getting a job in the aid sector can bring net wage gains, and in some cases public sector staff leave their position and join relief agencies.[40] The indirect labor market impact can be larger, as the presence of humanitarian workers creates trading opportunities.

Who is affected?
The labor market impact of forced displacement is unevenly distributed across socioeconomic groups within host communities. Employers and capital owners, as well as people whose skills are distinct from those of the incomers, may gain, while those whose skills put them in direct competition with the forcibly displaced can be negatively affected. In countries with a dual labor market, those in formally protected positions often benefit, while others may be exposed to negative effects. The response hence needs to include measures to help create jobs as well as mitigation policies to support specific socioeconomic groups within host communities.

BOX 3.6 Refugees as employers in Turkey[a]

In Turkey's open business environment, Syrian refugees have demonstrated their entrepreneurship. Syrian firms account for over a quarter of all new foreign-owned firms established annually. According to the latest figures from the Turkish Union of Chambers and Commodity Exchanges of Turkey, the number of Syrian-partnered firms established annually in Turkey increased from 30 in 2010 to 1,599 in 2015. A further 227 were set up in January 2016 alone.

Over the last four years, about 4,000 formal tax-paying Syrian-led firms (and an unknown number of informal businesses) have emerged in a broad range of sectors. Such firms are employing thousands of workers,

mostly Turks. They tend to concentrate in the restaurant, construction, trade, textile, real estate, travel, transportation, and foodstuffs industries.

The impact of these firms is greatest in provinces near the Syrian Arab Republic. In Hatay, Syrian firms numbered less than 1 percent of newly established firms in 2010; that number was 10.4 percent in 2014. In Kilis, no firms had Syrian partners in 2010; by 2014, 34 percent of new firms in the city had Syrian partners. The equivalent figure for Mersin was 15.7 percent. In Gaziantep, an economic hub in the southeast, the number of new Syrian firms rose from 3 in 2010 to 222 in 2014 (about 17 percent of the total), and reached over 600 in 2015.

a. Karasapan 2016b.

For instance, the abundance of refugee labor in the Karagwe district of western Tanzania enabled farmers to expand and increase production: between 1993 and 1996 cultivated areas doubled, as did banana and bean harvests.[41] In Guinea, the presence of Liberian refugees made it possible to push out rice cultivation to the lower swamp areas.[42] In Kenya, the Dadaab camp has evolved into a market with relatively solid purchasing power: this benefits those engaged in trade as well as pastoralists from within the host communities who produce milk and livestock,[43] and local wages are reportedly about 60 percent higher than in other comparable parts of the country.[44] Where there is a sufficiently conducive economic environment, such as in Turkey, host community workers can upgrade their skills, and specialize in more complex tasks that are associated with a higher set of competencies and provide higher incomes.[45]

In contrast, in western Tanzania in the mid-1990s, subsistence farmers were unable to compete with refugees in the labor market, and wages paid to casual laborers dropped by up to 50 percent in some areas.[46] Economic opportunities for women also dried up.[47] In Turkey, the presence of Syrian refugees has led to the "displacement" (within the labor market) of informal, low-educated, and female host community workers, especially in agriculture.[48] In Colombia, the inflow of IDPs led to a wage reduction of 28.4 percent among low-skilled workers, while wages and employment were not affected in the highly regulated formal sector.[49]

The factors that determine who gains and who is negatively affected from an inflow of forcibly displaced are multifold (box 3.7). They include the initial conditions in the host community, such as unemployment levels, skills, demographics, and labor market flexibility; the size and composition of the flow of displaced persons, including the extent to which their skills are complementary to, or overlapping with, those in the host community; and the policy response of the host government, including rural encampment, urban self-settlement, geographic mobility, and the right to work.[50] Often, the impact of the forcibly displaced is conflated with other factors that may have equally important or even larger effects, such as fluctuations in international prices of key commodities and global economic conditions.

BOX 3.7 The impact of Cuban refugees on Miami's labor market

In 1990, David Card published his classic analysis of the influx of Cuban migrants to Miami during the 1980 Mariel Boatlift.[a] Card found that, although the Mariel immigrants increased the labor force of the Miami metropolitan area by 7 percent, they had virtually no effect on the wage rates or unemployment levels of less-skilled non-Cuban workers, including other Hispanics and African-Americans. In fact, the Miami labor market was able to rapidly absorb the inflow of predominantly low-skilled Cuban immigrants. The presence of industries (e.g., garments) that could expand and provide jobs to unskilled migrants may have played an important role in this result. Interestingly, the arrival of Cuban refugees led to a reduction in the rate of migration into Miami from the rest of the United States: in other words, Cuban refugees may have taken the place of potential internal economic migrants who would have otherwise gone to Miami.

Following Card, many other instances of sudden migration surges have been analyzed and results have been similar, although some studies found somewhat greater effects on native wages in the range of 1 to 2 percent.[b] Studies of the Soviet Jews' immigration to Israel over the period of 1989–1997, yield particularly interesting conclusions.[c] The arrival of about 710,000 Soviet Jews from 1989 to 1997 increased Israel's working-age population by 15 percent over the eight-year period. The average effective wages of native Israelis initially fell and the return to capital increased in 1990 and 1991, while the current account deficit widened. An investment and construction boom, partly financed by foreign borrowing, followed. By 1997, both average wages and the return to capital had returned to pre-immigration levels.[d]

a. Card 1990.
b. See Hunt 1992; Carrington and De Lima 1996.
c. See Cohen and Hsieh 2000; Hercowitz and Yashiv 2001.
d. Friedberg 2001.

Where forcibly displaced persons heighten the competition for scarce job opportunities, governments are often tempted to respond by restricting their economic rights, especially for refugees since they are not citizens, in the hope that this will provide some degree of "protection" for nationals.[51] While such policies are largely detrimental to the forcibly displaced, the question is whether they are beneficial to host communities.

In fact, the debate over the right to work is largely an issue of political economy. Where there are opportunities, forcibly displaced persons often engage in the labor market, whether de jure or de facto. The discussion is often approached from a legal perspective, but most host countries have a very large informal sector, where people (including nationals) work regardless of formal rights. The informal market is estimated to account for about one-third of nonagricultural employment in Turkey, two-thirds of the economy in Sub-Saharan Africa, and over three-quarters in Pakistan.[52] In such contexts, the (lack of) "right to work" may not be much enforced.

In fact, the "right to work" determines not so much the economic engagement of refugees, but rather who within the host community is most likely to be negatively affected.[53] In situations where forcibly displaced persons are not permitted to work, or where their qualifications are not recognized, they compete in the informal labor market. This can negatively affect low-skilled and uneducated workers, as well as female workers, who tend to be over-represented in the informal sector. Where forcibly displaced persons are permitted to work (and where their qualifications are recognized), they tend to engage across the full spectrum of occupations. As a result they make a stronger (and taxable) contribution to the economy, but they may "displace" (within the labor market) other host community workers, including some who are more educated and often have a stronger voice in the political decision-making process.

Prices

A local impact

Changes in prices constitute one of the key channels for forced displacement to affect host communities. They may significantly alter the welfare of the poorest among host populations.[54] On the whole, the inflationary impact of forced displacement flows is primarily local, and mainly affects communities that host large numbers of refugees or IDPs. A large inflow of forcibly displaced often drives up inflation in the short term, as the demand for goods and services rapidly increases. In the medium term, however, the market often responds by increasing supply, so that prices return to an equilibrium.

The inflow of forcibly displaced is, however, taking place within a broader context. The formation of prices largely depends on the extent to which market forces are allowed to play their role. For instance, in economies with large consumption subsidies, the prices of the corresponding goods may not vary despite increased demand (which may entail heavy costs for the host government). In economies where there are controls on prices (for example, on rents), the market adjustments necessary to cope with an increase in population may not happen easily. The disruption of trade routes may also have a large impact. In Lebanon, for example, hosting communities in border areas have been hit by a decline in traditional agriculture and food trade with Syria.[55] And as with the economy more widely, global trends, including food and commodity prices, may have a far deeper effect on local prices than forced displacement.

Within host communities, those with better access to resources are more likely to benefit from forced displacement inflows, while the more disadvantaged become increasingly vulnerable, reinforcing inequalities.[56] Specific support may be needed for certain socioeconomic groups within host communities.

Food aid can push some prices down

The arrival of forcibly displaced can have a sharp impact on prices, but the tradable goods market can often respond quickly. Several factors may, however, hamper or delay the adjustment. In particular, the remoteness of hosting areas can complicate matters, and where markets do not function well, short-term impacts may be substantial and lasting. For example, in Darfur, Sudan, a study found strong correlations between the inflow of IDPs in 2004 and changes in food prices, with a strong increase in average prices for preferred items (sorghum and millet);[57] in Tanzania's refugee-hosting areas, prices of beans and carrots climbed respectively by 83 and 13 percent between 1993 and 1996.[58]

Price changes can be exacerbated by the provision of food aid, which distorts relative prices and may depress local production. Food aid and humanitarian rations are often resold on the local market, which can cause a drop in the price of aid items and an increase in the relative price of non-aid items. In a study of Kenya's Dadaab camp, the price of commodities such as maize, rice, wheat, sugar, and cooking oil reportedly stood at least 20 percent below prices in other arid and semi-arid towns in the country.[59] A study in Tanzania found a slump in the price of aid-delivered goods, such as maize, and an increase in the price of locally produced goods, such as beans, milk, and cooking bananas.[60] The overall impact of such variations on host communities is mixed, and various groups are affected in different ways. Consumers, for instance, typically benefit from lower prices, while local producers are hurt when aid lowers the demand for their products.

There have been intense debates over the relative merits of food aid and cash transfers to support poor and vulnerable groups. Cash aid has been shown to have large positive effects on household welfare, including multiplier effects for households other than the direct recipients, while food aid often acts as a disincentive to local production. This, however, assumes an effective functioning of the markets. When this is not the case, cash transfers can prompt a rise in food prices, and those who are neither targeted nor indirect beneficiaries may suffer welfare losses.[61] People living in remote areas are especially at risk if the shift from food to cash transfer programs is not accompanied by complementary measures.[62]

Housing and land—Prices go up

For nontradable goods like housing and land, the increase in demand usually results in higher prices, and the impact can be substantial.[63] This is especially so where forcibly displaced are concentrated in certain areas and are able to rent or buy property.[64] The inflow of the displaced tends to put pressure on the market for affordable housing, with detrimental effects for low-income host households.[65] In most cases, owners or those who can afford to sublet gain, while buyers or renters are negatively affected by the change in prices.[66]

In Colombia for instance, the arrival of IDPs increased demand for housing in urban areas, triggering a hike in prices. This benefited landlords but it also rendered home ownership inaccessible for many people who live in the slums of Bogota.[67] In Nyala, Sudan, the rental market expanded close to IDP camps, with clear distributional effects within the host community, depending on initial housing ownership.[68]

In the Arab Republic of Egypt, Iraq, Jordan, Lebanon, and Turkey, the influx of Syrian refugees has led to a housing shortage, which is driving up rents, especially for lower-income housing.[69] In Turkey, there is a widespread perception that rental prices have almost doubled in provinces along the border and that housing has become scarcer due to high demand. Surveys consistently conclude that along with food prices, rising house prices are the largest contributor to the inflation that has been experienced in the refugee-hosting areas.[70] Yet once again, initial conditions may play a large role: Turkey was already experiencing rising costs for affordable housing before the arrival of Syrian refugees;[71] and rent controls are causing a shortage of cheap accommodation in Egypt, which largely predated the arrival of refugees. Conversely, the relatively high prevalence of home ownership in Lebanon has meant that increases in rents affected primarily refugees rather than hosts.

Strains on local capacity for service delivery

The impact of forced displacement on service provision can be considerable, for both social services, where access can be controlled, and urban services where it is less easy to do so. Competition for services is also a frequent source of tension between forcibly displaced persons and their hosts.[72] The increase in demand has to be matched by a supply response, through external assistance or country systems (box 3.8).

Education: More kids to school

Because large numbers of refugees and IDPs are children and youth, their arrival increases demand for educational services, which may place a strain on public education systems. Urgent action is often needed to prevent the emergence of a "lost generation" and social tensions.[73]

In camp settings, the provision of services by humanitarian actors can lead to an increase in access that also benefits host communities. Humanitarian and government investment can successfully meet the new demand for education services while at the same time increasing access for host communities. For instance, a long term empirical study in Uganda found that private education is more prevalent in areas where refugees are

located.[74] In Zambia host children benefited from the presence of Mozambican refugees, as it improved their access to primary level education.[75] Meanwhile in the Dadaab camp in Kenya, host population's access to education increased significantly.[76]

Outside of camps, however, studies in both rural and urban hosting areas show that an inflow of forcibly displaced persons may be correlated with a decline in enrollment, educational attainment, and literacy among the hosts—unless significant amounts of assistance are provided. For example, in Colombia, the arrival of IDPs brought down educational enrollment in host areas: interestingly, the effect was three times higher for children from earlier waves of IDPs than for host children.[77] In Lebanon, to cope with the inflow of large numbers of Syrian refugees, the authorities established a two-shift system in public schools, which reduced school hours for Lebanese children.[78] In Amman and Irbid, Jordan, nearly half of schools suffer from overcrowding and they have very little capacity to absorb more students.[79] Meanwhile, in Iraq, the recent humanitarian crisis has put the education system under

BOX 3.8 Camps or country systems?

Host governments often have to decide whether to isolate forcibly displaced persons, typically in camps, or to integrate them into country systems.[a] Camps can offer an effective short-term response to avoid overwhelming existing services in the hosting area: additional services are typically provided by humanitarian agencies outside of regular country systems.[b] But such a solution is not sustainable unless continued flows of humanitarian assistance can be secured. On the other hand, refugees

and IDPs who are not in camps tend to receive services through country systems. This extra load may exacerbate pressures on delivery mechanisms which are often already under stress, including because of parallel demographic changes and internal economic migration.

Which approach works better? For the forcibly displaced who are in camps, services provided by humanitarian agencies may be superior to what is available locally, in terms of both accessibility and quality: shifting to country

systems may result in a net loss of welfare. But the overwhelming majority of refugees and IDPs do not have access to such services and their welfare depends on the strengthening of country systems. In the medium-term, scaling up such systems and including forcibly displaced persons (both refugees and IDPs) into them is likely to be the most cost-effective and equitable option, but the transition needs to be managed carefully, especially in those poor and remote regions where national systems are very weak.

a. Some hybrid approaches also exist such as the settlement model in Uganda.
b. In many cases, services provided in camps serve also members of the national population resident in or around the camps. In recent times, closer work with ministries of health and education, among others, are encouraging the use of humanitarian resources to support national service upscaling and provision.

considerable pressure, including through the use of schools as temporary shelters for IDPs.[80] In Kagera, Tanzania, the arrival of Burundian and Rwandese refugees in the 1990s led to a 7.1 percent reduction in schooling and an 8.6 percent drop in literacy in host communities.[81]

Health: More patients to treat

The impact on health service delivery can also be significant. The increased demand for health services can stretch local systems, creating a shortage in personnel and medical supplies and worsening the quality of care.[82] In Jordan, the refugee crisis resulted in steep increases in caseloads and in shortages of medicines in primary healthcare centers.[83] As a result, many Jordanians have turned to private healthcare providers, which is not easily affordable for the poorest.

The medium-term impact depends largely on the supply response. Investments by humanitarian agencies or host governments can help increase access, especially in rural areas where health services were not accessible. In Guinea, assistance programs increased health coverage for communities.[84] In Dadaab, Kenya, the availability of health services has been boosted thanks to humanitarian programs, and host communities' access levels are higher than in comparable arid parts of the country.[85] Yet, without adequate investments to meet the escalating needs caused by an inflow of refugees and IDPs, the risks are significant.[86] For example, in host regions in Tanzania in the mid-1990s, the presence of displaced persons has been linked to a 15 to 20 percent increase in the incidence of infectious diseases and a 7 percent rise in the under-five child mortality among hosts.[87] Aid can also substitute government programs and hence have limited effect: for example, in Uganda, a study found that communities hosting a larger number of refugees were less likely to have a government-funded health center because of the humanitarian presence.[88]

The spread of disease is also a potential danger. Forcibly displaced populations tend to face heightened risk of communicable diseases due to insalubrious living conditions such as low access to safe or adequate water and sanitation, poor vector control, and substandard housing, as well as limited access to basic health services, such as immunization for children.[89] For instance, the arrival of Syrian refugees to Jordan has led to an outbreak of hitherto eradicated communicable diseases such as tuberculosis and measles.[90] Outbreaks of polio in northern Syria and Iraq required a regional response of mass immunization in high-risk areas in Egypt, Iraq, Jordan, Lebanon, Syria, and Turkey throughout 2014.[91] Other diseases are also increasingly prevalent, such as acute respiratory infections and diarrhea among Iraqi children.[92]

Urban services: A clogged infrastructure

About 60 percent of the forcibly displaced—an estimated 35 million people—live in urban areas. This accounts for a relatively large share of urban growth in many host countries. For example, in Colombia, the urban population increased by an estimated 7 million people between 2002 and 2013, while the number of (largely urbanized) IDPs rose by about 2.9 million in the same period,[93] accounting for over 40 percent of total growth. The inflow of Syrian refugees in Lebanon also resulted in a significant increase in the population of urban centers. The impact is less pronounced in Sub-Saharan Africa where forcibly displaced persons predominantly live in rural settings or in camps.

Refugees and IDPs living in urban areas tend to cluster in densely populated and poorly serviced environments. Their arrival is typically accompanied by an expansion of slums, and by increased pressure on urban services. Heightened competition and conflicts over limited urban resources such as land and water affects the most vulnerable among the hosts and can generate tensions.[94] Depending on the concentration of new arrivals and the state of existing infrastructure, challenges range from public transportation to urban pollution, from solid waste management to availability of water and electricity, from the management of cemeteries to that of cell phone networks. Like other poor migrants, the forcibly displaced may also settle on land prone to natural disasters such as flooding and earthquakes.[95]

In many respects, from a host city perspective, the challenges are identical whether the newly arrived are rural migrants or forcibly displaced persons (box 3.9). In countries where there is adequate capacity to manage urban growth the shock can be absorbed. Where such capacity is lacking the shock may further destabilize an already precarious situation. Substantial investments may be needed, as well as proactive policies to provide land, housing, and services for the new residents. Urban planning can help match physical expansion with access to jobs, affordable housing and shopping, public transportation, and health and education services, including for disadvantaged communities.

The environment: Overtaxed resources

The sudden arrival of large numbers of forcibly displaced often causes severe environmental impacts on land, water, and natural resources. Some of the immediate effects include fuel wood shortages and water pollution around camps or other areas of high concentration. As the emergency period passes and refugees become more settled, the nature of the impact changes, but can still be significant. For example, in arid areas, the continued presence of the forcibly displaced may accelerate the depletion of water resources; in some urban settings, solid waste management can become an issue where

---

BOX 3.9 Regional development

Can refugee and IDP camps or settlements become poles of growth in hosting areas, and in the process facilitate the economic development of lagging regions? Some host countries accommodate forcibly displaced persons in marginalized, borderland regions, which are sparsely inhabited and economically struggling. Camps or settlements can become the main medium-size population centers in such areas. The argument has hence been made that the inflow of forcibly displaced persons, and the corresponding flows of aid, can provide an opportunity for local development.

There is indeed ample evidence that camps and settlements located in remote areas can become the epicenter of regional life, especially when situations become protracted. They tend to draw in local people (especially among the poor) on account of the increased economic opportunities and access to humanitarian services. They can hence become poles of growth in otherwise

destitute regions. For example, Dadaab town in Kenya has developed significantly over the last two decades from a cluster of rudimentary shelters to a busy regional center. This growth has been accompanied by a rapid rise in property prices where roadside plots are changing hands at premium rates due to speculation by developers. The total annual benefits of the camp operation for the local host community (direct and indirect) were estimated at around US$82 million in 2009.[a] In Tanzania, the increase in the size of the local markets due to the presence of refugees also boosted business and trade activities for both hosts and refugees, and the welfare of neighboring host communities improved, as measured by indicators such as electricity, televisions, and refrigerators.[b]

Such a growth model, however, has serious flaws. It relies on large flows of external assistance, with limited development of any capacity to produce goods and services that

can be marketed outside of the humanitarian context. In other words, it is often artificial and unsustainable once international flows of aid dry up. Indeed, there is no single example of a large refugee or IDP camp that has continued to act as a pole of regional growth after the termination of aid programs.

Infrastructure developed to deliver humanitarian aid can have long-lasting positive effects on the welfare of communities, for example, where roads are built that connect previously isolated areas.[c] Such side effects of external assistance are welcome and may be durable. Yet, from a broader development perspective, the question is whether using scarce resources to build infrastructure in remote areas is most efficient. There is evidence that this may not be the case, and that investing in "people" (i.e. skills, etc.) so that they can move to areas where there are economic opportunities may be more effective than investing in "places."[d]

a. NORDECO 2010.
b. Whitaker 2002.
c. Maystadt and Verwimp 2009.
d. World Bank 2009.

existing systems cannot cope with a large increase in the quantity of waste.

Several studies on deforestation provide an illustration of the environmental impact of forced displacement. In eastern Democratic Republic of Congo, the presence of Rwandese refugees in the 1990s severely deteriorated forests, soil, wildlife, and water supplies. An estimated 3,800 hectares of forestland were lost within three weeks of the arrival of refugees, especially in Goma and at the Virunga National Park.[96] A study on some 600,000 Sierra Leonean and Liberian refugees who fled into southern Guinea found that in rural host areas the hunger for arable land contributed to deforestation, a shortening of fallow periods (leading to a decrease in soil fertility), and the conversion of swamps into agricultural areas.[97] This environmental impact has direct consequences for the welfare of the host population. For example, in some hosting areas in Tanzania, deforestation means that women have had to spend 23 percent more time on wood collection and 18 percent more time on water collection.[98]

Such impacts are closely associated with settlement patterns: camps pose the biggest threat to the environment,[99] while the pressure and demands imposed on local resources are more diffuse when the forcibly displaced are more dispersed.[100] In Dadaab, Kenya, the existence and location of the camp has put enormous stress on the natural resources of the surrounding areas, specifically water resources and wood.[101] In contrast, where refugees are distributed between small settlements or in existing villages, such as in the Dedza and Ntcheu districts in Malawi, the impact on local firewood resources has been less extreme.[102] Where the forcibly displaced interact with their hosts, the local population also has sway over whether and how refugees use communal land and local resources, and how these resources are controlled.[103]

An agenda for development actors

Host countries and host communities lead their own development agenda. To help them manage the shock and make further progress in their own development and poverty reduction efforts in a transformed environment, development actors should engage in several areas: to help deal with preexisting issues through "traditional" development programs; to support the most vulnerable among the hosts and those who are negatively affected; to help strengthen and expand service delivery; and to support sound policies on right to work, encampment, and aid delivery.

Development partners need to help design a response that is not only technically sound, but that can also be implemented in a complex political context. They have a role to play in helping to shape the policy-making environment, for instance through analytics and contributions to the public debate. But they also have to take a pragmatic stance that takes into account the political realities on the ground.

Help tackle long-standing development problems

Development actors should support a broad-based, "traditional" development agenda, as a critical element of the response to the crisis. In many situations this may be one of their most important contributions. Refugees and IDPs are predominantly hosted in low- and middle-income countries, which typically face a wide array of development challenges. This can include a high degree of fragility, a poor business environment, an inadequate social protection system, a limited access to services, etc.

Development actors should also help ensure that forced displacement considerations are included in host countries' development strategies. The inflow of forcibly displaced persons often calls for a redefinition of priorities, to reflect changing needs and political economy considerations. Shifting priorities often include the need for a stronger focus on hosting areas, especially for lagging regions or where there are large regional inequalities. Actions may be needed to strengthen the infrastructure or to equip people within host communities with the skills they need to prosper.

Most importantly, the development response must include an emphasis on jobs. Public works programs and other subsidized schemes may provide temporary relief but they need to be rapidly followed by private sector-led job creation. Private sector investment in refugee-hosting areas is likely to be largely driven by business considerations: the regulatory environment, the demand from local and international markets, the quality of infrastructure, the availability of adequately skilled workers, etc. Development actors can both help tackle these issues and provide guarantees and loans or equity investments to private firms. The agricultural sector, in particular, can provide important opportunities for investments to help create jobs, including for low-skilled native workers.

Support those who are negatively affected

The impact of forced displacement on host communities is unevenly distributed. As a first step, development actors need to identify the groups who may require support, evaluate their vulnerabilities and their coping strategies (which may vary across subgroups), assess the political economy, and select entry points to provide assistance.

Deveopment actors should place an emphasis on labor market interventions. Those who are competing with the forcibly displaced for scarce jobs can benefit from programs designed to upgrade their skills or to otherwise enhance their employment opportunities. Efforts to improve productivity, for example in the rural sector, may also help maintain or even increase incomes in an altered environment. Development actors have significant experience with such programs across a broad range of countries at various development stages: from agricultural productivity and extensions services programs in low-income countries affected by climate change to the retraining of industrial workers in the wake of restructurings in upper middle-income countries.

Parallel action is needed to strengthen social protection programs. Labor market programs typically take time to yield results. And some people may face difficulties in upgrading their skills, for example among the illiterate or older workers. Some groups are likely to remain highly vulnerable, including minorities and female-headed households.

Social protection programs need to be tailored to each situation: the level of development of the host country, the availability of fiscal or other resources, and the expectations placed by society on the authorities.

Assist in expanding services

Development actors need to help provide for a supply response that can match the increased demand caused by the forcibly displaced for social as well as urban and environmental services. This typically requires major investment, as well as sustained support for operations and maintenance. External assistance may be needed to mobilize resources within a short time frame, so as to rapidly scale up delivery and to minimize (or even to avoid) any period of severe disruption. Recent experience, including that in OECD countries, suggests that managing such a scaling up in a relatively short period of time can be challenging.

Support may be required to help expand infrastructure (such as schools, dispensaries, sanitation, and power distribution), to strengthen systems, and to cover operating costs. Part of this can be financed through public resources, including external assistance. In some contexts, there may be an opportunity to use the skills of refugees and IDPs to expand services. Efforts may also be needed to attract private sector providers, including through public–private partnerships, as well as to support the provision of specific services through civil society organizations.

Investing large amounts of resources in infrastructure may appear to be a risky decision, considering that the presence of forcibly displaced persons is in principle temporary. Some host authorities may also be reluctant to engage in activities which suggest that refugees and IDPs may stay: this is a signal that their constituencies may find unwelcome. Yet, the risks of investing are often outweighed by the risks of inaction. A number of situations become protracted and the lack of sustainable support to host communities is likely to lead to prolonged negative outcomes. Furthermore, hosting areas are often relatively underserviced, and the investments needed to upgrade delivery are likely to help remedy preexisting shortages. In countries and regions where demographic growth is often significant, they are unlikely to be left unused even if and when forcibly displaced persons eventually move on.

Providing support for operations and maintenance is also challenging. Services often benefit the forcibly displaced and their hosts, especially urban services which typically have a public good element. National systems should cover the costs tied to the services that benefit host communities, although there may be a need for external support to smoothen the transition if the scaling up of delivery is rapid (that is, if amortization cannot be properly scheduled over time, or if cost-recovery mechanisms are not yet in place). There may also be an argument that external support is needed over the medium-term to cover expenditure that benefits the forcibly displaced, especially refugees who are not nationals.

Support freedom of movement, the right to work, and improvements in aid delivery

Development actors should encourage relevant stakeholders, both host governments and external agencies, to adopt "host-friendly" solutions: policies and aid delivery approaches that can have positive economic effects on host communities. Such solutions should be tailored to each situation. Yet, in a few areas, "default options" can be identified which should generally lead to positive outcomes, although in some contexts an alternative course of action might be preferable.

For governments, restrictive policies on refugees and IDPs—whether encampment or denial of the right to work or otherwise engage in economic activity—have proven largely unnecessary or ineffective to address concerns over security and employment issues. Wherever appropriate, development actors should support an agenda of free movement and participation in the labor market through a combination of analytics, to help inform public debate, and financing, to smoothen the transitions (box 3.10).

For aid agencies, a multi-fold shift is required to strengthen effectiveness and to ensure that programs can benefit and support the most vulnerable in host countries, not only among the forcibly displaced but also among the poorest hosts.

First, continued efforts are needed to ensure that assistance targets both forcibly displaced persons and their hosts in a given area. This is critical to the success of aid efforts.[104] Aid programs that also target host communities and that build links between both groups have a track record of reducing perceptions of injustice. For example, in Uganda, area-based programs have been supported by the United Nations High Commissioner for Refugees (UNHCR), as part of a comprehensive approach that responds to the needs of both refugees and host communities: this has been seen as successful in promoting peaceful coexistence.[105]

Second, the use of cash rather than in-kind assistance has proven more effective in areas where markets are functioning. It can become a critical instrument to boost local production, and hence to create economic opportunities in host communities. This typically benefits both the hosts and the displaced.

Third, a gradual transition of aid delivery mechanisms towards using country systems (for example for the delivery of education services) can both strengthen the sustainability of assistance programs and ensure a better degree of fairness between the hosts and the displaced. It can also facilitate interactions between both groups, and as such reduce the scope for social tensions. Such a transition should be managed effectively, however, so as to ensure that country systems are upgraded before they take on the extra load.

BOX 3.10 Support for formalizing Syrian refugees in Jordan

The World Bank Group is finalizing the preparation of a project in support of Syrian refugees in Jordan. Among other features, this operation will provide support to Jordanian authorities for the issuance of up to 200,000 work permits for Syrian refugees. This is the outcome of a positive and proactive dialogue with the government, in a country where many refugees are already engaged in the informal labor market. Allowing the refugees to work is seen as a solution that can benefit not only the displaced, but hosting Jordanian communities, too. The operation is also financing support for developing private sector activities, to create opportunities that the refugees—and their hosts—may well seize.

Notes

1. For example, UNHCR's policy has for a long time been to ensure that the services established for refugees and IDPs—even in camp settings—are available to the local population.
2. For the purposes of this chapter, when referring to "host community" we mean the populations living in the vicinity of areas hosting refugees and IDPs, irrespective of whether their welfare is affected by the arrival of forcibly displaced.
3. Chambers 1979, 1986.
4. Chambers 1986; Ruiz and Vargas-Silva 2013.
5. Chambers 1986.
6. Jacobsen and Bakewell 2013.
7. Kriebaum 2016.
8. Hammerstadt 2014.
9. In the post-Cold War era, the existence of a connection between the presence of refugees and the onset of conflict in the host country has been controversial. See for example Zolberg, Suhrke, and Aguayo 1989; Salehyan and Gleditsch 2006; Loescher 1992. See also Sambanis 2002; Fearon and Laitin 2003; Marshall and Gurr 2003; Beissinger 2007; Gleditsch 2007; Salehyan and Gleditsch 2006; Salehyan 2007, 2009; Choi and Salehyan, 2013. Some studies have found a correlation between hosting refugees and increased odds of conflict. This is attributed to refugees exacerbating ethnic tensions, intensifying economic competition, and expanding insurgent networks. See Salehyan and Gleditsch 2006. Also see Salehyan 2007, 2009. It is a narrative which is often echoed in media reports, see Herszenhorn 2015; Erlanger and Smale 2015; Shafy 2013; Shinkman 2013; Harrigan and Easen 2001. However, other studies contest these findings, noting that the majority of refugees are often noncombatants who do not engage in conflict: children (who typically account for about half of the total), women, and people who are incapable of, or disinterested in, fighting, see Matthews 1972;

Whitaker 2003; Onoma 2013; Hazlett 2013. Indeed, recent findings from camps find no support for claims that refugees degrade security conditions in their host communities: on the contrary, areas hosting large numbers of refugees are comparatively more secure than the rest of the country, see Shaver and Zhou 2015.

10. Authors' calculations. These cases were: the destabilization of host countries (Côte d'Ivoire, Guinea, Sierra Leone) by Liberian refugees in the mid-1990s / early 2000s; the destabilization of Eastern Zaire in 1994, and the subsequent civil war in what became the Democratic Republic of Congo; the inflow of refugees from Darfur and the subsequent 2005 war in Chad; population movements between Burundi and Rwanda which preceded the 1993 and 1994 genocides; and the increase in civil strife in Northwest Pakistan which is hosting large numbers of Afghan refugees.
11. Lischer 2005.
12. Whitaker 2003.
13. Zolberg, Suhrke, and Aguayo 1989.
14. The impact of refugee camps may have been higher during the Cold War, when large groups of people often followed leaders in exile and formed an alternative state in the host country. Camps could then constitute military bases for refugee-warriors to continue opposition activities, as described by Zolberg, Suhrke, and Aguayo 1989.
15. Authors' calculations. These cases were: the destabilization of host countries (Côte d'Ivoire, Guinea, Sierra Leone) by Liberian refugees in the mid-1990s / early 2000s; the destabilization of Eastern Zaire in 1994, and the subsequent civil war in what became the Democratic Republic of Congo; the inflow of refugees from Darfur and the subsequent 2005 war in Chad; population movements between Burundi and Rwanda which preceded the 1993 and 1994 genocides; and the increase in civil strife in Northwest Pakistan which is hosting large numbers of Afghan refugees.

16. World Bank 2011a.
17. See Bohnet, Cottier, and Hug 2013. The data sets used in such studies, however, are weak (in the absence of solid data on IDPs and their locations), and the results are hence open to controversy.
18. As UNHCR makes clear in Addressing Security Concerns Without Undermining Refugee Protection—UNHCR's Perspective any consideration of displaced persons' involvement in criminal activity generally and in terrorism needs to start with the recognition that refugees and IDPs "are themselves escaping persecution and violence, including terrorist acts. International refugee instruments do not provide a safe haven to terrorists and do not protect them from criminal prosecution. On the contrary, they render the identification of persons engaged in terrorist activities possible and necessary, foresee their exclusion from refugee status and do not shield them against criminal prosecution, nor do they prevent extradition or expulsion. UNHCR 2015b, para. 7.
19. Crawley 2009.
20. Refugee Studies Centre 2011, p. 78.
21. Hovil 2014.
22. Mkandawire 2015.
23. Aiyar et al. 2016.
24. Aiyar et al. 2016.
25. Jacobsen 2001.
26. Chambers 1986; Kibreab 1985; Castles and Miller 1998.
27. Jacobsen and Bakewell 2013.
28. Agblorti 2011.
29. Lopez 2011.
30. Castles and Miller 1998; Partridge 2008; Jacobsen and Bakewell 2013.
31. Couttenier et al. 2016
32. Aiyar et al. 2016.
33. Government of Malawi et al. 1990.
34. World Bank 1999.
35. World Bank 2015a.
36. IMF 2014, 2015; World Bank 2013b.
37. World Bank 2016b.
38. These are: Turkey (55), Pakistan (138), Lebanon (123), the Islamic Republic of Iran (118), Ethiopia (146), Jordan (113), Kenya (108), Chad (183), Uganda (122), China (84), Afghanistan (177), Sudan (159).
39. Landau 2004.
40. Whitiker 2002; Buscher and Vlassenroot 2010; NORDECO 2010.
41. Whitiker 2002; Van Damme 1995.
42. Van Damme 1995.
43. NORDECO 2010.
44. NORDECO 2010.
45. Cattaneo, Fiorio, and Peri 2015; D'Amuri and Peri 2014; Foged and Peri 2015; Beerli and Peri 2015.
46. Whitiker 2002; Kibreab 1985.
47. Whitiker 2002.
48. Del Carpio and Wagner 2015; World Bank 2015a.
49. Calderón-Mejía and Ibáñez 2015.
50. Aiyar et al. 2016.
51. For the signatories of the 1951 Convention, this is a violation of their obligations: under the Convention, host countries are to grant economic rights to refugees akin to those enjoyed by nationals.
52. ILO 2012.
53. Ruiz and Vargas-Silva 2013; Chambers 1986.
54. Mabiso et al. 2014; Werker 2007.
55. UN 2016.
56. Mabiso et al. 2014; Maystadt and Verwimp 2009.
57. Alix-Garcia, Bartlett, and Saah 2012.
58. Landau 2004.
59. Alix-Garcia, Bartlett, and Saah 2012.
60. Alix-Garcia and Saah 2010; Alix-Garcia 2007.
61. Gelan 2006.
62. Kebede 2006.
63. A few authors have looked at the impact of the aid community on housing prices. The presence of aid workers tends to induce price hikes and alter the type of housing demanded, see Buscher and Vlassenroot 2010. Yet, these pressures do typically not affect the majority of hosts who overwhelmingly rely on in a different segment of the housing market.
64. Bakewell 2014.
65. Aiyar et al. 2016.
66. Norwegian Refugee Council 2014.
67. Lopez et al. 2011.

68. Alix-Garcia 2007.
69. UN 2016.
70. ORSAM 2015.
71. World Bank 2015b; Harild, Christensen, and Zetter 2015.
72. REACH 2014.
73. Aiyar et al. 2016.
74. Kreibaum 2016.
75. Black 1994.
76. NORDECO 2010.
77. Calderón-Mejía and Ibáñez 2015.
78. UN 2016.
79. Francis 2015.
80. UN 2016.
81. Baez 2011.
82. UN 2016.
83. Francis 2015.
84. Van Damme et al. 1998.
85. NORDECO 2010.
86. Baez 2011, Singh 2001.
87. Baez 2011.
88. Kreibaum 2016.
89. UN 2016.
90. Francis 2015.
91. UN 2016.
92. UN 2016.
93. IDMC 2015.
94. Zetter and Deikun 2010.
95. World Bank 2010, 2015d.
96. Biswas and Tortajada-Quiroz 1996.
97. UNEP 1999.
98. Whitaker 1999, 2002
99. Jacobsen 1997.
100. Jacobsen 1997.
101. NORDECO 2010.
102. Wilson, Cammack, and Shumba 1989.
103. Jacobsen 1997.
104. Betts 2009a.
105. World Bank 2016d.

Reducing the Vulnerabilities of the Forcibly Displaced

4

Development approaches are geared towards helping people escape poverty. The goal is no different when it comes to forcibly displaced persons. Whether forcibly displaced persons are fleeing conflict or are the targets of political violence, their lives are being turned upside down and their hopes are dashed. This can lead to a "poverty trap" from which it is hard to escape, and which can have a lasting impact across several generations. Self-reliance is key to restoring their dignity, as well as their ability to earn a living.

Specific development interventions may be needed. Forcibly displaced persons are often not able to take full advantage of existing opportunities for poverty reduction. This is because they have acquired specific vulnerabilities through their forced displacement experience, which make them less prone to successful socioeconomic inclusion and more exposed to risks. They may require targeted assistance to overcome these vulnerabilities, and to regain the capacity to improve their situation.[1] The scale of the challenge is particularly acute when the forcibly displaced are "in limbo," with uncertain prospects for the future. In such cases, the objective is to help strengthen their capacity to seize opportunities not only in the current environment, but also under likely scenarios for the future.

Acknowledging and analyzing the specific vulnerabilities of forcibly displaced persons is vital to provide effective support. Although socioeconomic outcomes vary, across situations and individuals in the same situation,[2] some traits and experiences are shared across most contexts. These set the forcibly displaced apart from other poor and vulnerable groups, and that is why it is valid to treat them as a distinct category.

Forced displacement is accompanied by loss and trauma. The losses are often catastrophic, including physical and monetary assets as well as human and social capital. They set back individuals, households, and communities in their efforts to escape poverty and can have lasting consequences. Many forcibly displaced persons also undergo traumatic experiences: there is increasing evidence that this can hamper an individual's ability to build relationships and to seize economic opportunities.

In some situations, the shock is such that it may even swamp differences in initial conditions. Each forcibly displaced person has his or her own set of skills, experiences, and social networks before fleeing, which can explain differences in outcomes once displaced. Yet forced displacement can also act as an equalizer of conditions, pushing people of different backgrounds into the same poverty trap, and those who fared well before displacement may end up among the poorest once in exile.[3]

Over time, the situation of the forcibly displaced and their vulnerabilities evolve. For a large majority, the shock has a lasting impact, sometimes extending across generations.[4] For some people, time is the best healer and there is continuous progress towards a relatively satisfactory socioeconomic outcome. For a few, the recovery is complete, and they even manage to achieve a degree of economic success in spite of dire circumstances, or they become part of societies far more affluent than the one they left. For large groups, however, an extended displacement translates into a gradual depletion of the few assets they had left and a shrinking of opportunities, forcing them to pursue increasingly dangerous strategies.[5]

Economic opportunities are critical to mitigating and eventually overcoming the impact of losses and trauma. They may not be sufficient in some cases, but they are necessary. Having a job and an income is critical to rebuild lost assets over time, to maintain or further develop human capital and dignity, and to reestablish social networks. It can also help overcome the impact of trauma.

The path to recovery is often constrained by host countries' policies and to a lesser extent by aid agencies' programs. Refugees and internally displaced persons (IDPs) are economic actors who through their resilience and their decisions can mitigate (or exacerbate) the impact of their displacement experience. But such decisions are not made in a vacuum. While vulnerabilities are initially caused by a shock, they are often aggravated (or in some cases offset) by policy decisions, which can be influenced by external actors, including development actors.

Key factors relate to rights, location, and prospects. Forcibly displaced persons, especially refugees, tend to have restricted rights in the place where they live. This can limit their ability to work, or to otherwise engage in socioeconomic activity. It often leads to heightened dependency on humanitarian support or to possible abuse in the informal labor market. A number of refugees and IDPs also find asylum in borderlands or in places where there are very few economic opportunities. Some are in environments that are culturally or linguistically foreign and in which socio-economic inclusion is difficult. Being in the "wrong place" can make it all but impossible to develop a successful self-reliance strategy and this can have a lasting impact if no remedy is found. For most of the forcibly displaced medium-term prospects can remain unclear for a relatively long period of time. This makes it difficult to invest efforts

and resources in endeavors that take time to yield their full benefits. It can also lead to suboptimal or even counterproductive decisions with lasting negative effects.

Development actors need to distinguish between the vulnerability factors that stem directly from displacement—losses and trauma—and those grounded in the policies and decisions of host countries and international agencies—primarily rights, location, and planning horizon. Once displacement is under way, development actors can do little to mitigate the direct impact, but they can help create a better environment for recovery.

The initial setback: Losses and trauma

Sudden and catastrophic losses

The sudden and often catastrophic loss of assets experienced by most refugees and IDPs is a critical cause of impoverishment and vulnerability. Being displaced by conflict and violence often implies seeing property being seized or stolen, leaving behind assets that cannot be easily transported, spending relatively large sums during the journey, losing access to social networks, and having to use available resources to sustain oneself once at destination. Such losses can be difficult to remedy. They can push people into destitution and create a "poverty trap" from which it is often difficult to escape.

The experience of losing assets is distinct from that of poverty. Most refugees and displaced persons see their incomes (and social status) shrink as a result of their flight. They are often unable to find adequate work and their savings are gradually depleted. This makes it difficult to maintain previous living standards. What was considered normal, no longer is so. What was considered affordable is now out of reach. While extreme poverty is always a tragedy, falling into poverty and even destitution may have an additional impact on the sense of dignity of the displaced.

The poverty impact of such losses can be shattering. For example, IDP households in Uganda experienced a 28 to 35 percent decrease in consumption, as well as a significant decrease in the value of their assets compared with nondisplaced households. These effects were still felt two years after displacement, and there was no recovery for the bottom quartile households, who appeared to be trapped in poverty.[6] In Colombia IDP household consumption and income fell by 53 and 28 percent respectively, taking the majority of the displaced below the extreme poverty line.[7] In Afghanistan, a study found a 37 percent decrease in ownership levels among Afghan IDPs,[8] and even after five years in displacement, 61 percent of them remained in temporary housing, wracked by insecurity.[9]

There are wide socioeconomic inequalities among the forcibly displaced.[10] The extent of losses, of assets as well as social networks, partly explains such differences in outcomes. Those who manage to flee with more capital or who have access to social networks in their host community may fare relatively better, while the ones who lost most of their property and resources and are isolated in their new environment are at a high risk of lasting destitution.

Some groups may find it particularly difficult to overcome losses. For instance, among pastoralists in the Sahel, the loss of cattle goes beyond the material impact: it affects status and alters an entire way of life.[11] Time also plays an important role. For instance, at the Dadaab camp in Kenya, longer-term Somali refugees tend to be better off than new arrivals.[12] In Colombia, there is a gradual divergence over time between those who manage to restore a degree of normalcy and those who go down a spiral of impoverishment and marginalization.[13]

Assets

The most widespread loss of assets is that of fixed capital, such as land and housing, whose destruction or loss is often the very trigger for displacement.[14] In Colombia, 83 percent of IDPs had their land confiscated or were forced to abandon it when they left.[15] The loss of land is often definitive, especially when legal ownership has never been formally documented, when land title deeds are missing or were never issued, or when laws are poorly enforced.[16]

Displacement also leads to losses of portable assets, such as livestock and financial resources. People may try to transfer or liquidate their assets before fleeing, but it is often hard to do so in an orderly manner. They typically engage in "fire sales" in markets that are dysfunctional and where they are unlikely to obtain much. When people have time to plan for their flight the losses can be smaller than when they have to leave suddenly.[17]

Displacement is costly, especially when people are displaced multiple times.[18] For example, 62 percent of IDPs in the Central African Republic have reportedly been displaced at least twice, with each new round of movement causing further losses.[19] The situation is aggravated when the forcibly displaced have little or no income to finance their consumption or onward movement. Savings can deplete fast.

Human capital

The forcibly displaced often have particular demographic characteristics, notably a large share of dependents and vulnerable persons (children under the age of 15 account for about half the total). This contrasts with economic migrants—who are often self-selected among able-bodied adults—which means that many forcibly displaced are less able to seize socioeconomic opportunities and to achieve a degree of self-reliance in the short term.

When refugees and IDPs cannot engage in productive activities, they gradually lose their skills—in a process similar to that of the long-term unemployed—which makes it harder for them to eventually reenter the workforce. In many situations, the forcibly displaced have little choice but to take positions for which they may be overqualified, especially when they are officially not allowed to work. This worsens their vulnerabilities and reduces their economic prospects.

Children and youth face specific difficulties. Many have missed schooling, sometimes for an extended period of time. Their reintegration in an education system may be complicated, especially where they do not speak the language or where they have to work for their families to make ends meet. This can have lasting consequences at the level of individuals, as well as for entire societies if a large part of a generation misses out on education opportunities.

Social capital

Social capital and social networks are critical to rebuilding economic prospects. They often largely explain the different tiers of vulnerability of the forcibly displaced.[20] Many Somali refugees for example do much better than their Burundian and Congolese counterparts in Uganda and than their South Sudanese counterparts in Kenya, mainly because of their social connections.[21] In Pakistan, social ties among refugees have facilitated their integration: networks can help with accommodation, informal employment, welfare support and liaison with local authorities and representatives.[22]

Successive displacements may make it difficult for the forcibly displaced to rebuild social networks. Many anecdotal reports suggest that it can take several movements before people "settle" (temporarily) in a given place: yet creating social capital takes time, generally years.

Counterproductive coping strategies

Having lost assets and having little or no economic opportunity, some of the forcibly displaced adopt coping mechanisms that are counterproductive over the long term. These include selling their remaining productive assets, at the risk of aggravating poverty and of making an eventual recovery more difficult. Such sales have been documented in many situations, including most recently for Syrian refugees in Jordan and Lebanon.[23] They often mark a further step in a downward spiral of impoverishment.

Coping strategies may also include child labor, even for young children, as seen among Somali refugees in Kenya and Syrian refugees in Turkey. These children are missing out on education opportunities, and risk being trapped in poverty for their entire adulthood. Some households in Afghanistan and elsewhere are also resorting to sending unaccompanied minors to faraway destinations, at great risk: several tens of thousands of children and teens have reportedly gone unaccompanied to the European Union over the last couple of years, with large numbers disappearing along the way.[24]

Refugee and IDP women may also have to engage in prostitution or other forms of transactional sex, leaving lasting mental scars and, often, social exclusion. Among the poorest Syrian refugees in Jordan, there has been a reported increase in early marriage of young girls aged 14–16 or less. While many poor families traditionally secure their financial status through the marriage of their daughters, the practice is accelerated in displacement as a way to cope with impoverishment. In this sense the loss of assets is not only a temporary setback: it can define the rest of one's life.[25]

Psychological trauma

The stress of forced displacement can provoke impacts that directly impair the ability to escape poverty. Psychological trauma and distress have long been neglected by development actors. Yet unless these issues are addressed, socioeconomic recovery may remain elusive.

Stress and violence

Living in war-torn areas is intensely stressful, and it can have profound impacts on the social, emotional, and psychological state of the individual. Over 30 percent of people living in conflict-affected regions suffer from post-traumatic stress disorder.[26] In the Central African Republic for instance, nearly half the displaced population had a direct experience with war (45 percent), a quarter had witnessed a killing (27 percent), and around 1 in 15 had been raped (6 percent).[27] Even when people flee before being victimized, they often suffer from a sense of general insecurity.

The ordeal of forced displacement adds to this stress, and it may be intensified by separation from family and the hardship of the journey. Once at destination, confusion and insecurity in unfamiliar surroundings, uncertainty about the future, and disruptive living conditions all make for a very stressful environment. A sudden impoverishment, lower access to basic services, and a loss of social status have also been correlated with a higher incidence of psychological disorders.[28] A large body of evidence shows a high prevalence of mood and anxiety disorders among refugees and IDPs (box 4.1).[29] While many individuals and communities demonstrate astonishing resilience, others experience continued psychological distress, which impairs their daily functioning.

When displacement is protracted, mental suffering increases. Continued exposure to stress in the aftermath of a traumatic event has been linked to an increased incidence of psychological disorders.[30] A lasting stay in limbo diminishes resilience, while the stress induced by the uncertainty of future prospects is not conducive to recovery.[31] A recent study of Azerbaijani IDPs, displaced over 20 years ago, shows that psychological impacts can be lasting.[32] Perhaps worse, they can extend to the core of a person's sense of identity, causing a loss of trust in society and confidence in oneself.[33]

Managing psychological disorders—a long-term undertaking under the best of conditions—is extremely difficult in displacement situations. Support is rarely available, and the stigma attached to psychological health often creates a barrier to treatment. Left untreated, such disorders can have debilitating effects, and affect prospects for the next generation.

Risk aversion and lowered expectations

The impact of trauma and psychological disorders is not limited to psychological well-being. It can impair an individual's social functioning and develop into anxiety and depressive disorders,[34] affecting the whole household.[35]

Psychological injury can permanently alter the mindset and behavior of the displaced and make them more risk averse and more fearful of potential future shocks.[36] As a result, they may make suboptimal decisions that increase their vulnerability to poverty.[37] In Afghanistan, entire population groups, regardless of income levels, were found to prefer secure outcomes over uncertain but potentially more profitable ones.[38] In Colombia, displaced persons were found to grow subsistence crops instead of more profitable agricultural products that required larger investments: having been displaced once, they feared this could happen again and were reluctant to make any investment that would not yield short-term results.[39] Similar evidence from Uganda shows that higher risk aversion among those exposed to violence affected the choice of livestock and crops. Such decisions accounted for half of all conflict-related economic losses.[40]

The experience of severe violence can also lower the aspirations of the forcibly displaced, magnifying victims' perceptions of their inability to move out of poverty.[41] In Colombia, violence was found to hurt the capacity even to hope for a better future. Such psychological conditions can set up barriers to recovery: behavioral economics have shown the importance of expectations and self-confidence in economic development.[42]

When a large group of people suffers from trauma, collective norms and behaviors can be altered. Some victims of violence have been found to reenact traumatic events and later perpetrate violence against others, often in

---

BOX 4.1 Trauma and the displaced: An example from Syria

Trauma and psychological disorders affect many Syrian refugees.[a] A 2015 study by the German Federal Chamber of Psychotherapists estimated that half the Syrian refugees in Germany suffered from such disorders, with 70 percent having witnessed violence and 50 percent having been victims of violence. Turkish authorities report that 55 percent of the Syrian refugees they are hosting need psychological support, and nearly half of Syrian refugees think that they or their families need psychological support. The United Nations High Commissioner for Refugees (UNHCR) notes that "the most prevalent and most significant clinical problems among Syrians are emotional disorders, such as: depression, prolonged grief disorder, posttraumatic stress disorder and various forms of anxiety disorders." Lack of treatment and continuing high levels of stress worsen their situation.

Women and children face particular vulnerabilities. In the Syrian Arab Republic, as well as in host countries, they often face or feel threatened by gender-based violence, including domestic violence, sexual violence, increasing incidence of early marriage, harassment and isolation, exploitation, and survival sex. A quarter of Syrian refugee households are headed by women, who have to fend for themselves and their families, often away from their communities and traditional sources of support. Close to 50 percent of children suffer from post-traumatic stress disorder, and 27 percent face developmental challenges stemming from their experience.[b]

Only 5 percent of the needed support services are available for Syrian refugees in Jordan, Lebanon, and Turkey.

a. This largely draws on Karasapan 2016a.
b. IMC 2015.

much the same form they experienced it.[43] IDP and refugee camps concentrate people who have gone through horrific ordeals, and who may continue to feel threatened and unsafe. These feelings can lead to volatile and defensive behavior, which contributes to persistent uncertainty and insecurity in the camps.[44]

A particular shock for women and girls

Vulnerabilities linked to forced displacement often have an important gender dimension: men and women experience forced displacement very differently.

Shifting gender norms

Forced displacement can transform gender norms, especially where cultural norms differ between the host and origin countries. Women displaced into a more liberal environment can benefit from greater access to education and economic opportunities, as do rural Afghan women who are refugees in the Islamic Republic of Iran.[45] In some situations, their skills might be more transferable than men's, enabling them to find work more easily, for example as domestic workers.[46] If men cannot find employment, they can be unable to fulfill their traditional role of protector and provider.[47] The disruption of traditional social systems and the reconfiguration of the gendered division of labor can trigger broader changes in gender norms and provide space for gender empowerment.[48]

Displaced populations often face discrimination that affects women and men differently. In a number of host countries, women do not have the same socioeconomic rights as men,[49] but men are seen as direct competitors in already crowded labor markets.[50] Men, especially young men, may also be seen as potential sources of disorder, and as such face rejection. They can also be seen as possible (often forced) recruits for militias.

Prevalent gender-based violence

Women and girls are at a greater risk of rape and sexual abuse before and during flight, and at destination. Rape is prevalent in modern conflicts, including in many of the situations that are the main drivers of forced displacement, such as in Syria,[51] Afghanistan,[52] Somalia, the Democratic Republic of Congo,[53] Sudan, South Sudan, Uganda, Central America, Myanmar, and Nepal.[54] In many cases, rape is perpetrated in a manner that aims to physically injure or psychologically torture victims.[55] At times, it is also inflicted on men or young boys.[56] A number of the forcibly displaced, especially women, have undergone such experiences before they flee as refugees or IDPs.

The journey often heightens vulnerability to sexual exploitation, as traditional protection mechanisms weaken. Recent stories about the sexual exploitation of refugee women during their passage to Europe reveal only a glimpse of these issues, which are common across many displacement situations.[57] In transit, women and girls risk gender-based violence perpetrated by smugglers, strangers, as well as border patrol guards and detention-center authorities.[58] Some may also have to engage in prostitution or other forms of transactional sex as they seek to provide for their families or to pay for their passage.[59]

The ordeal does not always end at destination. According to the International Labour Organization (ILO), one out of every six irregular female migrants is coerced into sex at destination,[60] and the incidence among the forcibly displaced may be comparable. In some situations, displacement can isolate women, and leave them bereft of traditional mechanisms by which to seek protection or recourse. In camps, the lack of privacy and basic protection, as when people live in tents, can expose women and girls to high risks of sexual violence, especially if they have been separated from their family or community group. Unlit common areas can make a walk to latrines at night extremely risky.[61] Outside the camps, women can be exposed to abuse, for example by their landlords.[62] And access to sexual and reproductive health services is rarely available at the very time it is needed.[63]

Women may also be abused in their own households. In a recent study, almost two-thirds of displaced Afghan women reported domestic violence during displacement, with nearly a third reporting that it occurred often, very often, or every day, and far more frequently than before displacement.[64] In societies with strong gender norms that disempower women, widows or female-headed households are particularly at risk of exclusion.[65]

The environment for recovery: Rights, location, and planning horizon

Rights

In nearly all host countries, refugees have a separate legal or administrative status, which brings a degree of protection (box 4.2). Depending on whether host countries fully embrace the 1951 Convention and other applicable international legal instruments, refugees may enjoy such protection and other rights, to a greater or lesser degree. The lack of rights, or their poor enforcement, can be a key source of vulnerability and a critical bind on socioeconomic recovery.

In most countries, this issue does not affect IDPs (who are full citizens and theoretically enjoy the same rights as other nationals). IDPs are usually free to move within their own country and they have the right to work. Exceptions include temporary restrictions or de facto discriminatory practices. In Azerbaijan for example, IDPs are "institutionalized": they are granted special rights, but are subject to constraints on employment, accommodation, and schooling, etc., which is a major impediment to the normalization of their socioeconomic situation.

From a development perspective, and in addition to legal protection, two sets of socioeconomic rights are fundamental to preventing refugees from falling into lasting poverty: freedom of movement and the right to work (and more broadly to engage in economic activity). There are, of course, huge differences across host countries in the applicable legal framework and in its effective enforcement. Such differences play an important role in explaining the divergent socioeconomic situation of refugees across host countries.

There is currently no exhaustive review of the socioeconomic rights of the forcibly displaced in all large host countries.[66] Such a review is inherently difficult as laws are usually

---

BOX 4.2 Institutions

Some host countries establish a separate branch of government to manage refugee-related issues, often a ministry or a commissioner for refugee or IDP affairs. These authorities are typically in charge of liaising with sectoral ministries and institutions and of providing an interface in the discussions with humanitarian actors. In some cases, they also provide services directly to the displaced. To carry out such work, they often establish relatively large administrative institutions, which are typically partly funded by humanitarian agencies.

The impact of such arrangements varies across countries, and it changes over time. At the start of a crisis, having a focal point within the government with dedicated administrative resources to help deal with an influx of forcibly displaced is often a source of efficiency and effectiveness. But when the situation becomes protracted, the existence of a separate bureaucracy can complicate matters and institutionalize the separation between the forcibly displaced and their hosts. This in turn can cause inefficiencies, such as the establishment of parallel systems, which duplicate or bypass technical ministries.

In poor governance environments, some government ministries for refugee or IDP affairs may also face counterproductive incentives. This is for example the case when they receive financing from external partners and are reluctant to let it go, or where an end to the crisis would translate into a loss of power and prestige.

---

complemented by a host of additional regulations, which can be more or less restrictive, and have a significant impact on eventual outcomes. It is hence difficult to assess the degree to which some difficulties are general or isolated. A much more thorough understanding of the legal socioeconomic constraints faced by refugees and sometimes IDPs is needed.

Protection

For refugees, the most essential rights are those related to international protection, in particular the principle of non-refoulement. While most host countries respect their international obligations toward refugees, a number of them have not signed or ratified the 1951 Convention and the 1967 Protocol, including Jordan, Lebanon, and Pakistan, and others, like Turkey, apply geographic restrictions on the origin of refugees.[67] In addition, some asylum systems (and corresponding institutions) remain weak. This can provide refugees with inadequate protection, including entry restrictions, and it may leave a number of asylum-seekers undocumented and potentially vulnerable to detention, deportation, or even refoulement.[68]

Even when their presence is tolerated, those who flee violence and conflict and remain undocumented are among the most vulnerable groups of the forcibly displaced. They have no legal protection and are often out of reach of any assistance. Profiling exercises consistently highlight how the difference in migratory status influences living conditions. For example in Bangladesh, many Rohingya refugees from Myanmar remain at the mercy of local politics and extortion rackets, because the authorities do not recognize their refugee status.

Freedom of movement

Restrictions on freedom of movement can severely limit refugees' ability to seize socioeconomic opportunities.[69] Restrictions on movement are in principle in contravention of the 1951 Convention, and they are often the result of poor regulations and practices.[70]

For refugees living in camps, spatial segregation is a permanent reality. Camp inhabitants may be restricted from leaving the camp or they may be required to obtain permits to do so. Even where they are allowed to move, they have to deal with high transport and information costs, given their distance from economic hubs.[71] For instance despite having the right to move, many camp residents in Uganda do not have the means to pay for transportation. In República Bolivariana de Venezuela, refugees were reportedly restricted by military and security checks from leaving remote areas.[72] Assistance is also often only available in camps, and refugees have to move back and forth between the remote camp location and potential employment opportunities if they cannot immediately settle somewhere else.

In urban areas, although mobility may be allowed by the law, it may be discouraged in practice. In Kabul for example, authorities long opposed the provision of any form of assistance to the displaced, although this recently changed.[73] The displaced may also lack protection from state security services or suffer from discrimination.[74] They can be denied access to public services such

as health and education.[75] They can also be prevented from accessing such services by police harassment, as was reported in Nairobi.[76] When they have access, refugees may have to pay higher rents and school fees due to their tenuous legal status—on top of the time and money spent registering as refugees and acquiring legal documents.[77] In some situations, IDPs may face similar problems, for example if they are unable to replace lost or destroyed documents (or if procedures for replacing them are prohibitively expensive or compliance is impossible).[78]

Right to work and to engage in economic activity

The 1951 Convention stipulates that refugees should be granted "the most favorable treatment accorded to nationals of a foreign country in the same circumstances, as regards the right to engage in wage-earning employment" (article 18) and a "treatment as favorable as possible and, in any event, not less favorable than that accorded to aliens generally in the same circumstances, as regards the right to engage on his own account in agriculture, industry, handicrafts and commerce and to establish commercial and industrial companies" (article 19). Yet the actual exercise of this right is often restricted by national laws, regulations, practices, and poor enforcement.

In many countries, refugee status does not automatically confer a right to work, and in some, refugee status is incompatible with labor market access. For instance, in Lebanon, Syrians who renew their residency permit based on a United Nations High Commissioner for Refugees (UNHCR) certificate must sign a pledge not to work.[79] In many other countries, including Germany, South Africa, and the United Kingdom, asylum-seekers have to wait for a determination of their status, which can be long, before they can enter the labor market.

Where refugees have the right to work, regulations may hinder them from exercising that right, such as work permits, restrictions to certain sectors or activities, or limitations on property and land ownership.[80] The cost of work permits may be prohibitive against refugees' generally low incomes.[81] In most countries, refugees are excluded from professions related to security and defense, and often from government employment. In a few, the list of professions open to refugees is much shorter: only 16 in the Islamic Republic of Iran, for example.[82]

There may also be legal limitations to open a business, own property, or sign contracts. In Pakistan, to run a business or access financial services, refugees have to register their companies through Pakistani acquaintances;[83] in Ecuador and Turkey, refugees have little access to financial institutions to secure loans; in Bangladesh, procedures make it impossible to access credit and prohibit refugees from engaging in trading or owning property; in India and Sudan, the law does not permit refugees to purchase land.[84] The displaced are also often excluded from financial services either because they lack the requisite formal documents or because they are regarded as a high credit risk.[85] Women may face additional obstacles (box 4.3).

In addition, the recognition and validation of professional qualifications is often difficult. This makes it difficult for qualified and semiskilled refugees to find work that matches their experience.[86] Yet, some countries have adopted or are in the process of adopting procedures to provide for such recognition, for example in Ecuador or Zambia.

Surviving without socioeconomic rights

The majority of refugees and IDPs try to find means to provide for themselves and their families, including by overcoming the legal restrictions that largely determine the kind of opportunities they can officially engage in.

FIGURE 4.1 Number of legal restrictions on women seeking jobs in the 15 largest refugee-hosting countries, 2014

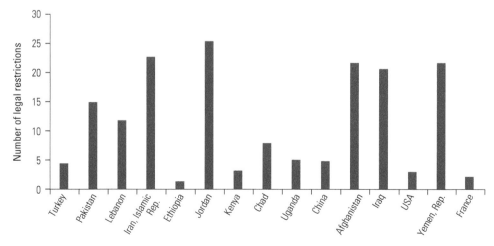

Source: World Bank 2016a.

Where they have the right to work, the displaced can access the formal sector; where they do not, they try to work informally to the extent opportunities are available: only a minority depend fully on humanitarian assistance over the long term.

In many host countries, de facto inclusion in the labor market is widespread.[87] The formal right to work is not effectively enforced, and the informal sector accounts for a large share of the economy. In such contexts, economic and social integration is often taking place despite rather than because of government policy.[88] The extent to which such informality is detrimental depends on the context, but refugees and IDPs are often even more vulnerable than poor people in host communities.[89] For example, in Tanzania, three-quarters of the Rwandese, Burundian and Congolese refugees working in agriculture, construction, housekeeping, and catering were paid with food rather than money.[90] In Bangladesh, undocumented refugees engage in jobs considered dangerous, such as deep-sea fishing.[91]

In countries where labor laws are more strictly enforced, work in the informal sector may be more discriminatory. Economic migration literature suggests that illegal workers tend to be paid less and to be subject to harsher working conditions than legal immigrants.[92] Skilled workers often have to accept low-wage menial positions. Anecdotal evidence suggests that refugees who work illegally are often exposed to abuse, including exploitation, violence, detention, and even threats of forced return.

The situations of Palestinian refugees in Jordan and in Lebanon illustrate the way differences in rights can translate into diverging socioeconomic outcomes. Palestinians have fared relatively well over the decades in Jordan, where they are allowed to work, use public services, and own businesses and property.[93] A majority has been granted citizenship and they now play a large role in the private sector and account for a large part of Jordan's middle class.[94] In contrast, Palestinian refugees in Lebanon have been largely hosted in camps, with limited socioeconomic rights. Their welfare indicators are significantly worse.[95]

Unfavorable locations

Having the right to work is one thing, being able to get a job is another. In marked contrast to economic migrants, the forcibly displaced do not necessarily go where there are economic opportunities: they move to the easiest place to reach where they will find safety. Although some of them manage to get to places where socioeconomic conditions are relatively favorable, large numbers lack the resources necessary for a long journey and they settle in regions close to home.[96] They may end up in a place where there are few opportunities for them regardless of their rights, a "wrong place."

Place and opportunities

A "wrong place" is not an objective definition. It is linked to each individual's skills and abilities, and it is largely a function of the way they can meet demand in the labor market. The job market mismatch is generally more severe in developing countries absorbing large numbers of refugees relative to their population (or experiencing large IDP movements) than in high-income economies absorbing small numbers of refugees.[97]

The first characteristic of a "wrong place" relates to language and social norms. In a culturally foreign environment, it is hard to achieve economic and social inclusion. Fortunately, most people flee to places that are fairly close geographically and that often have a degree of familiarity: of the 12 million people in large refugee situations at the end of 2014, 70 to 80 percent were living in countries or in regions whose language and cultural norms were familiar.[98] Exceptions include Syrian refugees in Turkey and relatively large numbers hosted in other Organisation for Economic Co-operation and Development (OECD) countries.

While it could be assumed that almost all IDPs live in culturally familiar environments because they are in their own country, the reality is sometimes more complex. Once displaced, IDPs may find themselves in areas that are under the control of people with whom they have little in common, or even with whom there is a history of mutual suspicion. They might, for example, share a similar trading language, such as Arabic, Swahili, or French, but not their mother tongue: this can make it a difficult environment in which to reestablish their lives.

Another potential source of vulnerability is the lack of economic opportunities in the hosting environment. The overwhelming share of refugees, and virtually all IDPs, are hosted in developing countries. Some of these economies, for example in the Middle East, are characterized by a dual labor market, with a relatively large public sector and slow private sector growth. In such contexts, economic opportunities for forcibly displaced persons are few. This typically leads to high unemployment and low earnings. For example, an ILO survey in Jordan found that wages for unskilled and semiskilled workers among Syrian refugees were below subsistence levels.[99]

In addition refugee-hosting economies are often struggling in relative terms. Of the 12 million refugees in large situations at the end of 2014, 15 percent lived in countries where the average growth of GDP per capita had been negative over the period 2010–2014, and 88 percent of them lived in countries that had fared worse than the global average of developing countries over this period.[100] Among IDPs, the equivalent figures were 30 percent and 94 percent.[101]

Within countries, refugees and IDPs are also often hosted in relatively lagging regions. Disaggregated data on location is available for only about 30 million forcibly displaced persons.[102] Of this group, at the end of 2014, about 72 percent lived in parts of the country where GDP per capita was lower than national average, including 13 percent who lived where it was less than half of the national average. Among those who lived in camps, 22 percent were in parts of the country where GDP per capita was less than half of national average.

Refugee and IDP camps provide an extreme version of a "wrong place" from a socioeconomic perspective. The Dadaab camp in Kenya, and more recently Zaatari in Jordan, illustrate how entrepreneurial refugees can develop their own businesses.[103] Yet for the overwhelming majority of refugees and IDPs, the isolation of the camps results in a lack of employment opportunities. In time this can even create a "culture of idleness" which can have long-term negative outcomes in terms of employability and social inclusion.[104] It also leads to a very low level of self-reliance and is often one of the main reasons given by refugees for leaving or avoiding camp life altogether.[105]

Large numbers of forcibly displaced persons, especially in Africa, are hosted in rural areas. In some countries, such as Chad and Uganda, they are provided with access to arable land, which is greatly contributing to their social and economic integration.[106] Where such resources are not available, however, refugees and IDPs may be trapped in undesirable and unsustainable situations as landless people in the midst of farming communities. This can have a severe impact on their ability to escape from extreme poverty, an impact that can be carried across generations.

Moving on to a "better place"

To try and reach a "better place," large numbers of forcibly displaced persons move into cities.[107] Refugees and IDPs in urban areas are generally better off as they can access a broader variety of jobs, including in the informal sector. For instance, forcibly displaced persons in Nairobi reported that they were generally able to find sufficient work to feed themselves and their families in the city, unlike in the rural areas they came from.[108] In Afghanistan, the longer IDPs had settled in major cities, the better their economic conditions.[109]

Still, the incidence and depth of poverty among these groups remain high. Urban displaced populations face the same challenges as poor host communities do, in terms of inadequate housing and insecure tenure, insufficient access to social services, potential discrimination, and persistent food insecurity.[110] There may also remain a mismatch between their skills and the opportunities that are available in urban environments, since many of them originate from rural settings. In Colombia the unemployment rate of IDPs at the reception site is significantly higher than that of the poor host population.[111] In Bosnia, the displaced had a 15 percent higher probability of being unemployed, even six years post conflict.[112] Discrimination, lack of social ties, and weak political influence in the host community are all factors that limit access to jobs.[113]

In most camps, a self-selection process comes into play, gradually. Where they can do so, the more mobile and capable among the displaced move on and look for opportunities elsewhere. This creates a vicious cycle, where the lack of opportunities and the departure of the ablest have mutually reinforcing effects, all too often making camps a locus for the most vulnerable refugees and IDPs, and sometimes even attracting destitute people from host communities.[114]

Short planning horizon

For the forcibly displaced, the future is uncertain. They often live in some form of limbo, which can be transitory or last for an extended period of time. Uncertainty about the future stems from a number of factors, ranging from the temporary nature of their legal or administrative status, to the absence of a predictable source of income, to the enduring hope for an eventual return. As a result, many forcibly displaced persons often lack the ability to plan and to make sound investment decisions. This can have large detrimental effects.

For instance, the forcibly displaced often make critical decisions based on an assumption that their exile will be transitory and relatively short. They tend to live in temporary settings as they await the termination of hostilities, and they continue to do so even in protracted situations. They do not invest in acquiring skills that are in demand in the host labor market as much as they would do if they were planning for a longer stay.[115] In a very concrete case, some Syrian refugees living in Turkey decided that it was not necessary to make their children learn Turkish so they could go to public schools: they thought their exile would be only temporary. These children have now missed an extensive amount of schooling.[116] Had the forcibly displaced known in advance that they would be in limbo for a long period of time, they may have made a different decision.

An agenda for development actors

The purpose of a development response is to help forcibly displaced persons overcome the displacement-induced vulnerabilities which impinge on their ability to seize opportunities and which put them at high risk of falling into lasting poverty. It is not directly aimed at providing for basic needs, but at restoring self-reliance (box 4.4).

Jobs and economic opportunities are critical to mitigating the impact of displacement-induced vulnerabilities. They may not suffice, but they are necessary, not only once a durable solution is in place, but also in the interim period, and especially in the short term. Any delay in accessing them can further exacerbate vulnerabilities, as people who stay out of the labor force for long periods have more difficulty engaging effectively in a social context as well as performing in a job.

To help refugees and IDPs access socioeconomic opportunities, development actors should support three sets of interventions: help the forcibly displaced (or at least let them) move to a place where there are such opportunities; help create opportunities in their place of exile (including by removing the barriers and obstacles to access the labor market); or help them develop new skills more attuned to the needs of the local labor market—in other words, change place, change the place, or change the people. Still some people

---

BOX 4.4 The "Wilton Park Principles"?

At a workshop co-chaired by the United Kingdom, the World Bank, and UNHCR and held in Wilton Park on April 4 to 6, 2016, a number of stakeholders including international institutions, bilateral donor agencies, host country governments, and civil society agreed on a set of five core and mutually reinforcing principles to forge new partnerships for delivery. These "Wilton Park Principles" include: work through national and local systems; support host communities and build social cohesion; enable economic participation and stimulate growth; provide impactful and innovative financing; and improve the data and evidence base.

may not be able to immediately recover from their experience: they may need dedicated support over the medium-term to help them gradually regain a degree of self-reliance.

This agenda is predicated on the assumption that continued humanitarian assistance is provided in parallel to ensure that the basic needs of the forcibly displaced (including food, health, etc.) are met until they can achieve self-reliance. The scope of such aid largely depends on the pace at which refugees and IDPs can gain employment or access other sources of incomes, which in turn is often a reflection of host government policies and of the success of development interventions.

Support freedom of movement and the right to work

Supporting freedom of movement is especially important in situations where refugees and IDPs are in unsustainable and undesirable situations. Access to opportunities requires changing place. Allowing the forcibly displaced to do so is politically sensitive, especially in a context of restrictive policies. Yet, the economic benefits of such secondary movements are real, whether they involve a move towards urban centers or, in the case of refugees, to another country where there may be more opportunities. They essentially imply that refugees and IDPs end up in places where there is a demand for their skills. Under such a scenario, the forcibly displaced are allowed to act in the same way economic migrants do: as a result all stakeholders can accrue the benefits of economic migration, including both forcibly displaced persons and their hosts.

Development actors should emphasize the benefits and feasibility of letting the forcibly displaced decide on their place of temporary settlement. They should also discourage programs designed to support them to stay in locations where their situation is neither desirable nor sustainable. At the global level, they should advocate for a more generous set of policies and support, especially from high-income countries, as part of a broader effort to secure not only enhanced well-being of the forcibly displaced, but also economic gains for their potential hosts. This can be a difficult discussion and development actors should be mindful of the perspective of host countries and communities.

To date, such discussions, when they have taken place, have mainly focused on the right to work. This remains an important agenda, but its relevance largely depends on the actual enforcement of labor laws. In countries with a very large informal sector, having the right to work, while important, may not necessarily translate into enhanced socioeconomic opportunities. The reciprocal proposition is, however, also true: for these host countries, granting the right to work does not necessarily have a significant impact on the labor market, especially when the number of refugees in relation to the population is limited. It does allow national authorities, however, to prevent a further expansion of unregulated activities and to tax the corresponding production.

Overall, many host countries are concerned that granting rights to the forcibly displaced, especially refugees, may increase inflows. They fear that they would be sending a signal that may make their country a preferred destination for potential asylum-seekers. This may be oversimplifying a complex issue, as the primary factor for forced displacement remains the fear of violence and as the large majority of refugees move to neighboring countries regardless of socioeconomic rights (while IDPs remain in their own country). It suggests, however, that a degree of international cooperation is needed to avoid a low-level equilibrium where most potential host countries would be reluctant to grant basic rights unless they know that others may also do so.

Create opportunities in the place of exile

Development actors should help create economic opportunities in places where there are large numbers of forcibly displaced persons. This may require significant financial resources, and it should be done in such a manner that it can also benefit host communities. Over the years, there have been a number of externally funded aid programs aimed at creating jobs or enhancing livelihoods, but results have been mixed.

To be successful and sustainable, such activities should take place within the context of a private sector-led, market-driven program. Public works and other heavily subsidized schemes may provide temporary relief but they are unlikely to be sufficient and durable. Activities for which there is no clear market are unlikely to provide an effective way to allocate scarce resources.[117]

Development actors should hence focus on attracting the private sector. Private sector decisions to invest depend first and foremost on business considerations, such as the regulatory environment, infrastructure, and access to markets. Getting the private sector involved is likely to be easier where refugees and IDPs are in or near large urban centers, or otherwise well-equipped regions. Conversely, it is more difficult in remote areas, devoid of adequate energy or transport systems, and in countries with a poor track record of business regulations. Development actors could usefully provide support through investments in key infrastructure (although these take time to yield results), via guarantees or other risk-sharing mechanisms, and through efforts to improve the investment climate (box 4.5).

Additional efforts may be needed to help foster entrepreneurship among both forcibly displaced persons (where it is legal for them to create jobs) and their hosts. This may include a broad range of activities to support small and medium enterprises, including training, access to credit, equity investments, etc. The feasibility of such activities depends largely on the overall business environment and on location. It is far harder in remote and isolated areas. It also depends on the skills and experiences of the forcibly displaced, and on their ability to adjust in a new environment. Experience (for example with Afghan refugees in Pakistan, Syrian refugees in Turkey, and Somali refugees in Nairobi) suggests that there is a vast reservoir of initiatives which can be tapped, with potentially large gains for the displaced and their hosts.

Finally, as many refugees and IDPs come from rural regions and have a farming background, development actors should provide support to engaging them in agricultural activities where land can be made available. This is likely to be helpful, especially in some African host countries, but overall it may benefit only a relatively small share of the forcibly displaced.

Build skills attuned to local labor market needs

To reduce the mismatch between opportunities in the labor market and the skills of the displaced, development actors should help upgrade the forcibly displaced's skills. To be effective, such support should be driven by a careful analysis of the demand in the labor market where people can be

BOX 4.5 Special economic zones in Jordan

The government of Jordan has developed a program to address the refugee crisis with the support of external partners, which includes developing jobs for Jordanians and Syrians. This Compact was presented at the Supporting Syria and the Region Conference, which was held in London on February 4, 2016.

The program rests on developing new economic opportunities, in particular through enhanced access to the European Union (EU) market, including through the relaxation of rules-of-origin requirements for products manufactured in designated special economic zones. Investors in these zones would be expected, or required, to employ a certain proportion of Syrian refugees in their workforce.

A core challenge is to attract new investment into Jordan, and hence to improve the business environment (Jordan ranks 113 on the World Bank Group's Doing Business index). The government has committed to provide a number of work permits for Syrian refugees to be employed in the zones. Additional support may be needed to train or retrain Syrian refugees for jobs that may become available.

employed under realistic scenarios. This is difficult in places where there are very few, if any opportunities. It is particularly challenging when the forcibly displaced are in limbo, and do not know what the eventual outcome of their displacement will be. In such cases, development actors should aim to strengthen the capacity to seize opportunities not only in the current environment but also in possible future destinations. This often implies focusing on portable skills, which can be of use in many places, rather than on location-specific skills, such as agricultural skills, which assume a return or a further move to a place where land is available. Investing in language skills early on is also likely to have a significant pay off for both host countries and refugees.

In parallel, development actors should make determined efforts to provide adequate education services to refugee and IDP children. In protracted situations, these children may spend their entire formative years in displacement. Ensuring that they can be rapidly reinserted in a functioning education system is hence critical, though very challenging. The difficulties are manifold, from a lack of financial resources which may force some parents to have their children work, to the challenges inherent in the rapid and massive expansion of an education system, to differences of languages between the displaced and their hosts, to the specific needs of children who have gone through traumatic ordeals, etc. Including refugee and IDP children in national education systems in host countries is often the most effective and sustainable way to prevent the emergence of a "lost generation," especially when the forcibly displaced live out of camps, and development actors should support such efforts (box 4.6).

Continue supporting the most vulnerable

Development actors should provide dedicated support—akin to social assistance—to those who may not be able to access opportunities, even when they are available (box 4.7). This is the case of a number of groups with specific needs or heightened risk, such

as persons with disabilities, elderly, or unaccompanied children. To ensure both cost effectiveness and sustainability, the use of country systems should be set as a common medium-term goal for all external stakeholders, but short-term efforts are needed to strengthen such systems and build the corresponding capacity before a shift can be considered. Continued external financing may also be needed over the medium term, in particular to cover the needs of nonnationals such as refugees.

Development actors should also share some of the lessons learned in modernizing

---

BOX 4.6 Providing education to Syrian refugees in Turkey

The Turkish Ministry of Education estimated in fall 2015 that the country hosted 589,500 school-age Syrian children, and that up to 250,000 of them were enrolled in school; an additional 138,000 were expected to be enrolled by the end of the 2015/16 school year.[a] School enrollment rates have been high inside camps (around 86 percent), but far lower outside them, where options for Arabic-language education are limited.

The government has made an enormous effort to provide education to Syrian refugees, along three main lines: integrating Syrian children into the Turkish education system; allowing community-based education programs run from within the Syrian community (these programs follow several curricula, with the most popular the Libyan curriculum and religious education); and facilitating access to temporary education centers (which are supervised by the Ministry of Education and have Turkish senior administrators, but are staffed by Syrian teachers

and use a modified version of the Syrian curriculum).[a] The comparative performance of the three options has yet to be assessed.

The ministry has asked all provincial directorates to register Syrian children of preschool and first-year primary school age in Turkish schools, but full registration is likely to take time. It has also begun to provide Turkish preparatory courses at public education centers to facilitate the transition of Syrian children into Turkish schools. It aims to address persistent issues such as the high degree of mobility, and thus school dropouts, among refugees; high rates of psychosocial trauma; difficulties in retaining Syrian teachers (most are not allowed to register for work permits and are paid only modest stipends); lack of quality control of community-based services; and overcrowding and disruption in Turkish schools that provide double shifts. Demand for vocational, remedial, and higher education among adolescent refugees is still large and unmet.

a. This is recognized in the humanitarian sector including the evidence from UNHCR's Operational Guidelines on the Minimum Criteria for Livelihoods Programming emphasizes the market and data driven approach to programming. UNHCR 2015e.

BOX 4.7 Forced displacement and the graduation approach

The "graduation approach" supports people living in extreme poverty and helps them graduate out of it.[a] It is aimed at people who are so poor that they typically cannot engage in activities that are supported through micro credit. It was first implemented by a Bangladeshi nongovernmental organization, BRAC, in 2002. It has now been tested in eight countries with support from the World Bank Group and the Ford Foundation, and it covers over half a million households.

The graduation approach includes a carefully sequenced 18- to 36-month set of interventions. It relies on a few core building blocks: consumption stipends to ensure food security until incomes are generated from economic activities; asset transfers and training to kick start economic activities; financial education; and weekly home visits for monitoring, building confidence and providing health, nutrition and other social information

Six rigorous randomized impact assessments conducted by Innovations for Poverty Action (IPA) between 2006 and 2014 demonstrated that the graduation approach increased incomes and household consumption at all but one site.[b] Evidence from the BRAC program in Bangladesh shows the poorest who participated in the program were truly breaking free of the poverty trap. Overall earnings increased 37 percent over the seven years surveyed (five years after the program ended), with significant rises in consumption and savings. Households not only earned and saved more but they also diversified their assets and income sources.[c] The total cost of running pilots (consumption support, asset transfer, training, coaching, staffing, monitoring, and head office overhead) ranged from US$330 to US$700 per participant in India, the Republic of Yemen, Ethiopia, and Pakistan, to around US$1,250

in Honduras, and from US$1,750 to US$2,500 in Ghana, Haiti, and Peru.[d] The cost-effectiveness of the program was high, with annual household income gains as a percentage of total program costs ranging from about 7 percent to 25 percent.[e]

UNHCR has recognized the potential of the graduation approach for refugees and IDPs, provided it is adapted for this specific group, e.g., with the addition of legal assistance and psycho-social counseling components. The model is currently tested in five sites, in Burkina Faso, Costa Rica, Ecuador, the Arab Republic of Egypt, and Zambia, in rural, urban and camp settings, as well as in both emergency and protracted situations.[f] Results thus far have been encouraging, and the graduation approach provides a means to link somewhat disparate program inputs (livelihoods, protection and others) in a coherent program.

a. UNHCR has put the graduation approach at the center of its 2014–2018 Global Strategy for livelihoods. UNHCR 2014b.
b. World Bank 2012.
c. Banerjee et al. 2015.
d. *Economist* 2015.
e. Differences stem mainly from local salary scales, population density, and status of infrastructure, as well as the site's emphasis on each of the building blocks (e.g., size and duration of consumption support).
f. At BRAC the total cost of running the program is US$325 with a cost-benefit ratio of 5.07. See Sinha, Gidwani, and Das 2008.

social protection systems to further inform the debate on aid effectiveness. The situation of forcibly displaced has specific characteristics and not all lessons may apply: for example, where the forcibly displaced do not have the right to work, the scope for promoting self-reliance is necessarily limited. Still, some of the key elements of modern social protection systems may be relevant, including: improved targeting (often based on proxy indicators, which are easily monitored and provide for an adequate prediction of poverty and vulnerability levels), conditionality (for example through conditional cash transfers, which have been adopted in many countries to

link social assistance payments with the adoption of positive behaviors, such as children immunization or school attendance), and activation (to provide support so that beneficiaries can eventually return to the labor market).[118] Interventions should be tailored to each situation: for example, in low-income, low-capacity countries, responses have to be different from those in middle- and high-income countries.[119]

Finally, development actors should consider expanding their programs to areas where there is no strong track record of interventions yet, but which are critical to success. This includes issues related to mental health and psychosocial support (box 4.8).

BOX 4.8 Supporting psychosocial and post-traumatic care?

Helping to address trauma-related issues is critical to achieve a lasting solution, yet this is an area where development actors have limited experience and expertise.[a]

Over the last few years, small-scale pilots have tested innovative approaches, for example in working with very young mothers who were part of armed groups in Liberia, Sierra Leone, and northern Uganda, or in supporting youth inclusion programs for disenfranchised groups in Liberia. These programs typically combined livelihood-related activities like training and social reintegration, for example through participation in peer groups. They were often accompanied by mentoring or support services.

Emerging lessons suggest that community-based activities (and not only individual treatment) can be effective to help restore psychological well-being; that psychological and economic support can be complementary and achieve in combination more than what any single set of interventions would; and that time and patience are needed for durable results. Yet randomized control trials for such interventions in Burundi, the Democratic Republic of Congo, Liberia, and Uganda also suggest that there is still much to learn.

A critical area on which development institutions can already take action is in preventing aggravation of stresses and trauma-related issues. At a minimum, projects targeted at refugees and IDPs should be

designed with awareness of psychosocial issues and of factors that may exacerbate them, particularly among interventions for children and youth. For example, education programs need to reflect the emotional and social impact of violence on their pupils, and to include activities to help address them.

Addressing trauma requires a comprehensive strategy with efforts to recreate and nurture the social fabric in affected communities, especially as there are no or very few doctors, and far fewer psychiatrists in many host countries. The United Nations (UN) Inter-Agency Standing Committee has published mental health and psychosocial support guidelines that offer a useful framework to that effect.[b]

a. Drawn from World Bank 2014.
b. IASC 2007.

Notes

1. This is distinct from a strict focus on attaining a specific welfare target (for example as compared with the situation of the host community or their predisplacement status). It is consistent with the strategies that are adopted to support other groups which face specific vulnerabilities in developing countries, for example in the case of gender issues or for indigenous people and minorities.
2. Verme et al. 2015; Kamau and Fox 2013.
3. Verme et al. 2015.
4. Geller and Latek 2013; Mosel and Jackson 2013; Fielden 2008; Crawford at al. 2015.
5. De Vriese 2006; Durieux 2009; Young, Jacobsen, and Osman 2009; Crawford et al. 2015.
6. Fiala 2002, p. 1.
7. Ibañez and Moya 2016.
8. JIPS 2012a.
9. World Bank and UNHCR 2011.
10. Betts et al. 2014.
11. World Bank 2013a.
12. Kamau and Fox 2013.
13. Aysa-Lastra 2011; Crawford et al. 2015.
14. Justino 2009.
15. Kirchhoff and Ibañez 2001.
16. JIPS 2011, p. 11.
17. Ibañez and Moya 2010.
18. World Bank 2014, p.22.
19. JIPS 2011.
20. Crawford et al. 2015, p. 31.

21. Oamata 2012a; Buscher 2011.
22. Banki 2004.
23. Verme et al. 2015; UNHCR 2014d, 2015i.
24. Townsend 2016.
25. Buscher, forthcoming, p. 5.
26. Steel et al. 2009.
27. JIPS 2012b.
28. World Bank 2014.
29. Gorst-Unsworth and Goldenberg 1998; Hinton et al. 2000; Hinton et al. 2001; Turner et al. 2003.
30. Beiser and Hou 2001; Porter and Haslam 2005; Schweitzer et al. 2006.
31. Beiser and Hou 2001; Porter and Haslam 2005; Schweitzer et al. 2006.
32. World Bank 2014.
33. Cernea 1997.
34. Mollica, Wyshack, and Lavelle 1987; Vinck et al. 2007.
35. World Bank 2014.
36. Rockmore 2011, 2012.
37. Ibañez and Moya 2016.
38. Callen et al. 2014; Bundervoet 2006.
39. Ibañez and Moya 2016.
40. Rockmore 2011, 2012.
41. Moya and Carter 2014, p. 38–39.
42. World Bank 2015e.
43. Van der Kolk 1996.
44. IDMC 2013.
45. Monsutti 2006.
46. Buscher 2009, p. 90.
47. Buscher, forthcoming, p. 5.
48. Fiddian-Qasmiyeh et al. 2014, p. 403.
49. World Bank 2016a.
50. World Bank 2016a.
51. Atlantic 2013.
52. Ruiz 2004.
53. Merger 2010.
54. For an extensive review see Bastick, Grimm, and Kunz 2007.
55. Farr 2009.
56. New York Times 2015.
57. New York Times 2016.
58. IOM 2013.
59. Ghosh 2009; Crush and Ramachandran 2009.
60. ILO 2003.
61. Bangura 2016.
62. Bangura 2016.
63. Buscher 2009.
64. JIPS 2012a, p. 15.
65. Crawford et al. 2015, p. 32.
66. Zetter and Ruaudel, forthcoming, is a first and important step in this direction.
67. Zetter and Ruaudel, forthcoming.
68. Zetter and Ruaudel, forthcoming.
69. Smith 2004; Milner 2013.
70. Some states have made reservations to Article 26 of the 1951 Convention on freedom of movement.
71. Werker 2007.
72. Zetter and Ruaudel, forthcoming, p. 12.
73. Metcalfe et al. 2011; Harild, Christensen, and Zetter 2015.
74. UNHCR 2009.
75. JIPS 2011.
76. Campbell, Crisp, and Kiragu 2011.
77. Pavanello, Elhawary, and Pantuliano 2010; Anderson 2012.
78. This is the case, for example, when IDPs have to rely on testimony from leaders of opposing ethnic groups.
79. Zetter and Ruaudel, forthcoming.
80. Zetter and Ruaudel, forthcoming.
81. Zetter and Ruaudel, forthcoming.
82. Zetter and Ruaudel, forthcoming.
83. Mosel and Jackson 2013.
84. Zetter and Ruaudel, forthcoming.
85. Jacobsen 2014.
86. Refugees also often lack documentation of the diplomas or qualifications obtained as they were not able to bring them with them during the flight. Zetter and Ruaudel, forthcoming, p. 9.
87. Bakewell 2014; Hovil 2014.
88. Hovil 2014.
89. Chen 2007.
90. Whitaker 2002.
91. Zetter and Ruaudel, forthcoming, p. 9.
92. See Rivera-Batiz 1997.
93. Harild, Christensen, and Zetter 2015.
94. Harild, Christensen, and Zetter 2015.
95. Chabaan et al. 2010.
96. Some might also opt to stay as close as possible because they hope to return soon.
97. Dadush and Niebuhr 2016.
98. Calculations based on UNHCR data (end-2014). A large refugee situations is defined as a situation involving 25,000 people and more.
99. Aljuni and Kawar 2014.

100. Calculations based on UNHCR refugee data (end-2014) and World Bank Group economic indicators.
101. Calculations based on IDMC IDP data (end-2014) and World Bank Group economic indicators.
102. UNHCR data as of end-2014. Among key "missing" countries are Colombia and Nigeria (for IDPs) and the Islamic Republic of Iran (for refugees). Disaggregated data by category (refugees vs. IDPs) and by region are not available.
103. Verwimp and Maystadt 2015; Verme et al. 2015.
104. Lehrer 2010.
105. Zetter and Ruaudel, forthcoming, p. 12.
106. Zetter and Ruaudel, forthcoming, p. 9.
107. Harild, Christensen, and Zetter 2015, p. 9.
108. Harild, Christensen, and Zetter 2015, p. 10.
109. Harild, Christensen, and Zetter 2015, p. 10.
110. Here the story loops back to the question of status. Whereas registered forcibly displaced with the right to work usually work in higher-skilled work, the unregistered ones are forced into precarious work which is usually at the lowest end of the income spectrum even compared to poor hosts.
111. Ibáñez and Moya 2006, 2016.
112. Kondylis 2010.
113. World Bank 2015b, p. 11–12.
114. Kamau and Fox 2013 find that 27 percent of the Dadaab camp was made up of Kenyan nationals.
115. Chin and Cortes 2014.
116. Human Rights Watch 2015.
117. This largely draws from World Bank 2015a.
118. This curriculum has been developed by the Syrian Commission of Education under the Syrian Interim Ministry of Education.
119. World Bank 2012.

Rebuilding Lives

5

The traditional definition of the "end" of forced displacement is based on a framework of rights and legal protection. For refugees, forced displacement comes to an end when they can once again enjoy the protection of a state in a durable and effective manner, whether through voluntary return to their country of origin, integration in their host country, or resettlement to a third country.[1] For internally displaced persons (IDPs), a durable solution is achieved when IDPs "no longer have specific assistance and protection needs that are linked to their displacement" and "when they can enjoy their human rights in a nondiscriminatory manner vis-à-vis citizens who have never been displaced."[2] This can be achieved through sustainable integration in their place of origin (return), sustainable integration where they took refuge (local integration), and sustainable integration in another part of the country (settlement elsewhere).[3]

For development actors, such legal definitions may be somewhat difficult to operationalize within the strictures of their mandate. Development actors are part of a broad effort to promote comprehensive solutions to the plight of the forcibly displaced but their comparative advantage (and hence their contribution to the overall agenda) is focused on the socioeconomic dimensions of the crisis.

A possible approach is to define the "end point" of engagement through a practical prism: it is the moment when the forcibly displaced no longer require dedicated development support. The need for such support arises from the specific vulnerabilities that the forcibly displaced are struggling with due to their displacement. The "end-point" is the moment when these vulnerabilities have been offset so that the displaced can take full advantage of available poverty reduction programs and reestablish their lives in a manner that is genuinely durable from a socioeconomic perspective. For development actors, the primary focus is hence not on where people live (which may change over time) but on whether they have specific vulnerabilities that hamper their ability to seize development opportunities (box 5.1).

Forced displacement and its resolution take place against a backdrop of human mobility. The notion that return and sustainable reintegration—a "re-emplacement"—constitute the most natural end point to the crisis may need to be reconsidered. In fact, in every situation some people return, but others do not, and return is rarely a simple and straightforward solution.

Rather, return is a complex and difficult process, and support is often needed to ensure it is successful and sustainable. In most situations, security and economic opportunities are the two main parameters. Returnees who have assets (financial

The "specific vulnerabilities" approach to resolving forced displacement situations is both distinct from, and complementary to, the focus on legal protection. For example, refugees who have been living out of camp for several decades in a hospitable and culturally familiar place may still lack citizenship rights, and thus remain refugees, but they may no longer have economic and social vulnerabilities that are markedly different from those of the host communities.[a] While they may need continued legal protection, they may no longer require dedicated development support. Conversely, recently naturalized refugees may no longer require legal protection, but they may still need development support to overcome specific vulnerabilities they acquired through their displacement experience, such as trauma.

This approach is also distinct from a needs-based agenda. For instance, IDPs impoverished by their displacement and living in an informal settlement may still have needs related to their experience, but they may no longer have vulnerabilities that differ from those of other people in the area where they live. They can be supported as part of a broader poverty reduction program, and no longer require dedicated development support.

The focus on vulnerabilities, as opposed to needs, may also help address the thorny issue of defining an equity benchmark. "Needs" can depend on individuals' expectations and on the environment in which they live. It is often difficult to gauge the level at which the needs of the forcibly displaced should be met. It could, to cite just a few possibilities, range from a subsistence benchmark (measured by a daily calorific intake); "decent-living" conditions (which may be out of reach for many poor people in the world); a level equivalent to the host community (which would suggest that the forcibly displaced should be treated differently depending on where they are); or standards of living comparable to the preconflict situation (which would imply that more support should go to those fleeing middle-income rather than low-income countries). The focus on vulnerabilities—reequipping the forcibly displaced with the ability to seize socioeconomic opportunities where they live—may still be difficult to define with precision, but is clearer from an equity perspective.

This focus should not conceal the importance of achieving a satisfactory legal solution to the plight of forced displacement. This remains essential for the forcibly displaced to be able to fully engage as contributing members of the society they belong to, and to ensure the full sustainability of any socioeconomic solution. Within this broader context, development institutions can best contribute to this agenda by focusing on the socioeconomic dimensions of the resolution.

a. Bakewell 2000.

resources, human capital, and social capital) tend to fare better upon return: this suggests that policies that enable refugees and IDPs to earn an income and to maintain or further develop their skills while in displacement can help during the resolution phase of the crisis.

Local integration is also a complex process. For IDPs it is about settling in their new environment in a sustainable manner. For refugees, it also requires securing a legal status that can provide predictable and reliable terms of stay, such as renewable residence and work permits. This is politically difficult, and support may be needed to develop adequate legal solutions, even if they fall short of naturalization.

The integration outcomes for refugees and asylum-seekers in high-income countries are contrasted. Refugees generally face many difficulties integrating into the labor market, in spite of considerable support. This highlights the depth of their vulnerability, including when compared with economic migrants—and their need for continued support.

Any discussion of durable solutions to forced displacement ought to incorporate the concerns of host countries. Most host countries and communities are unwilling to accept, at least explicitly, the continuing presence of large numbers of forcibly displaced other than as a "temporary" occurrence, even when the situation is long lasting. Political considerations often require leaders to emphasize that the forcibly displaced will eventually return to their places of origin. The fact that it does not always happen is fraught with sensitivity and should be discussed carefully to avoid the adoption of counterproductive policy positions.

Stay, return, or move on?

A complicated issue

Whether to stay, to return, or to move on: refugees and IDPs often have little choice—one of the key markers of their situation. Yet when they do have options, their decision-making process may be partly similar to that of economic migrants: they compare their welfare in their place of displacement with their likely welfare in the place they could move to, including back home. Among safe destinations, they choose the place where they believe they will maximize their welfare (once the cost of the transition is deducted), based on economic considerations as well as on a host of other factors, including social, cultural, and political. Recognizing that in resolving their situation the forcibly displaced act in some part like economic migrants is critical to supporting solutions that can be durable: They have distinct protection needs and vulnerabilities, but share migrants' desire and economic need for a better life.[4]

In these calculations, once security is ensured, economic considerations are likely to be essential. Accessing economic opportunities is key to reconstituting assets (including social capital) after a sudden and catastrophic loss, to overcoming trauma, and to restoring a planning horizon. It is a necessary (though not sufficient) condition to achieve a durable solution from a socioeconomic angle. It requires both enjoying socioeconomic rights and living in a place where there are opportunities.

For refugees, there can be a tension between legal rights and location. In the absence of large-scale naturalization, resettlement, or permanent residency status, the only way to recover durable legal status is often to return to the country of origin, but that often means going to a place where there are no or very few economic opportunities. On the other hand, staying in a host country or moving on (even irregularly) may provide economic opportunities, but not formal legal status. In other words, refugees may have to make a choice between status and location: this tension is at the root of the "insolvability" of many forced displacement situations. A brief reflection on economic migration, and on the large number of illegal migrants across the world suggests that, at least in some situations, people may prioritize location over legal status. The question is thus to determine what it would take to align status and location in each case: staying, returning, or moving on.

In this context, return is rarely a simple solution (box 5.2). It is in fact a new movement. That refugees want to return is sometimes taken as a given, and in many public debates their motivation for repatriating is assumed.[5] Yet the decision to repatriate is complex: rather than an easy homecoming or a return to the preexisting order of things, repatriation is better described as "a new life cycle in a challenging environment."[6] The place of origin, affected by conflict and violence, has often undergone wrenching social, economic, and political changes. The forcibly displaced, too, are not who they were when they left: women may have acquired more rights, children born in exile may not be literate in the language of the country of origin, and youth may have adopted new norms and values.[7] The reintegration of returnees in their country or place of origin can be almost as complicated as the experience of adjusting to a host society.[8]

Mobile livelihoods and urbanization

Solutions are often thought of as a final process, such that forcibly displaced are reestablished with enough safety and economic opportunities to preclude further movement.[9] Yet in some cases, movements and temporary migrations (including to places that have become asylum) were an integral part of livelihood strategies well before the conflict started. For example, for many Afghans migration has long been a way of life: just prior to the Soviet occupation, between 500,000 and 1,000,000 Afghans worked in the Islamic Republic of Iran, nomads used to cross the Pakistan border every year, and many poor families engaged in seasonal migration to complement low agricultural incomes.[10] Similarly, Lebanese officials estimate that about 300,000 Syrians were living in Lebanon as economic migrants before the conflict:[11] they became the first refugees,

BOX 5.2 The complexities of return and reintegration

Return is often regarded in public debates as the most natural solution to forced displacement, especially for refugees: the forcibly displaced are seen as "out of place" and return is a way to restore the natural order of things.[a] Repatriation is often discussed in terms of a return "home" even a generation or more after the flight from conflict and even when the descendants of the original refugees may never have seen their "homeland."

This focus on return is relatively recent.[b] When the 1951 Convention was drafted, its language suggested that it expected refugees to slowly integrate into host communities with adequate protection in the meantime. Given the redrawing of borders and alliances, no one expected the millions of ethnic Germans displaced from Eastern Europe to go home, nor was this considered desirable. During the Cold War, refugees who had "chosen freedom" were not expected by their Western hosts to go back to the Soviet-dominated bloc. The focus on repatriation started in the 1980s, when millions of Africans and Central Americans became displaced by postcolonial wars and proxy conflicts in the Cold War and started to be

integrated in official refugee statistics.[c] It sharpened in the 1990s, when the number of refugees and asylum-seekers reached a peak, and restrictive policies became more widespread. At the same time, with the end of the Cold War, direct humanitarian interventions in countries of origin became politically and operationally more feasible, which facilitated the international community's involvement in voluntary repatriation.[d]

The focus on return is also underpinned by a world view in which the place of birth, to which one aims to return, is a primary factor of one's identity. Modern psychology suggests, however, that the construction of one's identity is more complex, and that it is a function of many factors beyond the place of origin. There is a wide acceptance that many groups of people who have moved (such as internal or international migrants) will not return to their place of origin nor that they necessarily want to do so.

What is traditionally seen as "return" by host authorities and international agencies can be perceived very differently by the forcibly displaced themselves. For example, among Angolan refugees

living in Zambia, most of those perceived as repatriating refugees by the government and the international community actually saw themselves as villagers moving in search of better livelihoods in resource-rich Angola.[e] From their perspective, repatriation was taking place in the context of the normal movement of the ethnic Lunda people across their traditional land, which straddles the border.[f] Some people originally from Zambia were interested in being "repatriated" into Angola while some refugees were not.

Reintegration is also a difficult concept. It assumes that there is a somewhat stable and functioning society to reintegrate into. Yet many refugees are returning to a post conflict environment, where violence has often been accompanied by social dislocation and where risks of renewed fighting can be high. Reintegration is not about reentering a condition that existed in the past, but rather about taking part in the emergence of a new social fabric and a new social contract.[g] But this is particularly fraught for those who return after a long exile, including for younger generations that have no knowledge of their parents' place of origin.

a. Hammond 1999.
b. This process began with two conferences in Africa, the International Conference on Assistance to Refugees in Africa (ICARA) I and II, which discussed durable solutions—return, local integration, and resettlement—and identified return as the best option. Then, in Central America, the International Conference on Central American Refugees (CIREFCA) supported efforts to combine repatriation with post-conflict rehabilitation and peace consolidation. These initiatives led to more recent attempts to engage development actors in the repatriation process and extend the United Nations High Commissioner for Refugees' (UNHCR's) mandate from protecting refugees to promoting durable solutions. Hammond 2014a.
c. Hammond 2014a.
d. Ghanem 2003; Amore 2002; Allen and Morsink 1994.
e. Bakewell 2000. Such perceptions are not inconsistent with their status as repatriates: although they described their return in economic terms they no longer needed international protection.
f. Bakewell 2000.
g. Duffied, Diagne, and Tennant 2008.

bringing in their families as insecurity grew. In central Peru, people rotated for decades between villages and cities to complement their incomes: from their perspective, the valleys from which IDPs fled and the cities to which they went constituted complementary spaces.[12] The simple notions of return or integration do not fit well with such livelihoods.

Displacement is also taking place against the backdrop of global urbanization trends: it is an accelerator of movements that were already in the making or would have happened anyway, although in far less traumatic circumstances and with far less impact on the vulnerability of those affected. Urbanization induces profound transformations.

Many with a rural background no longer want to return to their villages of origin, for reasons that typically include security concerns, lack of job opportunities, and inadequate access to services.[13] Others may not have the option to return at all. And a return to a relatively poor rural area is often no more likely than the return of a rural economic migrant. Under such circumstances, defining an "end point" of forced displacement can become murky, especially for rural IDPs now in cities.

For some forcibly displaced, what was initially forced may eventually transmute into other forms of movement (box 5.3).[14] Some see onward labor migration as offering not only a chance of economic betterment but also the possibility of a more dignified life, because access to employment allows self-sufficiency and autonomous decision making.[15]

These movements raised difficult legal and ethical questions, and introduced a degree of confusion between forced displacement and economic migration. When engaging in a secondary movement, refugees remain refugees (continuing to need international protection) but behave like migrants (moving to places that will use their skills and offer more opportunities). Such secondary movements are not new (and were common, for example, among those who fled the Nazi regime before and during World War II) but the size of the flow in a context of restrictive policies has brought the issue to the fore. It highlights the complexity of human migration and the mismatch between the way durable solutions have been traditionally conceived and the aspirations of some of the forcibly displaced.

What the numbers say

Any new movement entails a substantial element of risk for the forcibly displaced. In a post conflict environment, peace and security are often uncertain, and economic prospects dire, at least in the short term. The forcibly displaced, with limited resources and a vivid experience of past trials, are unlikely to take such risks easily (box 5.4). The fundamental uncertainty of the situation is built into the entire decision-making process.[16]

In every situation some people return, others do not, and the proportions vary across countries. Durable solutions are often described as either/or categories: a one-off repatriation process, a forever integration, or a rare resettlement opportunity. Yet in practice the forcibly displaced have to negotiate a complex process of belonging based on a multiplicity of factors.[17] Many try to keep their options open.

Solutions are worked out through an iterative process, and movements are often staggered or even cyclical.[18] For example, displaced households (or groups of households) may split themselves up, sending an advance party to explore conditions, reclaim assets, and prepare for a permanent return (or secondary movement).[19] In some situations, for example among Afghans and South Sudanese, solutions can involve a temporary or permanent dispersal of family members between exile and return locations to maximize the family's overall prospects:[20] some adult men may repatriate to retrieve land and livelihoods, children may stay in camps in the care of relatives to access educations services, and some family members may try to migrate to a high-income country from where

BOX 5.4   Do the forcibly displaced want to return?

A number of studies has found that return is not always the preferred solution for many refugees and IDPs. Those who wanted to return accounted for 11 percent of IDPs in Colombia in 2014;[a] for 16 percent of Afghan refugees in Pakistan in 2011 (with major concerns over security, employment, and housing);[b] for 32 percent of Somali refugees living in Ethiopian and Kenyan camps in 2013 (with preconditions like stability, health and education, livelihood opportunities, and continued humanitarian assistance);[c] and about 10 percent of Iraqi refugees in 2008.[d]

Different groups usually express distinct preferences, which reflect their conditions in the place of exile and their expectations for the place of return. Their decision making is complex and can divide households, as exemplified in the case of Iraqi returnees from Denmark.[e] Preferences vary based on criteria such as age and gender, duration of exile, remoteness of the place of origin, education level, economic status, occupation, and political affiliations.[f]

In particular prospects can be very different for men and women. Both tend to see return as going back to preflight gender relations after an exile during which women may have enjoyed enhanced opportunities. Men and women also tend to consider different factors in making their decision: women may give more weight to health and education, while men may be more concerned about employment.[g] In a 2004–05 survey, women were far less willing than men to return to Afghanistan from Pakistan and the Islamic Republic of Iran, and they were apprehensive about security and mobility restrictions there.[h] Similarly among IDPs in Colombia, female-headed households were less willing to return.

Prospects can also vary across age groups. The younger generation may not know their country of origin, and may be anxious about leaving the familiar environment in which they grew up. In a 2004–05 survey of Afghans, youth were far less interested in return than older generations, and they were mainly concerned about access to education and employment.[i]

Security concerns are critical, yet play out differently across various groups. They tend to be highly related to personal experiences during the conflict. In some cases, the original "home" is a place of trauma, where people have been victimized. Minorities and victims of direct violence are typically less willing to consider return.[j] The formal signing of a peace agreement does not necessarily mean that the country of origin has become safe for all. For example, in the Buduburam settlement of Liberian refugees in Ghana, some women expressed a fear of being "hunted" by warlords and ex-soldiers if they returned.[k] There may also be continued or new persecution risks for some groups. And a simple reduction of the threats to physical safety is rarely reason enough for people to want to return.[l]

Economic conditions are also important in shaping intentions. For Afghans, those who had set up lucrative businesses in exile were reluctant to repatriate, even though they often maintained high levels of commercial activities and social ties with Afghanistan.[m] In Colombia, IDPs with access to land, social networks, or job opportunities in their places of origin were more willing to return.

Finally, social networks and peer decisions may be important (even if little studied). Anecdotal evidence suggests that in some camps of Afghan refugees in Pakistan, leaders exercised considerable influence in deciding for an entire group whether, and when, to return.

a. Arias, Ibañez, and Querubin 2014.
b. UNHCR 2012.
c. Danish and Norwegian Refugee Councils 2013.
d. UNHCR 2008.
e. Riiskjaer and Nielsson 2008.
f. Stepputat 2004; Monsutti 2006.
g. Stepputat 2004.
h. Monsutti 2006.
i. Monsutti 2006.
j. Arias, Ibañez, and Querubin 2014.
k. Hardgrove 2009.
l. Monsutti 2006.
m. Monsutti 2006.

they can provide remittances.[21] In Uganda, many South Sudanese refugees opted out of official repatriation schemes at first instance: they chose to return on their own while leaving some relatives behind, so as to keep their refugee status active in case the return failed.

Other strategies can include cyclical return, with household members moving back and forth between their place of origin and a place of exile, as was documented among Somali refugees.[22] In the Central Sierra in Peru, IDPs involved in return programs similarly wanted to keep the option of moving back to their place of asylum or splitting up their residence between city and rural communities.[23]

Overall, large numbers of refugees end up with a solution that is not one of the traditional "protection-focused" durable solutions. Of the 7.7 million people who exited United Nations High Commissioner for Refugees (UNHCR) refugee statistics in 2009–14, 61 percent were in the "others" category (figure 5.1), presumably reflecting a variety of further movements or de facto integration.[24] By contrast, returns accounted for 27 percent of the total, resettlement 6 percent, and naturalization 4 percent.[25]

From return to successful return

When and where people return

Return often takes place against the backdrop of political calculations: by the host country, which may encourage refugees to leave, by the country of origin, for whom returnees can be a critical stake in political processes such as an election or census, and by donors, who prefer repatriation to expensive support programs or to large number of refugees for resettlement (box 5.5).

From the end of the Cold War in 1991 to 2014, 25 million refugees returned to their countries of origin (figure 5.2), with the pace of returns far higher before 2005 (almost 20 million) than after (5.2 million). Four situations accounted for over 65 percent of the total: Afghanistan following the withdrawal of Soviet troops in 1989 and the collapse of the Taliban regime in 2001 (36 percent of the total), Rwanda immediately after the 1994 genocide and then after the entry of Rwandese troops in Zaire in 1997 (13 percent), Iraq mainly after the 1991 Gulf War (9 percent), and Mozambique after peace was concluded in the early 1990s (7 percent).[26]

Refugee returns tend to happen in peaks, typically about one to three years after the end of a conflict. Past this period, the pace of returns is much slower. This suggests that people who have made the decision not to return in the immediate aftermath of a peace settlement are unlikely to return in large numbers later on. It may be the situation of a number of refugees who are currently in protracted situations, and for whom the odds of return may be relatively low.

The duration of forced displacement does not seem to be a major impediment to return: a number of major episodes of return correspond to situations where refugees had been in protracted displacement (for example for Afghanistan in 2001, or Mozambique in the early 1990s). Cultural and linguistic proximity with the host country does also not seem

FIGURE 5.1 Exits from UNHCR statistics

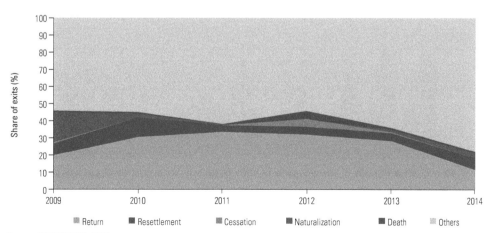

Sources: UNHCR 2016b, 2016c.
Note: UNHCR = United Nations High Commissioner for Refugees.

Rebuilding Lives   **105**

BOX 5.5 The politics of return

Repatriation is often regarded as a visible vote of confidence in the country's political and economic prospects. For example, the return of Cambodian refugees from Thailand was governed by agreements that aimed to have them participate in the 1993 national elections.[a] In Southern Sudan, efforts were made to ensure that as many of the displaced persons as possible would be back in time for the 2008 census.[b] In Bosnia and Herzegovina, pressures by European Union (EU) countries that had hosted refugees played a key role in the early timing of return.[c] This often imposes an urgency on the process that may leave little time to ensure that the socioeconomic conditions for successful reintegration are in place.[d]

In such a politicized environment, there have been controversies over the "voluntary" dimension of some returns.[e] For example, for the return of Cambodian refugees from Thailand in the 1990s, there were reports that many refugees did not have much of a choice.[f] Large numbers of Burundian refugees were also sent back home, from Tanzania, in 1996. Return under such circumstances greatly impedes the ability of returning refugees to rebuild their lives and contribute to society.

The return of IDPs can also be very politicized, to signal the end of an insurgency or the return to normalcy in regions previously torn by conflict. IDPs may be returned to their areas of origin with little choice but to accept, even when their prospects are dim. There have been allegations, for example, of such situations in the case of minority returns in Bosnia and Herzegovina or IDP returns in pacified areas of Pakistan.

Returnees with accumulated capital and exposure to new social, economic, and political ideas can, however, make a significant contribution to reconstructing their country, as with returns from the Rwandese diaspora after the 1994 genocide. More widely, successful return can be a critical element of sustainable recovery after conflict, and it is important to consider explicitly the fate of refugees and IDPs as part of peace settlements.[g]

It is often taken for granted that return is beneficial for the host country or region. Because of the political rhetoric calling for return, it is often assumed that the economic impacts on host communities are positive, and that any negative consequence is minimal or transitory. Yet these impacts have not been studied systematically. It is likely that at least in some cases the departure of large numbers of people reduces demand dramatically. Those who benefited from the presence of forcibly displaced are likely to be negatively affected. Some former host communities may need support to overcome an economic slowdown, which may be long lasting in areas with few economic opportunities.

a. Ballard 2002.
b. Pantuliano et al. 2008.
c. Harild, Christensen, and Zetter 2015.
d. Harild, Christensen, and Zetter 2015.
e. Harild, Christensen, and Zetter 2015.
f. Harild, Christensen, and Zetter 2015.
g. Long 2009.

FIGURE 5.2 Returns of refugees by country

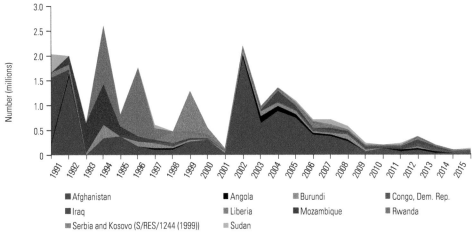

Sources: UNHCR 2016b, 2016c.

FIGURE 5.3 Returns of IDPs by country

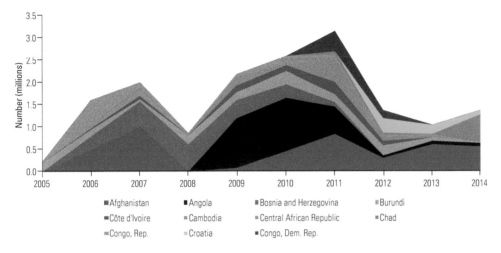

Source: UNHCR 2015c.
Note: Includes only internally displaced persons (IDPs) assisted or protected by the United Nations High Commissioner for Refugees.

to play a major role: most large returns originated from relatively familiar environments.

Data suggest comparable trends for IDPs.[27] About 19 million IDPs returned with some assistance or protection from UNHCR in 2005–14.[28] Once again, this is largely concentrated in a few countries: Afghanistan (19 percent of the total), Angola (14 percent), Bosnia and Herzegovina (10 percent), and Burundi (7 percent). Cambodia, the Central African Republic, Chad, the Democratic Republic of Congo, the Republic of Congo, Côte d'Ivoire, and Croatia accounted for 2 to 4 percent each (figure 5.3). As with refugees, returns also take place in peaks, but these are paced over a much longer period of time. In a given situation, the peak return of IDPs is also typically later than the peak of refugees, usually several years after a peace settlement.

A large share of returnees do not go back to their place of origin but settle in other areas in their home country, often in urban areas. This caused sharp growth in cities such as Kabul in Afghanistan (where returnees and IDPs may account for up to 70 percent of the population), Juba in South Sudan (where the population doubled between the signing of the Comprehensive Peace Agreement in 2005 and independence in 2011), Luanda in Angola,[29] and Monrovia in Liberia.[30] For those who have been exposed to

urban lifestyles during displacement or who do not have access to land in the countryside, the lure of urban centers includes expectations of better security, more anonymity, employment opportunities, and access to services.[31] Even where returnees move to rural areas, they may be looking for better opportunities. Some Cambodian refugees, for instance, "returned" to areas known for having higher agricultural potential than to their places of origin, as did many refugees from Guatemala.[32]

The risk of failed return

Not all returns have a happy ending. For example, eight years after their return in 1991–97, former Eritrean refugees were still living with very few assets: only 41 percent of them owned land (against 73 percent before flight) with an average lot size a quarter of the previous average; almost no one owned cattle (66 percent before flight); and only 24 percent owned goats (67 percent before flight).[33] Women and girls may face particular challenges on return as they generally have fewer opportunities, fewer resources, lower status, and less power and influence than men in their country of origin (box 5.6).[34]

There have been many reports of returnees becoming IDPs in their country of return. This suggests not only that they did not return to their place of origin, but also that their new situation remains unsatisfactory and uncertain, so that they need continued assistance and protection. Over the last 15 years, large-scale returns were paralleled by a sizable increase in the number of IDPs in 46 percent of cases.[35]

Returnees may even have to flee again after returning to their country of origin, a telling sign that their return was unsuccessful. The total number of returns exceeds the peak number of refugees in nine of the ten largest return countries, typically by about 30 percent.[36] For example, the total number of returnees from Afghanistan over 1979–2014 was 40 percent higher than the peak number of refugees during the period. Such numbers are difficult to explain in an unambiguous manner, but they confirm anecdotal reports that a good number of people had to leave again after having returned. In other words, from the perspective of the forcibly displaced themselves, their return was a failure.

In some cases, large-scale returns have also been followed by a renewed round of fighting. Of the 15 largest episodes of return since 1991, about one-third were followed by a new round of fighting within a couple of years.[37] This is especially the case in

situations where peace remained fragile and economic prospects limited, as in Afghanistan after the 1989–91 and 2001–03 returns or in the Democratic Republic of Congo after the 1997–98 returns. It is consistent with broader statistics about the risks of renewed conflict within a few years of a peace settlement.[38] In some cases, there may however be an element of causality, with the massive and relatively rapid return of large numbers of people having a destabilizing effect in an already fragile environment. This suggests that return is not always a blessing, and that risks need to be carefully analyzed as external actors design support programs. From the perspective of host countries as well, too early a return process may prove counterproductive by causing further instability in a neighboring country.

The impact on return communities

The impact of return on receiving communities is in many respects similar to the impact of forced displacement on host communities. In both cases, a relatively sudden and large demographic shock has to be managed. The ultimate effect depends on the initial conditions, the nature and magnitude of the shock, and the response. What makes it easier in the case of return is that returnees are nationals with full socioeconomic rights and are usually familiar with the culture and environment. What can make it more difficult is that the initial conditions in the return communities tend to be very dire, especially when the overall environment continues to be politically fragile and economically depressed, and when there remain tensions, such as identity and land conflicts. External support to returnees and return communities also tends to be smaller than that provided to the forcibly displaced during their exile, and to a lesser extent to their host communities.

Return communities are hence likely to face considerable economic and social difficulties, which typically affect both the returnees and those who stayed throughout the conflict. At the national level, the presence of large numbers of returnees may add to the country's fragility and further complicate economic management, at least in the short term. At the local level, their presence may put additional pressure on services, cause an increase in prices of nontradables and create competition for jobs in some segments of the labor market. Social cohesion challenges can also be significant, whether the returns reignite tensions that caused displacement in the first place or lead to resentment between the returnees and those who stayed behind. The ultimate impact of such shocks is largely dependent on initial conditions, and these are typically very poor in the aftermath of conflict, which is when most returns take place.

What makes return successful?

From a development perspective, return is not an end in itself: the main goal is to mitigate the specific vulnerabilities of those who have been forcibly displaced. The focus is not on return, but on *successful* return. Considering the relatively large number of "twice displaced," this is in the interest of the host country, too. Available studies show that security and economic opportunities are the two main parameters that influence the success of return.

Security and social acceptance

For people who have been displaced by violence, security is paramount. People with traumatic experiences in their country of origin, or people who are perceived as having sided with the party that lost the conflict tend to be particularly reluctant to return, as documented for Iraqi and Liberian refugees.[39] In some cases, memories of the conflict, during which the government, neighbors, and friends became the most feared enemy (as happened in former Yugoslavia or Rwanda) remain overwhelming.[40] In Bosnia and Herzegovina, for example, many returnees sold or rented their properties, preferring not to live in ethnically mixed neighborhoods. In Afghanistan, discrimination in otherwise relatively stable areas in the north of the country prevented the return, whether spontaneous or assisted, of large groups of refugees belonging to ethnic minorities.

There are also many potential sources of tension between the returnees and people already living in return communities. Because

the returnee and the home country have both changed considerably during the intervening years, the "reconnecting" is often complex.[41] Large-scale repatriation may be perceived as a threat to a local community, especially when there is some competition for limited resources.[42] Those who stayed in war-torn areas can resent the provision of aid to returnees, as they see themselves as having endured the effects of conflict and violence with little assistance for many years.[43] Eritrean refugees who returned between 1991 and 1997 reported receiving very little help from the community: networks developed while in exile proved much stronger than those built in the first eight years of return.[44] Returnees may also encounter hostility, or become vulnerable to crime when they are viewed as having become wealthier while in exile.[45] The urgency of the material dimensions of reintegration should not overshadow the short- and long-term emotional challenges that refugees face upon return.[46]

Financial resources, social networks, and human capital

Return is the prelude to a difficult process of socioeconomic reintegration and it can be a great deal easier for those who come back with resources, skills, and networks. Refugees are more likely to repatriate successfully where they have portable assets (mainly capital to rebuild their homes and to provide a cushion in case of adverse developments) and marketable skills.[47] Those who do not have such assets or skills tend to face economic hardship, and their vulnerability may be exacerbated by repatriation.[48] Social networks in the country of origin also seem to play an important role in return and reintegration,[49] and can be critical for finding a job, as exemplified in the case of Liberian[50] and Afghan[51] returnees: those with strong social ties in the country of origin found employment more quickly than other returnees.[52]

There has long been a debate as to whether a harsh treatment of refugees by host countries is likely to accelerate their return. The reality is complex, as the decision to stay or return is informed by a comparison of conditions in exile and in the country of origin. In some cases, repatriation can be induced by difficult living conditions in the host country: for example, in Mexico, Guatemalan refugees in camps in Chiapas were much more likely to return at the end of the conflict than the refugees in Yucatan, who were better integrated.[53] Yet in many instances, returnees who left their place of displacement because of "push factors" such as strong discrimination or overt hostility by host authorities or host communities, required special assistance and protection even after return.[54] This in turn can lead to a failed return and a new cycle of displacement and exile.

More benevolent policies in host countries may in fact be more successful. In some cases, economic success while in displacement may facilitate return:[55] among Liberian refugees in Ghana, households who were better off while in displacement were keener on returning than poorer ones;[56] similarly, over 300,000 Angolan refugees who were relatively well established in Zambia returned spontaneously once peace was restored.[57] Such returns, with financial resources and human capital accumulated during displacement, are more likely to be sustainable. The extent to which life in exile provides space to build up assets and skills can therefore be critical to successful return.[58]

Access to economic opportunities

Access to economic opportunities in the country or region of origin, along with the prospects of recovering lost assets such as land and property, are key factors that influence successful return (box 5.7).[59] Refugees who can recover assets are often among the first to return: this is especially true for rural households that are able to reclaim their land or to gain access to land elsewhere.[60] Remittances can also be important, as was the case for Afghan and Liberian refugees, since they provide a cushion in the early stage of repatriation and initial capital for new income-generating activities.

The way this plays out is also a function of the sociocultural and political environment, including whether agricultural land is held privately or in common, whether laws give precedence to original owners or long-term users, whether authorities play a neutral role or engage in land grabbing, and whether the confiscation of property is part of a deliberate process of spatial segregation along ethnic and sectarian lines.[61] Support programs for return and reintegration have generally struggled with such difficulties and most have not been very successful, as illustrated by experiences in Afghanistan, Burundi, and Cambodia.[62] This was typically due to a range of factors such as lack of cadastral surveys, lack of ownership documents, poor land administration and arbitration, and weak law enforcement and justice systems. The result has been that most returnees have been left to fend for themselves when trying to reclaim their property or to find alternative land, and that they have often failed to do so.

External support

Return is often assisted by humanitarian agencies, in the form of transportation and "return kits," including cash, which provide returnees with a modicum of resources for the immediate period after their return (box 5.8). Common sense and anecdotal reports suggest that these programs are often instrumental in enabling returns that would otherwise not have taken place, but no empirical study has examined whether they are more likely to lead to sustainable reintegration than when returns are spontaneous.

BOX 5.7 Return and access to land

For forcibly displaced from rural areas, the ability to reclaim their land or to obtain access to land elsewhere is critical.[a] Land belonging to the forcibly displaced may have been appropriated by others during exile, especially in protracted situations or where land is scarce. Restitution raises thorny issues, including a risk of impoverishment for those who had settled on abandoned land, sometimes for many years, and are ejected.

Land disputes can become major impediments to a successful return and a key reason for rural returnees to move to urban areas in search of opportunities. For example, Eritrean returnees who described themselves as "not accepted" by the community cited land disputes as the main reason.[b] Such disputes have also been on the rise in Afghanistan, leading many returnees to settle in cities.[c] Unless institutions and mechanisms are in place to deal with these issues effectively, they can rapidly escalate into conflict.[d]

a. Harild, Christensen, and Zetter 2015.
b. Bascom 2005.
c. Monsutti 2006.
d. Rogge and Lippman 2004.

In Sudan for example, assisted returnees were seen by return communities as being in a difficult position, because they only returned with a reintegration package, while those who self-repatriated had enough resources to sustain themselves for some time and to restart their lives.[63]

Integration in host countries: Location vs. rights

A politically difficult solution

Forcibly displaced are considered locally integrated from a socioeconomic perspective when they are not in physical danger (and not at risk of *refoulement*); when they are not confined to camps and settlements; when they have basic socioeconomic rights; when they can sustain themselves and their families; when they have access to education and other services; and when they are socially networked in the host community.[64] To be sustainable, such socioeconomic integration needs to be underpinned by a legal status that provides security and some planning horizon. In other words, forcibly displaced are locally integrated when they have overcome their specific vulnerabilities to the point that they and their hosts show little difference in access to opportunities.

Local integration is in many respects the continuation and culmination of a successful process of inclusion in the host community during the episode of displacement. For most IDPs it is a relatively straightforward development, which mainly entails socioeconomic elements. For refugees it is more complicated, as it implies that they may remain indefinitely in their country of asylum and find a solution to their plights in that country: ideally but not necessarily this includes acquiring citizenship.[65]

Local integration depends on the goodwill of key groups in the host country and in the host community, for without it socioeconomic inclusion will remain an elusive prospect.[66] Such goodwill largely depends on the predisplacement relationships between the hosts and the displaced, including cultural, linguistic, as well as political dynamics. Some Afghan refugees and Pakistani hosts, for example, are connected by kinship, ethnic,

---

BOX 5.8 Assisting return

Large programs of assisted returns include the repatriation of about 370,000 Cambodians from Thailand in 1992–93, about 1.7 million Mozambicans from six countries in 1992–96, and about 1.5 million Afghans from Pakistan in 2002.[a] Efforts were often made to try and implement development projects in return areas (such as "quick-impact projects"), although there were typically difficulties associated with targeting (that is, effective identification of areas where people return) and timing (activities typically take time to yield their full impact). Such programs are largely focused on refugees and cover IDPs only to a much lesser extent.

But not all returns are assisted. For example, after the withdrawal of Soviet troops in 1989, about 55 percent of the 550,000 Afghan refugees who returned from Pakistan did so spontaneously.[b] Another wave of about 300,000 unassisted returns took place following the fall of the Taliban in 2001.[c] Large numbers of Rwandese refugees returned spontaneously from eastern Zaire in 1997. The 2002 Luena Accords in Angola were followed by rapid and large-scale refugee return of about 335,000 refugees.[d] A large majority of the returnees to South Sudan were also unsupported.[e] Overall, unassisted returns accounted for about 33 percent of the total in 2006–14.

The rationale for refugees to return spontaneously when assistance programs are available is multifold. It can be a lack of information, difficulties in accessing the programs, or social or peer pressure to move at a certain time. It can also be linked to the refugees' preference to keep refugee status even after return (which they would forfeit through an assisted process), as insurance in case peace does not hold and they have to go into exile again.[f] Importantly, those who return spontaneously may not be the same as those who return with assistance, and may in particular have access to more resources to start with.

a. Harild, Christensen, and Zetter 2015.
b. Harild, Christensen, and Zetter 2015.
c. Harild, Christensen, and Zetter 2015.
d. Harild, Christensen, and Zetter 2015.
e. Harild, Christensen, and Zetter 2015.
f. Return programs can also be abused by refugees who do not intend to return, or who return several times, as illustrated by a survey of Afghan returns from Pakistan, which showed many instances of people getting a return package, crossing the border to return, but then reentering Pakistan to obtain additional return packages. See Turton and Marsden 2002.

---

religious, and political networks, which create a moral obligation of solidarity.[67] Conversely, there are instances where (foreign) refugees are more easily integrated than IDPs.[68] Whether the local population accepts de facto or de jure local integration of the refugees and IDPs depends on who benefits and who loses from their continued presence, and on whether the interests of the various actors, particularly the most powerful, are being sufficiently preserved or served.[69]

Local integration is often accompanied by an increase in inequality among the displaced. With time, some displaced are able to improve their socioeconomic situation, while others struggle in a downward spiral of impoverishment.[70] For example, among Afghan refugees in Peshawar, Pakistan, a small group is engaged in skilled professions or in large businesses (notably transport and import–export between the two countries) and is well off, while the majority works in unskilled and irregular positions.[71] Such inequalities often reflect the amount of assets refugees were able to bring with them, their skills, as well as their social networks in the host city.[72]

De facto integration—Without rights

For refugees, local integration ideally means acquiring a new national identity with the full range of legal, social, and economic rights. A few host governments, including Belize, Mexico, Tanzania (box 5.9), and Uganda, have offered this option to some refugees who cannot or do not wish to repatriate.[73] A number of OECD countries have done the same.

However, many host countries are reluctant to naturalize refugees for a number of political reasons: in such cases, social and economic integration often proceeds "de facto." Many host governments have permitted refugees to settle amongst the local host community without official assistance.[74] Even in situations where host governments do not support a policy of integration, informal integration is widespread. Except in a few situations where concerted efforts were made to round up and forcibly relocate refugees, most host governments and local authorities lack the will or the capacity to impede the integration process, especially for the displaced who live outside of camps. Most of the time self-settled refugees are simply ignored by the authorities and eventually they can become integrated into the community.

But unless they naturalize or manage to keep their protected status, many refugees live in a state of legal limbo, with limited rights in society. This impedes their development prospects, even though citizenship rights have different meanings across the world. In general, the stronger the rule of law in a country, the more difficult it is to live on the fringes of legality (box 5.10).

In some cases, de facto integration may even include de facto regularization, although this is typically achieved through fraudulent means. In one study, 40 percent of Angolans who had been hosted in border villages in Zambia had managed to obtain a national registration card (citizen documentation). Many described themselves as Zambians in their encounters with Zambian authorities and as Angolans when it was in their interest to be seen as refugees, and local villagers did the same.[75] Their perception of nationality was instrumental rather than definitional of who they were. Some Somali refugees have also reportedly obtained Kenyan national ID cards from corrupt officials, allowing them to move freely around the country and to access formal employment and higher education, while providing them with greater security.[76]

BOX 5.9 Tanzania's integration of Burundians

In 2007, Tanzania offered citizenship to the Burundian refugees who had fled their country in 1972, and their children. While some 400,000 returned to Burundi, 162,000 opted for naturalization. Another 12,000 were resettled to the United States as part of a comprehensive strategy.

Obtaining citizenship seemed the logical step for a group of self-reliant and taxpaying residents, especially as over 85 percent of them were actually born in Tanzania. The process was interrupted in 2010 when refugees were required to relocate from their settlements to other parts of Tanzania in order to become citizens: in essence they were forced to choose between local and national integration.[a] This issue was resolved in 2014 when the government allowed the new citizens to choose whether to stay in their settlements or to move to another party of the country. This is the only recent example of a large group of refugees being offered citizenship in a country of first asylum.[b]

a. Hovil 2014.
b. Markus 2014.

Residency vs. citizenship

Local integration can constitute an effective solution for IDPs. For refugees, however, de facto integration cannot be a panacea, and the restoration of full citizenship rights is a vital component of any durable solution.[77] Without formal status, people may remain in uncertainty, lack legal protection, be exposed to institutionalized discrimination, and eventually risk statelessness.[78]

There may be some intermediate solutions between an irregular status and full citizenship. For example, countries can open access to naturalization to specific groups, or provide enhanced rights short of full citizenship (e.g., permanent residency).[79] Providing formal legal migrant status to "de facto integrated" refugees may be a way to recognize the reality of their situation and the normality of human mobility.[80] Such an approach distinguishes between citizenship (formal political membership and associated rights) and residency (economic and social integration), and it prioritizes economic security over political membership. In doing so, it may alleviate some of the host countries' concerns about national identity and the political implications of a long-term stay. At the same time, it may have only a small impact on host communities and the labor market when socioeconomic integration has already proceeded de facto.[81]

Many high-income countries are familiar with such situations, as they accept relatively large numbers of economic migrants (figure 5.4). Immigration countries and refugee-hosting countries often face similar anxieties over the medium-term impact of integration on their economy, social fabric, and even national identity.[82] Yet immigration countries have been regularizing or naturalizing large numbers of migrants over the years and this has been largely successful. For example, in spite of a difficult economic situation, Italy regularized about 1.2 million illegal migrants (that is, about 2 percent of its population) in 2012; since 2000, the United States has naturalized on average a little over 700,000 foreigners every year adding up to close to 4 percent of its total population. In fact, the total number of naturalized immigrants in the United States over the last 15 years (about 10.5 million) is

similar to the total number of refugees hosted in developing countries (about 12 million).

Innovative solutions have been developed along these lines in a number of refugee situations. In both Central America and West Africa, regional agreements have been used to provide refugees with permanent residency in their host country, while they remain citizens of their origin country. Under such arrangements, former refugees can remain in their host country with a formal legal status. For example, in Costa Rica in the early 1980s, all registered Central American refugees were offered the opportunity to switch their status to temporary or permanent residency.[83] Other countries in Central

---

BOX 5.10   Does status matter? Lessons from economic migration

Some studies of economic migration in high-income countries suggest that the costs of informality can be high, although it would be risky to extrapolate these conclusions uncritically to refugee situations in developing countries.

For example, a comparison of documented and undocumented Mexican migrants in the United States in the late 1990s showed that legal migrants earned on average over 40 percent more than illegal immigrants, and that over half of this difference could be attributed to their legal status.[a] Unsurprisingly, illegal immigrants tend to be overrepresented in low-skill segments of the labor market.[b] Higher education does not easily translate into higher wages for them, but gaining legal status "activates" its positive influence.[c] The lack of proper documentation also very significantly increases instances of abuse, nonpayment or underpayment of wages, forced overtime, and unsafe working conditions.[d] Use of health care services, whether preventive, curative, or emergency, is also lower among undocumented adults and their children.[e]

Some authors, however, have proposed that the assumption on which we can distinguish between citizens and migrants in the North may apply differently in the South. For them, the understanding of citizenship is based overwhelmingly on the states of Western Europe and North America, in which the government has unquestioned power to regulate entry and residence.[f] The formalities for residing in a country are easier to circumvent in many countries of the South: what is regulatory and legal may not always be enforced where governments are overburdened with competing priorities, and where administrative capacity is stretched.[g]

a. Rivera-Batiz 1997.
b. Rivera-Batiz 1997.
c. Mehta et al. 2002.
d. Mehta et al. 2002.
e. Gusmano 2012.
f. Gagnon and Khgoudour-Casteras 2011; Sadiq 2009.
g. Gagnon and Khgoudour-Casteras 2011.

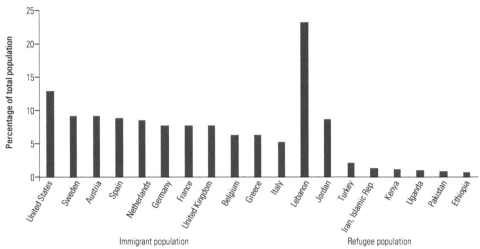

FIGURE 5.4 Immigrants in selected OECD countries and refugees in key host countries as a share of the total host population

Sources: UNHCR 2016c, OECD 2016a.
Note: Immigrant numbers in European Union (EU) countries do include refugees but do not include citizens from other EU countries.
OECD = Organisation for Economic Co-operation and Development.

America, including Belize and Mexico, have offered permanent residency to long-staying refugees who have opted not to repatriate.[84] Similarly, when the civil wars in Liberia and Sierra Leone ended in the early 2000s, some refugees were allowed to stay in their countries of asylum under an economic migration status thanks to the free movement protocols of the Economic Community of West African States (ECOWAS). For example, the Nigerian government issued renewable residence and work permits to refugees (and withdrew their refugee status) once the governments of Liberia and Sierra Leone provided them with passports.[85] This solution combined local integration with "legal" repatriation—a restoration of citizenship rights that does not include physical return (box 5.11).[86]

Integration in high-income countries: A difficult endeavor[87]

Fifteen years in Europe, and less than ten in North America

The recent inflow of refugees into the EU has drawn attention to the experience of refugees who are hosted or resettled in high-income countries. As of end-2015, about 2.4 million refugees lived in these countries, which is relatively low by historical standards but on an upward trend (figure 5.5). Six countries accounted for two-thirds of the total: the Russian Federation (13 percent), Germany (13 percent), the United States (11 percent), France (11

BOX 5.11 ECOWAS and labor migration

The 1979 Protocol Relating to the Free Movement of Persons, Residence, and Establishment signed by the 15 members of ECOWAS provides for freedom of movement for ECOWAS citizens across ECOWAS states.[a] Under this framework, ECOWAS citizens can apply for residence and work permits within the ECOWAS region. In principle, this also applies to ECOWAS refugees who are hosted in another ECOWAS country.[b]

In practice, implementation has been hampered by weak administrative capacity. Yet, such solutions have been implemented for some Liberian and Sierra Leonean refugees in several ECOWAS countries. International actors can play a role in facilitating access for refugees to resident-migrant status. They can support the waiving of residence-permit fees for refugees, as happened in Ghana, or arrange to pay them, as UNHCR did to support the integration of refugees from Liberia and Sierra Leone in Nigeria.[c]

a. Long 2009.
b. Long 2009.
c. Long 2009; Adepoju, Boulton, and Levin 2007.

FIGURE 5.5 Refugees in high-income countries

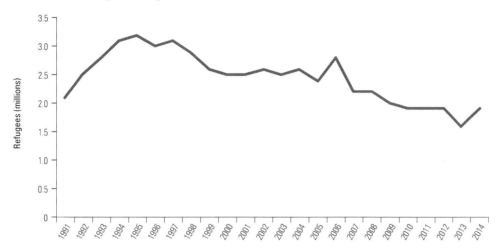

Source: UNHCR 2016c.
Note: High-income countries according to World Bank classification.

percent), Sweden (7 percent), and Canada (6 percent). Refugees reach Organisation for Economic Co-operation and Development (OECD) countries either through a secondary movement from their country of first asylum, or via an organized resettlement program. Most refugees arriving in the EU do so through secondary movement. Resettlement is mainly directed towards the United States (which accounts for 71 percent of the total since 1991), Canada (11 percent), and Australia (11 percent).

In the EU, it takes on average more than 15 years for refugees to reach the employment rate of economic migrants (figure 5.6). By contrast, in the United States, labor market performance of refugees overtakes that of economic migrants within ten years.[88] Differences in outcomes may be related to language issues or to distinct social models: for example,

FIGURE 5.6 Employment rate by immigrant category and duration of stay in European OECD countries, 2008

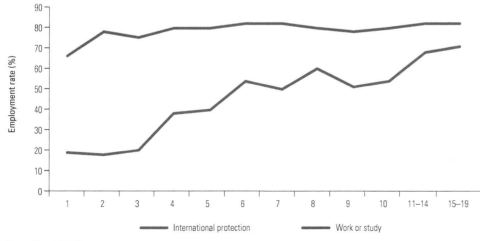

Source: Eurostat 2008.
Note: OECD = Organisation for Economic Co-operation and Development.

economic migrants in Europe face far higher unemployment rates than the population as a whole, while the difference is much smaller for Canada and nonexistent in Australia and the United States.[89] There may also be a difference between refugees who arrive on their own (typically in continental Europe) and those who have been screened through a formal resettlement program (the large majority of those who reach Australia, Canada, and the United States): findings and experiences may not be replicable across countries.

If the experience of economic migrants is any guide, integration challenges may persist across generations. In some countries, second-generation migrants continue to fare less well than native workers. For example, in Denmark in 2008, native workers had a 79 percent employment rate compared with 56 percent for first-generation migrants; second-generation migrants had a 67 percent employment rate—better than their parents but still far behind native workers.[90]

What makes integration successful?

Economic conditions

The economic conditions at the time of settlement have an impact on labor market participation and incomes. Evidence from Norway, Sweden, and the United States shows that employment rates for refugees who arrived or completed their integration program in the immediate aftermath of the 2008 financial crisis were lower than those of earlier cohorts.[91] In Norway for example, 63 percent of those graduating from the integration program in 2007 had a job 12 months later, but only 44 percent for the 2009 cohort.[92]

The first few years in a country have an outsized effect on later employment opportunities and wages. Refugees who are employed quickly and continuously after arrival end up on a trajectory that leads to higher incomes later.[93] Yet, in many countries, refugees face difficulties in getting a job. In Germany, for example, almost two-thirds of refugees remain unemployed two years after arrival.[94] In Canada, only 52 percent of those of working age were employed seven years after arrival.[95]

There are significant differences between refugees who arrive in OECD countries on their own ("approved asylum-seekers") and those benefiting from a formal resettlement program. For example in Sweden, resettled refugees start with a lower employment rate than approved asylum-seekers and it takes them more than fifteen years to catch up (figure 5.7).[96] Conversely, in Canada, approved asylum-seekers fare worse than resettled refugees with a gap in earning that persists

FIGURE 5.7 **Employment by years in Sweden for resettled refugees and approved asylum-seekers, 2007**

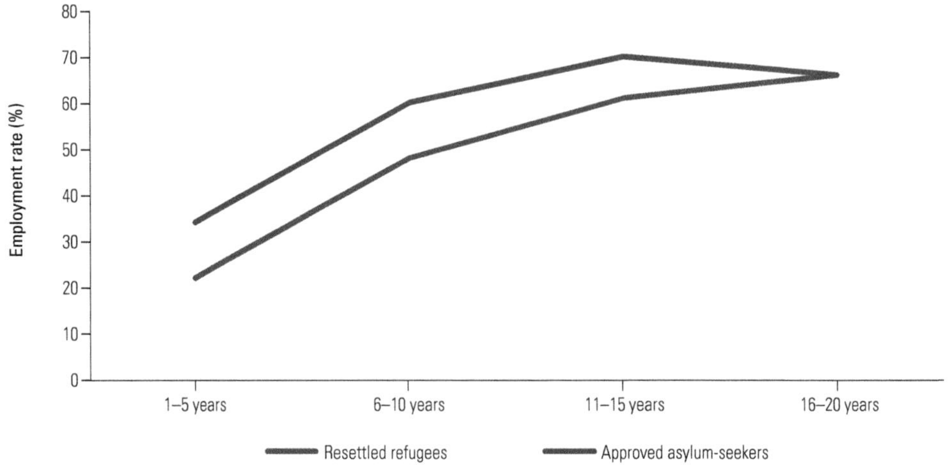

Source: Bevelander 2011.

five years after arrival.[97] Such differences may partly reflect the fact that each resettlement country uses its own set of screening criteria to select beneficiaries: some focus on the vulnerability of refugees, others on their likelihood of integrating successfully.

Human capital

Not surprisingly, the level of education and skills affects employment and earnings. For example, in Canada refugees with only a high school degree earned about 30 percent less than those with a university degree.[98] Language skills are also critical.[99] In the United Kingdom, 79 percent of people who spoke English very well were employed within two years of being granted refugee status, against only 18 percent of those who did not speak English at all.[100] In the United States, nearly 90 percent of refugees with no income had no English speakers in their household.[101]

Employment rates for refugee women are typically half those of men, sometimes less.[102] For example a 2006 study found that in the Netherlands female Afghan refugees had employment rates of 8 percent compared with 49 percent for men, with comparable figures among Somali refugees.[103] More recently, female Somali refugees' wages in the Netherlands have typically ranged from 60 to 75 percent of men's wages.[104]

Refugees' health also affects their employment prospects. Refugees generally have poorer health than the broader host population.[105] In the Netherlands, health problems, including depression, led to lower rates of employment and occupational status.[106] In the United States, a recent study found that the greatest barrier to employment among refugees (listed by a fifth of respondents) was health and disability.[107]

Legal status

The longer it takes for asylum-seekers to receive a response to their claim, the worse the integration outcomes. Obtaining refugee status can take anywhere from several months to several years.[108] The resulting uncertainty has negative consequences for integration. In the Netherlands, a group of asylum-seekers surveyed in a recent study had an average stay in temporary accommodation of 21 months, with some people staying for more than five years.[109] Unsurprisingly, the longer refugees remain in a reception center, the worse they do in employment.[110]

Gaining citizenship, as opposed to temporary refugee status, leads to a higher degree of integration. For refugees in the Netherlands, obtaining nationality is associated with higher employment rates, higher likelihood of holding a permanent job, and lower reliance on social welfare.[111] This pattern is consistent with studies of economic migrants, which show a strong correlation between employment rates and citizenship (although the causal links are unclear).[112] The issue of citizenship is particularly relevant as a large majority of refugees in high-income countries intend to remain: for example, in Germany, 76 percent of Syrians, 88 percent of Iraqis, and 89 percent of Afghans express a desire to stay.[113] Yet naturalization rates vary widely across countries.[114]

Location

Being in the "right place" is critical for successful socioeconomic integration. A number of countries put restrictions on the location of refugees (or otherwise provide incentives to settle in a given place). Yet, the availability of employment opportunities remains the critical criterion for success. For example, in 1985 Sweden adopted a policy of placing refugees according to housing availability rather than labor market conditions.[115] A comparison with earlier arrivals shows that this resulted in a 25 percent drop in refugee earnings, along with a 33 percent increase in idleness and a nearly 50 percent increase in the use of welfare.[116] The policy was subsequently altered to allow refugees to settle where they wished, with social support funds following them.

There is an intense debate, especially in the EU, about whether to disperse refugees as a means to facilitate integration. The concentration of refugees of a given origin in certain locales can help them establish social networks, which have proven key to accessing employment, especially in the early years after arrival.[117] However, it can also hamper their social and cultural integration, especially where there is an implicit expectation of assimilation. Austria, Belgium, Denmark, Germany, the Netherlands, Sweden, and the

United Kingdom all have elements of an active approach to dispersal.[118]

Support programs

Governments are implementing a range of support programs for refugees. In Europe, these concentrate on language acquisition and cultural competency (with mandatory language and integration programs in countries such as Belgium, the Czech Republic, Denmark, France, Germany, Greece, the Netherlands, and Norway), while in the United States, they tend to focus on helping refugees get a job quickly.

There is mixed evidence on the effectiveness of these efforts. A review of mandatory integration training in the EU found limited evidence that it leads to measurable or long-term changes in integration,[119] with of course differences across countries. Long integration programs which keep refugees out of the labor market for an extended period of time can have ambiguous effects on their likelihood of regaining employment:[120] in Sweden for example (where these programs can last up to two years), one study found that only 18 percent of program participants got a job soon after program completion, compared with 43 percent of non-enrollees.[121] Comprehensive and rigorous impact evaluations are needed to assess the effectiveness of these efforts and to determine the factors that allow for the successful integration of refugees.[122]

An agenda for development actors

The objective of development actors is to help the forcibly displaced overcome their specific vulnerabilities in a durable manner, without adversely affecting other groups. The focus is therefore not on return, but rather on regaining the ability to seize socioeconomic opportunities; not on where people live, but on whether they have specific vulnerabilities. This can only be achieved with the active engagement of host countries, which need to be supported in developing solutions that are acceptable to them.[123] It is part of a broader effort, spearheaded by UNHCR that aims to promote comprehensive solutions, including elements that go beyond the socioeconomic sphere.

In some situations an ad hoc solution is required. This is especially the case for countries that are hosting very large numbers of refugees relative to their population, such as Jordan and Lebanon. Solutions that may be adequate in countries with a smaller proportion of refugees may not be feasible (or even desirable) for these two countries.

For other situations, development actors should aim to provide access to socioeconomic opportunities, as a necessary condition for recovery. This is about rights, but also about the availability of jobs. The agenda for development actors is hence fourfold: first, in the case of return, provide support to both returnees and return communities; second, in the case of local integration, help resolve the tension between legal rights and socioeconomic opportunities; third, help deal with lasting "limbo" situations; and fourth, be engaged over the medium-term to help overcome lasting vulnerabilities.

Return: Support returnees and return communities

To support successful return, development actors should engage in a range of activities.

First, development actors should support other agencies, including UNHCR, in their efforts to advocate for an orderly process of return. Although part of the returns is spontaneous, there is some scope for governments and international actors to influence patterns. Pacing the return process, to the extent possible, may help mitigate the shock to communities of return. Preparing for, and managing, a rapid urbanization of returnees, and hence an explosion of urban centers, may be critical to medium-term stability. Monitoring the flow of returnees and their situation beyond the first few months of return may provide the information needed to determine the places that are most in need of support.

Second, development actors should support the country of return in its recovery efforts. This can build on the extensive experience of development actors in supporting post conflict recovery. Robust economic performance is essential to create a stable environment in which return can be successful and sustainable. It is also critical to generate socioeconomic opportunities for returnees, so that they can overcome the legacy of displacement.

Third, development actors should provide targeted support to the communities most profoundly affected by return. This support may be similar to that required by host communities. It includes in particular a dual focus on expanding service delivery and on providing support to those who may lose out with the arrival of returnees. It may also include support for private investment so as to help create jobs in the area. Development support ought to be provided with particular attention to fostering social cohesion and to preventing or reducing tensions between returnees and their communities.

Fourth, development actors should work with humanitarian agencies to ensure the complementarity of efforts. For example, quick-impact projects developed by humanitarian agencies to support areas of return may need to be complemented by longer-term development programs to support economic activity and job creation or to help cope with shortages of housing or services. Immediate support to returnees moving to urban centers may need to be accompanied by development assistance to manage the corresponding urban growth, and so on. Investments can also be complemented by a policy dialogue with the authorities, for example to help address difficulties in returnees reclaiming their land and other assets.

Integration: Help provide legal status and opportunities

Local integration is taking place often without government and international efforts. For IDPs, it constitutes an important solution, and it can help resolve the overwhelming majority of situations. For refugees, a degree of de facto integration is occurring, and this may indeed be a step toward a solution but it remains incomplete.[124]

Development actors should support countries that are willing to provide an adequate and durable status to refugees, even short of citizenship, such as permanent residency or formal migrant status. This may be more feasible in countries with relatively few refugees who have de facto integrated. A parallel effort may be needed in those situations where IDPs are institutionally discriminated against, under the guise of a "special status" that prevents their full integration in society. Wherever there may be opportunities, development actors should engage in a dialogue with the authorities, assess the feasibility of such solutions, and provide financial support as may be needed for implementation.[125]

In some situations, however, local integration may not be feasible for the host country. For example, where it appears that it would create or exacerbate fragility, other options must be developed.[126] A flexible approach is needed, one that addresses the needs and concerns of host governments and local populations as well as refugees.

Help close limbo situations

A number of forcibly displaced remain in limbo situations, even when return and local integration (and, for a small minority, resettlement) are possible. This is most often the case for people who have been in camps for a long time. It may be a consequence of having spent years in a state of dependency, or reflect the particular vulnerability of specific groups for whom the camps may provide a vital safety net and protective environment (such as the elderly, widows, and female-headed households).[127]

Dealing with such situations is extremely challenging. Developments actors could engage in two directions, as part of a comprehensive effort by a range of partners.

First, development partners should support initiatives to transform camps into settlements or at least to better integrate them in the local economy. This is part of a recent UNHCR policy.[128] It is being tested in countries such as Chad or Kenya. Development actors can provide socioeconomic expertise to design such solutions, as well as financing for some of the corresponding investments, while working hand in hand with humanitarian actors.

Second, development actors should help transform camps based on lessons learned in modernizing social protection systems. They should encourage all stakeholders to distinguish between highly vulnerable groups and people who could work but are disincentivized to do so because of aid, and to target assistance accordingly. For those who can work, efforts should focus on promoting inclusion into the labor market through activation programs, while gradually reducing aid so as to avoid counterproductive incentives. For the neediest, targeted social assistance may be required for a long period: development actors should help strengthen national social safety nets so they can absorb this group of people, and they may consider providing resources to make up for the corresponding expenditure over the medium-term.

Support over the medium to longer term

Ensuring that people have access to socioeconomic opportunities is a necessary condition to help them overcome their vulnerabilities, but in many contexts it is not sufficient. Both return and integration are processes rather than events. They are not only the end of a terrible ordeal, but also the beginning of a new process of social, political, and economic inclusion, which can take many years and in some cases may never be completely achieved.[129]

Development actors should be prepared to provide continued support over the long term, including assistance to help overcome traumatic events or destitution that may make the forcibly displaced unable to fully seize opportunities. The corresponding programs may be similar to those developed for marginalized or excluded groups in developing societies. Over the medium-term, success also depends on the acceptance of the forcibly displaced by the communities in which they live: specific support to these groups may be needed.

Notes

1. Under the 1951 Convention refugee status can also be ceased by the asylum state of the United Nations High Commissioner for Refugees (UNHCR) when it has been determined that "the circumstances in connection with which the person has been recognized as a refugee have ceased to exist" and that the individuals in question cannot claim international protection for reasons that fall outside the scope of the invocation of the cessation clause. The 1951 Convention relating to the Status of Refugees sets out the conditions under which refugee status can be ceased at Article, 1C (1)–(4) "This Convention shall cease to apply to any person falling under the terms of section A if: (1) He has voluntarily re-availed himself of the protection of the country of his nationality; or (2) Having lost his nationality, he has voluntarily reacquired it; or (3) He has acquired a new nationality, and enjoys the protection of the country of his new nationality; or (4) He has voluntarily re-established himself in the country which he left or outside which he remained owing to fear of persecution."
2. IASC 2010.
3. IASC 2010.
4. Long 2009.
5. Bakewell 2000.
6. Monsutti 2006; Long 2009; Crisp et al. 2009.
7. Riiskjaer and Nielsson 2008.
8. Omata 2011; Black and Koser 1999.
9. Stepputat 2004.
10. Monsutti 2006.
11. Statement by a representative of Lebanon's Ministry of Finance, Wilton Park, April 5, 2016.
12. Stepputat and Soerensen 2001.
13. Harild, Christensen, and Zetter 2015.
14. Van Hear 2003.
15. Long 2009.
16. Stepputat and Soerensen 2001.
17. Stepputat and Soerensen 2001.
18. Marsden 1999; Stepputat 2004; Lindley 2011.

19. Harild, Christensen, and Zetter 2015.
20. Harild, Christensen, and Zetter 2015; Monsutti 2006.
21. Stepputat and Soerensen 2001.
22. Lindley 2013.
23. Stepputat and Soerensen 2001.
24. Further movements may include irregular movements, family reunions, or use of migration channels without reference to refugee status.
25. Comparable data are not available for earlier years with the same level of details.
26. Other countries which experienced relatively large return include Burundi (1.2 million), Serbia and Kosovo (1 million), Liberia (1 million), Sudan (0.9 million), Angola (0.7 million), the Democratic Republic of Congo (0.6 million), Somalia (0.5 million), Bosnia and Herzegovina (0.5 million), Sierra Leone (0.5 million), and Togo (0.3 million).
27. Data are not available for IDPs in most situations. Some data are available from UNHCR but they are limited to the return of those IDPs assisted or protected by UNHCR, which are only a subset of those included in IDMC data.
28. UNHCR 2015c. Data are also available between 1997 and 2004 but are incomplete.
29. Harild, Christensen, and Zetter 2015.
30. Omata 2011.
31. Long 2009.
32. Stepputat 2004.
33. Bascom 2005.
34. Harild, Christensen, and Zetter 2015.
35. Calculations based on UNHCR data for refugees, and Internal Displacement Monitoring Centre (IDMC) data for IDPs. Since 2002, there have been 290 "country/year of large situations," and refugee returns in 63 of these cases. Out of these, there was a parallel increase in the number of IDPs in 29 cases.
36. Based on UNHCR data. The ratio cumulative number of returns over peak number of refugees (stock) is as follows: Afghanistan (1.4), Rwanda (1.5), Iraq (0.9), Mozambique (1.2), Burundi (1.3), Serbia and Kosovo (3.1), Liberia (1.2), Sudan (1.2), Angola (1.6), the Democratic Republic of Congo (1.2).
37. Based on UNHCR return data (as of end-2014). Cases of return followed by renewed bout of conflict include Afghanistan (returns in 2001 to 2005); Iraq (returns in 2003 to 2005), Burundi (returns in 1996 to 1997); the Democratic Republic of Congo (returns in 1997 to 1998); Somalia (returns in 1993 to 1995).
38. World Bank 2011a.
39. Omata 2012b; Chatty and Mansour 2011.
40. Ghanem 2003.
41. Ghanem 2003.
42. Bascom 2005.
43. Ghanem 2003; Riiskjaer and Nielsson 2008.
44. Bascom 2005.
45. Riiskjaer and Nielsson 2008.
46. Ghanem 2003.
47. Stepputat 2004.
48. Omata 2013.
49. Harild, Christensen, and Zetter 2015.
50. Omata 2013.
51. Monsutti 2006.
52. Omata 2013. Similar patterns can be observed in the case of economic migration where networks serve as a risk reduction tool for migrants in the destination area.
53. Jacobsen 2001.
54. Rogge and Lippman 2004.
55. Stepputat 2004.
56. Omata 2012b.
57. Harild, Christensen, and Zetter 2015.
58. Harild, Christensen, and Zetter 2015.
59. Harild, Christensen, and Zetter 2015.
60. Harild, Christensen, and Zetter 2015.
61. Harild, Christensen, and Zetter 2015.
62. Harild, Christensen, and Zetter 2015.
63. Stepputat and Soerensen 2001.
64. Jacobsen 2001.
65. Crisp 2004.
66. Jacobsen 2001.
67. Sturridge 2011.
68. Gagnon and Khgoudour-Casteras 2011.
69. Jacobsen 2001.
70. Harild, Christensen, and Zetter 2015; Metcalfe et al. 2011; Betts et al. 2014, p. 5.

71. Harild, Christensen, and Zetter 2015; UNHCR 2012.
72. Harild, Christensen, and Zetter 2015; Mosel and Jackson 2013.
73. Jacobsen 2001.
74. Jacobsen 2001.
75. Bakewell 2000.
76. Lindley 2011.
77. Long 2009.
78. Long 2009.
79. Adepoju, Boulton, and Levin 2007.
80. Long 2009.
81. Long 2009.
82. Numbers for the EU do not include foreigners with citizenship in another EU country.
83. Jacobsen 2001.
84. Jacobsen 2001.
85. Boulton 2009. Under this arrangement, refugees re-availed themselves of the protection of their country of nationality, in the sense of Article 1C(1) of the 1951 Convention.
86. Long 2014.
87. This section draws extensively on Sussman, forthcoming.
88. Eurostat 2008; Cortes 2004.
89. Poptcheva and Stuchlik 2015; Midtbøen 2015; Lemaître 2007.
90. Bijl and Verweij 2012.
91. GAO 2011; Bevelander and Irastorza 2014.
92. Lodovici 2010.
93. Fuller 2015.
94. Note that as measured here, unemployment represents those people who do not have a job, but are also not studying or actively looking for work. Worbs and Bund 2016.
95. DeVoretz, Beiser, and Pivnenko 2005.
96. Bevelander 2011.
97. Yu, Ouellet, and Warmington 2007.
98. Xue 2007.
99. See Khoo et al. 2007; Hiebert 2009; Cebulla, Daniel, and Zurawan 2010; Huddleston and Dag Tjaden 2012; Doerschler and Jackson 2010; Xue 2008. On the other hand, in Sweden, immigrants employed by co-nationals are more likely to end up with lower incomes than their peers, and half of the income earned by those in the private sector.
100. Cebulla, Daniel, and Zurawan 2010.
101. GAO 2011. Similar evidence was obtained in Australia, Canada, Germany, and Scandinavia.
102. Worbs and Bund 2016; Bevelander and Lundh 2007; Le Grand and Szulkin 2000; Cebulla, Daniel, and Zurawan 2010.
103. Bevelander and Veenman 2006.
104. Hiebert 2009; Fuller 2015.
105. Cebulla, Daniel, and Zurawan 2010.
106. De Vroome and Van Tubergen 2010.
107. Taintor and Lichtenstein 2016.
108. Edin, Fredriksson, and Åslund 2004; Mulvey 2015.
109. Bakker, Engbersen, and Dagevas 2014.
110. De Vroome and Van Tubergen 2010.
111. Bakker, Engbersen, and Dagevas 2014.
112. Bevelander and Pendakur 2011.
113. Worbs and Bund 2016.
114. Huddleston and Dag Tjaden 2012.
115. Lemaître 2007.
116. Edin, Fredriksson, and Åslund 2004.
117. Edin, Fredriksson, and Åslund 2004; Damm and Rosholm 2003; Damm 2009; Fuller and Martin 2012.
118. Hatton 2012.
119. Goodman and Wright 2015.
120. OECD 2015.
121. Wiesbrock 2011.
122. De Vroome and Van Tubergen 2010; Hatton 2012; Ott 2013; Bevelander and Pendakur 2014; Allsop, Sigona, and Phillimore 2014; Platts-Fowler and Robinson 2015.
123. Jacobsen 2001.
124. Long 2009.
125. The World Bank Group is preparing a project aimed at supporting the allocation of up to 200,000 work permits for Syrian refugees in Jordan.
126. Jacobsen 2001.
127. Sturridge 2011.
128. UNHCR 2014a.
129. Kjertum 1998. A study of the economic integration of about 8 million Germans who fled from Eastern Europe at the end of World War II found them to be worse off (in terms of income and unemployment) 25 years after their displacement to West

Germany, despite compensation for their lost property and tax incentives to lease or buy farms. Perhaps more surprisingly, their children did not fare better (in terms of incomes), suggesting that the impacts of displacement can last generations even with favorable integration policies, see Bauer et al. 2013). By contrast, being displaced increased the long-term incomes of the 430,000 Finns who were displaced from territory ceded to the Soviet Union during World War II. This was largely attributed to the ability of the displaced to transition faster from traditional (rural) to modern (urban) occupations, which was often made possible by a secondary movement within Finland.

Making the Most of Development Finance

6

Significant financing is necessary to respond to forced displacement crises. Most host governments count on external partners to support refugees because they are not nationals, and many make similar calls to assist internally displaced persons (IDPs). External actors are often expected to provide for the basic needs of large numbers of people over many years. But there is a critical flaw in this model: forcibly displaced persons have to be supported by the international community at such a high cost in large part because they are prevented from working. This is not sustainable in a global context of slow economic growth and fiscal pressure, where grants and highly concessional resources are limited.

In the period to come, humanitarian financing is expected to remain substantial, to meet essential needs, including interventions in emergency situations and continued protection of refugees and IDPs. Yet in spite of donors' generosity, there is a growing mismatch between requirements and available financing.

Development financing should be used to scale up the international response. This requires stepping up ongoing initiatives to mobilize and allocate resources. Financing should be used beyond investment finance, to support policy reforms, preparedness, and results. Dedicated interventions should be considered to attract and leverage private sector contributions, in particular through risk-sharing instruments.

The main elements of a major international effort

A complex financing picture

Host countries rely on a broad range of funding sources to cover their financing needs. However, there is no comprehensive picture of the resources provided to support forcibly displaced persons and host communities. This is partly due to the nature of such crises, to the large number of actors and funding channels involved, and to methodological issues.[1] Sources of finance include official development assistance (ODA), for both humanitarian and development financing, private donations, and private sector investment, including foreign direct investment (FDI), commercial lending, and remittances. Several host countries also report using domestic resources to cover refugee-related costs.[2] While all these resources do not necessarily translate into direct support to the forcibly displaced, they can be critical for creating economic opportunities (through private investment, for example) or in helping those who live in host communities to adjust in the initial period (such as through remittances).

In aggregate, for the ten largest humanitarian assistance recipients in 2013, remittances accounted for about 40 percent of total flows, ODA 21 percent, debt and commercial financing 13 percent, and FDI 14 percent. The proportions varied widely across countries. For example, the Islamic Republic of Iran, Lebanon, and Pakistan received large amounts of remittances, Turkey relied extensively on commercial borrowing, while Chad, Ethiopia, Kenya, and Uganda received relatively large amounts of ODA. As a group, developing host countries tend to receive less FDI than other low and middle-income countries, and they are more dependent on ODA and to a lesser extent on remittances.[3]

US$20 billion a year in humanitarian financing

Humanitarian assistance accounts for the largest share of direct external support to refugees and IDPs. It is financed by bilateral donors and private contributors. Private donors typically focus on responding to rapid-onset events like natural disasters rather than to chronic and conflict-related crises.[4]

Humanitarian assistance has grown rapidly over the last 15 years, from US$7.2 billion in 2000 to US$21.8 billion in 2015 (figure 6.1). This represents about one-sixth of total ODA financing, which stood at about US$130 billion in 2015. Private donors were incorporated in aggregate statistics from 2010, and they provide a relatively stable amount of resources, estimated at about US$6 billion a year. There are two factors

behind the continued increase. The number of people who are supported rose from 30–40 million in the early 2000s to 50–70 million in the mid-2010s. At the same time, the cost of individual responses to crises also increased, for example in middle-income countries such as Jordan and Lebanon or in the parts of South Sudan that are insecure and difficult to access.

A large share of this assistance is provided outside the United Nations (UN) appeals system, which aims to provide a framework for mobilizing resources. The requirements have dramatically increased over the last years, to a record US$19.3 billion in 2015. Contributions have increased but not at the same pace, and funding gaps are large and growing (figure 6.2). In 2014, only 49 percent of the required amount was funded: this is the largest shortfall to date in both volume and proportion. The level of donor response varied widely. For example, the Syrian crisis, South Sudan, Iraq, and the Ebola response were over 75 percent funded, while four regional refugee response plans (for Burundi, the Central African Republic, Nigeria, and the Republic of Yemen) received less than half of what was required.

Humanitarian aid is distributed broadly across countries. The largest recipient (Syria) accounts for less than 10 percent of the total,

FIGURE 6.1 Humanitarian assistance

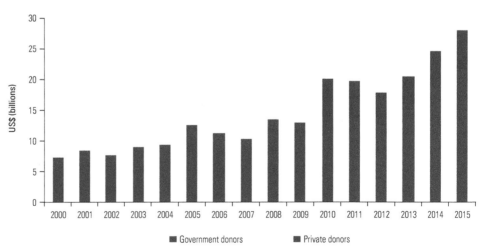

Source: GHA 2015, based on Organisation for Economic Co-operation and Development (OECD) Development Assistance Committee data, United Nations (UN) Office for the Coordination of Humanitarian Affairs Financial Tracking Service, UN Central Emergency Response Fund, and Development Initiatives' dataset for private voluntary contributions.

FIGURE 6.2 United Nations appeals: Needs and contributions

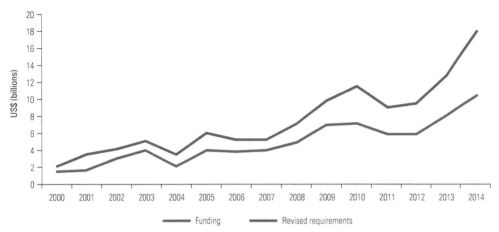

Source: UN OCHA Financial Tracking Service (FTS), https://fts.unocha.org/.

and the ten largest recipients (Syria, West Bank and Gaza, Sudan, South Sudan, Jordan, Lebanon, Somalia, Ethiopia, Afghanistan, and the Democratic Republic of Congo) for only 40 percent of the total.[5]

Still, humanitarian aid is increasingly provided to support protracted and lasting crises (figure 6.3). In 2013, 66 percent of it went to crises that had been going on for eight years or more, and an additional 23 percent to crises that had lasted three to eight years (figure 6.4).[6] Only 11 percent of humanitarian aid was directed to crises of less than three years. Six of the ten largest recipients in 2013 had been in the "top ten group" at least eight times in the previous decade.

Several hundred dollars a year per displaced person

Detailed data on the cost of caring for refugees and IDPs is critical to assess the

FIGURE 6.3 Share of long-, medium-, and short-term recipients of official humanitarian assistance from OECD-DAC donors

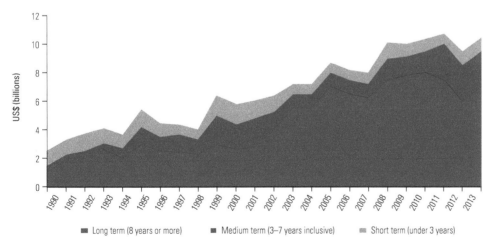

Source: GHA 2015, based on Organisation for Economic Co-operation and Development Assistance Committee and United Nations Central Emergency Response Fund data.
Note: Long-, medium- or short-term classification is determined by the length of time the country has received an above-average share of its official development assistance (ODA) in the form of humanitarian assistance. Calculations are based on shares of country-allocable humanitarian assistance.

cost-effectiveness of interventions and to make cross-country comparisons. Yet, no global data are available on the share of humanitarian resources that benefit forcibly displaced persons and their hosts.

The order of magnitude of the cost per displaced person can be estimated at around a few hundred US dollars per year.[7] This average seems to hold for low- and middle-income countries alike, though there seem to be large variations across countries.[8] It is calculated by comparing the number of refugees and IDPs in a given country with the total amount of humanitarian assistance that country receives. The distance of such estimates to the actual costs can, however, be significant.[9]

Such amounts are of the same order of magnitude as the extreme poverty line (US$1.25 a day or about US$450 a year), which suggests that they may be insufficient if the objective is to provide entirely for the needs of refugees and IDPs in a context where these people are not allowed (or are unable) to engage in economic activity. Yet, these amounts are significant if compared with the resources typically allocated by development partners on a per capita basis in a development model that relies on promoting self-reliance and access to economic opportunities.

The costs are much higher when refugees are hosted in high-income countries. Under rules of the Development Assistance Committee of the Organisation for Economic Co-operation and Development (OECD-DAC) donor countries can report, as part of their ODA, the expenditure they incur for hosting refugees themselves for the first 12 months after arrival (box 6.1). These costs are typically fairly large, averaging around US$13,000 per person per year. Yet because of wide variations across countries on the types of expenditure included in these figures, it is difficult to make cross-country comparisons.

BOX 6.1 In-donor refugee costs

"In-donor" spending has risen sharply over the last few years (figure 6.4), from US$3.4 billion in 2010 (2.7 percent of total ODA) to US$12 billion in 2015 (9.1 percent).[a] In several countries, in-donor refugee costs amount to a large share of ODA: 33.8 percent in Sweden, 26.8 percent in Austria, 25.5 percent in Italy, and 22.8 percent in the Netherlands. While these expenditures were mainly absorbed by an increase in overall ODA, several countries have indicated that their room for maneuver is now shrinking. Further increases in in-donor refugee costs could see funds diverted from development assistance and humanitarian aid, which in turn could aggravate the forced displacement crisis.

a. OECD 2016b.

FIGURE 6.4 **Net ODA expenditures on in-donor refugee costs**

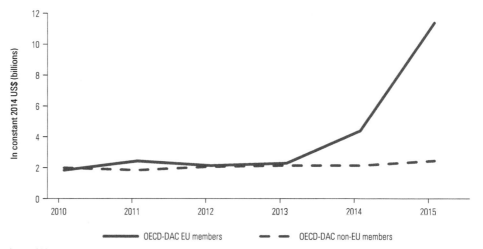

Source: OECD 2016a.
Note: Data for 2015 are projections. EU = European Union; ODA = official development assistance; OECD-DAC = Organisation for Economic Co-operation and Development–Development Assistance Committee.

The potential for development financing: Maximizing the use of public resources

The need for special mechanisms to mobilize and allocate resources

The financing model used by some development institutions, notably multilateral development banks (MDBs), is constraining their ability to engage at scale in forced displacement crises. These institutions typically provide their financing in the form of credits or loans, usually as part of fixed country allocations (box 6.2).

There is an inherent tension between such a country-based model and the situation of refugees who, by definition, do not live in their country. Host countries can be reluctant to borrow for non-nationals. Even when aid is provided in grant, there can be a trade-off: within a set allocation, what is used for refugees cannot be used for nationals. The situation is different for IDPs, who are nationals and fall squarely under the responsibility of the country's authorities.

Additional financing for host communities may also be required and justified in some situations, for instance, where the share of refugees to hosts is very large: people living in host communities are nationals, and can in principle be covered by borrowing, but their needs have been transformed by an external shock, which may lead to higher costs.

Development actors hence need to review both volume and borrowing terms to respond effectively to the crisis. This requires mobilizing further resources and adjusting allocation mechanisms. It is consistent with the argument put forward by many commentators that host countries are providing a global public good when they put in place a legal and regulatory environment that is conducive to refugees offsetting their vulnerabilities.

Bonds

Special-purpose bonds could help mobilize additional resources to respond to forced displacement. While fairly new instruments, they have already shown some successes (box 6.3). In principle, such bonds make it possible to access financiers interested in socially responsible investment, including foundations, pension funds, and Islamic investors.

Bonds guaranteed by donors could also provide innovative ways to mobilize resources. Under the conventional bond

---

BOX 6.2 The financing model of development banks

Development banks typically borrow financial resources on international markets, which they lend to developing countries (or to other stakeholders such as private sector operators or sub-national governments in developing countries). Because they have the backing of reputable shareholders, they enjoy strong credit ratings and can borrow on favorable terms, which they pass on to their clients. Their financing is hence cheaper and more attractive than what their clients could raise directly, if they have access to international markets at all.

Over the years, additional mechanisms have been put in place

for low-income countries. For such countries, traditional (aka non-concessional) development loans can often not be provided on an adequate scale without building up an unsustainable amount of debt. Some development banks have hence established mechanisms to raise donor resources so as to be able to lend at very low interest rates, typically close to nil (aka credit or concessional loan). Countries are expected to repay over an extended period of time and with a "grace period" during which no repayment is required. These mechanisms were further complemented by special windows for the poorest countries

where resources can be provided as grants based on debt sustainability criteria (some countries may also receive financing partly in the form of credit, and partly in the form of grants).

As an illustration, as of mid-2016, the World Bank Group lends to middle-income countries with maturities of up to 35 years and at an interest rate between LIBOR +0.41% and LIBOR +1.65%. Low-income countries can borrow with a 38-year maturity (that includes a 6-year grace period) at an interest rate of 0.75% (in special drawing right terms).

model, the repayment obligation rests with borrowing countries. Under these innovative approaches, bonds are either fully repaid or guaranteed by donors: this makes it possible to "frontload" donor financing when responding to a crisis.

BOX 6.3 Innovative bonds

Since 2008, MDBs have issued "green bonds" to mobilize private sector financing and help finance climate change adaptation and mitigation projects. A green bond allows investors to contribute to specific environmental goals, by financing projects that conform to bonds' offerings stipulations. The largest issuer is the World Bank Group, which has raised US$12.3 billion since 2008.[a] This green bond market has expanded exponentially in recent years as MDBs, public entities and increasingly private corporations have entered it. Developing countries can access funds raised through green bonds by submitting proposals for projects to issuing institutions.

The International Finance Facility for Immunization (IFFIm) has issued guaranteed bond

on behalf of GAVI, a vaccine alliance. IFFIm is a public–private partnership that works to increase access to vaccinations in developing countries. The bonds are intended to make a large volume of finance available for vaccine production and program implementation at the outset of a program. They are to be repaid by supporting countries that have made long-term pledges to that effect.[b] The availability of frontloaded resources helps reduce costs of production and helps beneficiary countries better plan their national programs. IFFIm bonds have raised more than US$5 billion from investors, including two sukuk issuances, which raised US$700 million for socially responsible investments compliant with Islamic law.

a. This includes US$8.5 billion for the International Bank for Reconstruction and Development (IBRD) and US$3.8 billion for the International Finance Corporation (IFC). For the World Bank, green bonds are part of its general funding program and projects financed through loans at regular IBRD rates.
b. Together, IFFIm's guarantors—the United Kingdom, France, Italy, Norway, Australia, Spain, the Netherlands, Sweden, and South Africa—have pledged to contribute more than US$6.5 billion to IFFIm over 23 years.

BOX 6.4 Climate investment funds

The Climate Investment Funds (CIF) provide a useful example of a complex MDTF. It is financed by a large group of donors, is implemented by a variety of parties, and aims to deal with aspects of a global problem, comprehensively. The US$8.3 billion CIF provides 72 low- and middle-income countries with resources to manage the impacts

of climate change and to reduce their greenhouse gas emissions. CIF concessional financing offers flexibility to test new business models and approaches, to build track records in unproven markets, and to boost investor confidence to unlock additional finance from other sources, including the private sector and the MDBs that implement CIF funding.

Multi-donor trust funds

Multi-donor trust funds (MDTFs) pool resources from partners into a single fund that is usually managed by a multilateral development institution as trustee. MDTFs typically benefit from the trustee's convening power, and from its fiduciary, management, and oversight systems. They provide a platform for broad-based partnerships, donor coordination, and harmonization. They can reduce transactions costs for donors and recipients, who are not subject to multiple fiduciary rules and reporting requirements. Their governance structure varies but it usually involves a combination of donors, stakeholders in beneficiary countries, and the fund administrator. MDTFs can be structured in many ways, and they provide a flexible vehicle to address global or regional issues. MDTFs also make it possible for development actors to engage outside the country-based model, allowing greater flexibility (box 6.4).

Special allocations

Some donors, including MDBs, are considering whether to establish special allocations or set-asides for forced displacement activities as part of their lending programs. In the past, such arrangements have proven effective in providing targeted support to address complex development challenges. They have been used for example for crisis response or regional projects, and current mechanisms could be expanded to address forced displacement challenges.

Blending arrangements and buy-downs

Blending arrangements and buy-downs can lower the costs of borrowing, especially for middle-income countries, which do not have access to concessional development finance. Blending entails combining a grant with a loan to lower the interest cost of the loan. Blending arrangements have been used in several contexts, typically where there are global or regional externalities that justify additional support, or where a country is in debt distress. Donor funds were either held in a trust fund or provided directly to the government.[10]

Buy-downs are a combination of a loan and a donor commitment to buy down the loan. Buy-downs can be linked to performance conditions, where a donor or third party provides a pay-off as agreed development results are achieved. In Nigeria for example, the World Bank Group provides resources to finance polio vaccinations, and on successful completion of the polio eradication program, donors buy down all or part of the net present value of the credit. An independent reviewer assesses whether the agreed results have been achieved, and if so, funds for the buy-down are released.

To date, blending and buy-downs have been used on an ad hoc basis rather than through a central pool of funds with well-defined qualification criteria. A structured and transparent mechanism for interested development partners to pool resources could simultaneously leverage MDBs' balance sheets and expand access to grants and loans. For middle-income countries it could enable access to funding on concessional terms, for low-income countries on grant terms. In both cases, funding could be linked to performance targets (box 6.5).

Delivery instruments

There is significant scope for expanding the range of financing instruments that can be used to respond to the forced displacement crisis. This should make it possible to achieve better outcomes. Most projects to date have been financed through investment projects, that is, the direct financing of activities (inputs) supporting the forcibly displaced or their hosts. But other modalities can be considered.

First, development policy financing: Policy loans (or grants) are generally provided in the form of support to a recipient government's general budget. They are linked to the adoption or effective implementation of policy measures, for example, to improve the business environment or to support sectoral reforms in the education sector. They could be useful where policy actions are critical to helping the forcibly displaced offset their vulnerabilities (for example by facilitating their economic inclusion) or to supporting host communities.

Second, outcome-based financing: Under such mechanisms, beneficiary authorities implement programs through their own systems, and donor funds are provided when pre-agreed targets are met, for example, numbers of children enrolled in primary education, or average transport time between two locations. This has proven an effective way to focus on results rather than inputs, and to promote the use of country systems. It could also support forced displacement activities by, for instance, linking external funding to issuance of work permits, as the World Bank Group is contemplating in Jordan.

Third, contingent financing: This gives countries access to liquidity immediately after an exogenous shock, such as financial shocks or natural disasters (box 6.6). Funds can be provided in the form of

---

BOX 6.5 The World Bank Group Concessional Financing Facility

The Concessional Financing Facility (CFF) aims to provide development assistance on concessional terms to middle-income host countries, with an initial focus on helping Jordan and Lebanon address the impact of Syrian refugees. Developed in partnership with the UN and the Islamic Development Bank Group, the facility brings together the UN and various MDBs to bridge the gap between humanitarian and development assistance and ensure a coordinated international response to refugee crises. Importantly, the CFF creates a sustainable, long-term, and predictable financing platform for host countries, in contrast to scattered bilateral and individual multilateral approaches.

The CFF combines grants from supporting countries with lending from MDBs to provide financing at concessional terms for projects supporting refugees and host communities. Through the facility, US$1 in grant contributions can leverage around US$3–4 in concessional

financing among recipient middle-income countries. The objective is to raise US$1 billion in grant contributions over the next five years for Jordan and Lebanon, and at a pledging conference on April 15, 2016, seven countries and the European Commission provided initial pledges in line with this objective.

The CFF is being expanded into a Global CFF to provide a structured international response to refugee crises in middle-income countries wherever they occur. The Global CFF would build on the coordinated platform established by the Middle East and North Africa (MENA) CFF. Financing for specific projects will be at the discretion of donors and determined by the commitment of host countries to policy reforms that contribute to long-term solutions that benefit both refugees and host communities. The Global CFF seeks to raise US$1.5 billion in grants over the next five years, which will provide middle-income countries an estimated US$4.5–6 billion in concessional financing.

budget support or investment finance. They are made available on the basis of policy commitments—for risk management, for example. This has proven effective to help prepare for, and respond rapidly to, shocks and to mitigate their overall costs. In forced displacement situations, such instruments could be used to help host countries weather the initial shock, including by strengthening preparedness. This could be supported through a regional or global pool of capital to allow for a comprehensive approach.

The potential for development financing: Leveraging private capital and expertise

Development finance should aim to attract and leverage private sector contributions of capital and expertise. The private sector has so far engaged in forced displacement crises primarily as a contractor, by delivering goods and services as part of agreements with UN agencies and donors. Further involvement, in human development and job-creating private investments for example, while widely discussed, has yet to materialize at scale.

The quality of the business environment is often a precondition for large-scale private sector engagement. To invest, to provide capital and know-how, private investors need a degree of predictability, which is often lacking in forced displacement situations. Political, and at times security, risks are high, and the regulatory environment is often not conducive to business. The economy in many host countries is also dominated by the public sector. Unless these challenges are addressed, the private sector response is likely to remain below its potential.

Risk-sharing and guarantees

Using ODA to support private investment, through equity investment or lending, has proven effective in a number of developing countries. There is also scope for such initiatives to be used in forced displacement contexts. This may require developing new approaches, risk profiles, and instruments to support job creation and service delivery, including expanding programs that target small and medium enterprises.

Guarantee instruments have considerable value in situations of high uncertainty (box 6.7). Investors can often purchase such guarantees for a fee, which provide them with protection against certain political risks (such as expropriation, breach of contract, currency inconvertibility, war and civil disturbance) or credit risks (such as default on payment obligations on bonds, loans, trade finance, and other financial instruments). Using ODA to provide guarantees has proven to leverage significant private investment.

Potential innovative products

A number of innovative products have been developed over the last few years, which could be relevant in situations of forced displacement. But more work is needed to refine these concepts and resolve thorny technical issues.

Development impact bonds provide an example of such instruments.[11] Under this approach socially motivated private investors provide upfront funding to an implementer for a development program, and they are repaid with a return only if pre-agreed social and economic outcomes are achieved.[12] This mechanism can allow implementers or

---

BOX 6.6   An example of contingent financing

The Development Policy Loan with Deferred Draw-Down Option, or "CAT-DDO," of the International Bank for Reconstruction and Development allows middle-income borrowing countries to secure immediate access to budget support of up to US$500 million, or 0.25 percent of GDP (whichever is lower), once a country declares a national emergency. Since the instrument was introduced in 2008, 11 countries have used a CAT-DDO. These loans have also provided a platform for policy reform to strengthen national risk management capacity.

As an example, in 2011 the government of the Philippines set up a contingent credit line with the World Bank through a US$500 million CAT-DDO. In the aftermath of Tropical Storm Sendong (Washi), which hit the country on December 29, 2011, the government was immediately able to access the full amount of the CAT-DDO for budget support and technical assistance in key areas, such as infrastructure and housing. In December 2015, the government signed a second CAT-DDO, which will provide US$500 million to strengthen investment planning and risk reduction, and help manage financial impacts when disaster strikes.

---

service providers to experiment with different intervention models while ensuring that resources are put to productive use (as private investors will be concerned about recovering their investment).[13] Experience is still shallow but such instruments could be considered, for example, to provide urban, social, or environmental services or jobs to the forcibly displaced and their hosts. This could include reimbursing private firms or nongovernmental organizations for the delivery of goods and services when results are achieved. It would, however, require a clear definition of the results to be achieved and of the corresponding metrics to assess performance.[14]

The past 15 years have seen growing demand for insurance solutions, which are now used in every sector of the economy to manage risks (box 6.8). The insurance industry has indicated that it may be possible to structure insurance contracts for refugee shocks, by combining guarantees, insurance instruments, and risk pooling—although the costs may be high. As a prerequisite, it would be necessary to define and model the nature of the "loss" against which insurance can be ascribed, and to carefully manage attendant moral hazard risks.

An agenda for development actors

The proposed agenda for development actors is threefold: encourage the search for cost-effective solutions; broaden the range of financing instruments and approaches; and help strengthen the framework for collective action.

Promote sustainability and cost-effectiveness

Development actors should focus on complementing humanitarian efforts. This should be based on the recognition that they have distinct yet consistent objectives and ways of operating. Rather than trying to align interventions, efforts should aim to identify areas of complementarity and potential synergies in a given context. For example, development actors can best contribute by helping address the socioeconomic dimensions of the forced displacement crisis as part of their

BOX 6.7 Guarantees and forced displacement

Guarantees for political risk have particular relevance for private investments, whether in origin or host countries. Political risk insurance can be purchased through the market at commercial rates, usually from reinsurance companies. The Multilateral Investment Guarantee Agency of the World Bank Group also provides a wide range of guarantee products, including political risk insurance. For example, in the West Bank and Gaza, 10-to-24-year political risk insurance guarantees have been provided to small and medium enterprises engaged in a range of sectors, such as export of dates, supply of clean water, and production of cheese, pharmaceuticals, packaging, or biogas energy.[a] These guarantees helped generate employment, directly and indirectly.

Credit guarantees have similar potential applications. Those offered by MDBs are designed to attract private financing for development projects that might otherwise be too risky. For example credit guarantees can protect a lender in case a country defaults on its repayment obligations. With such protection, the financing terms may be more favorable (that is, extending tenors for debt and lowering costs), which can make commercial financing possible.

a. The West Bank and Gaza Investment Guarantee Trust Fund was established by the Multilateral Investment Guarantee Agency in 1997 with the Palestinian Authority, the Japanese Ministry of Finance, and the European Investment Bank.

BOX 6.8 A precedent: Insurance against natural disasters

A broad menu of instruments in disaster risk insurance (derivative and insurance contracts, or catastrophe bonds) can now be used to transfer the risk of meteorological or geological events (droughts, hurricanes, earthquakes, and floods) to market actors (insurance and reinsurance companies, banks, and investors). These market-based insurance products use scientific information and actuarial modeling to estimate potential losses caused by a specific event. Such models allow the market to price the risk and set the premium.

The World Bank Group has helped develop this market over the last ten years. It has executed or arranged transactions, involving over 25 countries for close to US$1.5 billion in coverage. Regional risk pools have also been set up in the Caribbean (the Caribbean Catastrophe Risk Insurance Facility, covering 16 countries), the Pacific (the Pacific Catastrophe Risk Insurance Facility, six countries), and Africa (the African Risk Capacity, 26 member countries).

From a technical perspective, expanding such instruments to forced displacement situations would require the capacity to use statistical data for modeling the probability of forced displacement in certain places and the losses to be covered. If financially feasible, a public–private sector partnership would likely be needed to establish a platform for such a program, including modeling and quantitative analysis; triggers and rules for coverage (which would need to be managed by an independent agency); risk pooling across different geographic areas and types of risk (to help bring down the costs of coverage); and a reliable stream of funding for paying premiums.

broader poverty reduction mandate. This is partly distinct from some of the elements of a traditional refugee or IDP protection agenda, but it is an integral part of the search for comprehensive solutions.

Development actors should also focus on interventions that can be sustainable. Most of them aim to finance investment rather than consumption:[15] to simplify, the implementation of a development project (to fund an investment or support policy reform) is expected to eventually reduce the requirements for external assistance. Support to refugees, IDPs, and host communities should aim to gradually reduce needs by making durable improvements in their situations, as part of a broader effort to move toward sustainable solutions. Some host countries may wish to use development resources so as to be "compensated" for the public good they provide by hosting refugees. Yet any move by development actors to provide short-term "maintenance" support to refugees and IDPs or to simply offset the recurrent costs borne by host governments would likely be inefficient in the short-term and ineffective over the medium-run—a nonproductive use of scarce development resources.

With financing scarce, cost-effectiveness is key. The fundamental issue for governments and international partners alike is to determine the affordability of forced displacement programs and their value for money. The quality of support for refugees, IDPs, and host communities is largely a function of available resources and of the policy context. But for a given amount of financing, outcomes also depend on the choice of activities to be supported and on how they are implemented (box 6.9). Development actors have an important role to play in collecting and analyzing data and evidence on what works and at what cost. This would make it possible to calculate and compare the costs of interventions across countries.

Use the full range of development finance

Development actors should pursue their efforts to develop adequate instruments to support refugees, IDPs, and host countries. This remains critical for their effective engagement and it includes several elements.

First, development actors should continue their efforts to mobilize development resources and to allocate them in such a manner that they include a high degree of additionality and concessionality. This may include, particularly, establishing MDTFs to engage in countries of origin where the situation may be too unstable for traditional development programs or where lending instruments are not available or appropriate; tapping capital markets through special-purpose or guaranteed bonds; setting aside specific amounts of resources to provide additional support to host countries on grant or highly concessional terms; and further developing buy-down or blending mechanisms to leverage grant resources through concessional lending, especially for middle-income countries.

Second, development actors can greatly broaden the range of approaches and instruments used in forced displacement settings. They should give priority to funding mechanisms that have performed well in other situations. This includes: engaging with relevant authorities through development policy operations to stimulate key policy decisions; providing resources through outcome-based financing to focus efforts on the achievements of pre-agreed targets; developing guarantees and other risk-sharing mechanisms to support private sector investment;

BOX 6.9 Illustrative questions on cost-effectiveness

How much do forced displacement programs cost per capita? How does the ongoing annual expenditure in support of refugees, IDPs, or host communities in a given setting compare with potential alternative approaches?

What are the best ways to achieve desirable outcomes? Can possible options be identified and costed in a manner that makes it possible to determine the most cost-effective solution?

How are risks being assessed? Is there a way to determine the cost-effectiveness of potential upstream mitigation approaches?

Are country systems used effectively for providing support? Where implementation through external partners may perform better, what are the operating costs? Hence, where is the appropriate delineation between the assistance that can be more effectively provided through external actors vs. country systems?

and piloting contingent financing to help potential host countries prepare before a shock. Such instruments should be tailored to the specific context and based on the displacement situation, government capacity and policies towards the forcibly displaced.

Third, development actors should pursue further efforts to design, test, and bring to scale new financing mechanisms (box 6.10). These include innovative ideas for mobilizing resources and applying existing financial solutions in response to forced displacement crises.

Help strengthen collective action

The forced displacement challenge is global and calls for a global response. Events in origin and host countries are intrinsically linked. A partial response addressing only some of the problems will remain suboptimal. Similarly, individual initiatives or bilateral agreements are unlikely to provide more than temporary relief. What is needed is a comprehensive response, developed and supported by the international community at large and in line with the spirit and principles of international cooperation. This response would aim to provide for a complementary set of context-specific engagements within a comprehensive global framework.

Development actors should contribute to the ongoing debates on the global architecture to deal with forced displacement issues.[16] They should highlight the socioeconomic dimensions of the crisis, and delineate

---

BOX 6.10 Exploring new sources of financing

The Future of Humanitarian Financing report, published in June 2015 by the Catholic Aid Agency for England and Wales (CAFOD), the Food and Agriculture Organization of the United Nations, and World Vision, and the report from the UN Secretary General's High Level Panel on Humanitarian Financing, launched in January 2016, both took a comprehensive look at the landscape of existing financial tools and made recommendations.

Expand the donor base. As more countries achieve upper-middle-income or high-income status, there may be scope for contributions by new donors.

Raise a levy. Taxes on financial transactions and currency exchange could help direct resources toward social and global goods. Some climate finance funds are already financed partly or wholly through such mechanisms: for example, the Adaptation Fund is funded by a levy on international carbon market transactions. An airfare tax levy initiated by the governments of Brazil, Chile, France, Norway, and the United Kingdom in 2006 has also leveraged new funds for development and provides 70 percent of UNITAID funding, as well as additional funding to IFFIm. The political feasibility, costs, and benefits of a financial transaction tax are still debated, although some European Union (EU) countries have agreed to begin implementing a version of this.

Use crowd funding. A 2013 World Bank study estimating the global market for crowd funding at US$96 billion by 2025, that is, 1.8 times the size of the global venture capital industry. Crowd funding is typically used to finance small and medium projects of US$10,000–250,000, with some projects raising considerably more.[a] Crowd funding can be used for donations and investment funding, and both have relevance for forced displacement.

Develop matching funds. This can help mobilize additional voluntary contributions from private companies and citizens. The government of Canada, for example, set up a Pakistan Flood Relief Fund in 2010: for every donation from individual Canadians it contributed an equivalent amount. Due to their simplicity, matching funds can provide an attractive vehicle that brings together the credibility of a public sector financing partner and a pool of matching resources from the private sector.

Mobilize Islamic social finance—Zakat and awqaf. Islamic finance and services have been mainstreamed in for-profit capital markets, commercial banking, insurance, and microfinance. Islamic philanthropy and not-for-profit modalities are only starting to be considered to tackle social issues globally.

Mobilize resources from the diaspora. Bond offerings aimed at mobilizing remittances for refugee and host country assistance could be attractive. Such bonds could also help reduce the cost while increasing the security of remittances. The United Kingdom's Somalia Safer Corridor program may provide lessons on how to facilitate remittance flows to refugees.[b]

a. World Bank 2013e.
b. Government of the United Kingdom 2015.

the role that development solutions can play in complementing diplomatic, political, security, and humanitarian interventions. They should underline the need for solidarity and responsibility-sharing, as host countries are in effect providing a global public good when they provide an environment in which refugees and IDPs can offset their vulnerabilities. Finally, development actors can share their experiences in solving problems of collective action when providing such public goods (box 6.11).

Notes

1. For example, it can be difficult to determine the share of specific expenditure that is considered as benefiting refugees, such as when a refugee child is educated in a public school.
2. Estimating such expenditure is often difficult in the absence of a clear methodology to attribute specific sectoral expenditure to refugees.
3. GHA 2015.
4. Data on humanitarian financing varies widely across sources, in part due to different definitions and methodologies. For example, a comparison of the data published by the Organisation for Economic Co-operation and Development (OECD) Development Assistance Committee (DAC) and by the United Nations Office for Coordination of Humanitarian Affairs (OCHA) shows wide discrepancies, with OCHA estimates being up to three times larger than OECD's in some cases. All data is from the Global Humanitarian Assistance 2014 report (GHA 2014), which aims to consolidate across existing sources.
5. GHA 2014.
6. GHA 2014.
7. For example, the United Nations High Commissioner for Refugees (UNHCR) indicated that it costs about US$100 million a year to run the Dadaab camp in Kenya, with an estimated population around 300,000 people.
8. Calculations based on GHA numbers for end-2014 (GHA 2014).
9. A small proportion of beneficiaries would imply an underestimate of costs per person; the existence of other crises would imply an overestimate of costs per person.
10. In Botswana, for example, the European Commission provided funds directly to the Ministry of Finance and Development Planning for its HIV/AIDS Prevention Support Project that was financed with a US$50 million International Bank for Reconstruction and Development (IBRD) loan. Similar arrangements were used in countries such as China and Mexico.

11. Several development impact bonds (DIBs) are currently under development, including a project developed by the World Bank Group on youth training and employment in West Bank and Gaza. This initiative seeks to catalyze the role of the private sector by crowding in both private sector capital and expertise to better incentivize employment outcomes.

12. Impact bonds are not technically bond structures (that is, debt securities that pay a fixed interest rate until maturity): they are equity-like investment instruments that offer repayment only on the basis of results achieved, without getting involved in implementation modalities.

13. Center for Global Development and Social Finance 2013.

14. A variant of the model could also be an outcome fund that would provide pooled finance for impact bonds and other outcome-focused projects.

15. In practice, a number of humanitarian agencies are also funding development-type projects.

16. A number of reform proposals aim to strengthen the refugee regime and close financing gaps. These frequently revolve around the notion of quotas and financial transfers to host countries (Czaika 2005, 2009; Dennis 1993; Hoertz and GTZ 1995; Rapoport and Moraga 2014; Schuck 2010), with poorer countries agreeing to accept more refugees in return for funding from donor countries. Other proposals aim to establish a market for trading such quotas (Hathaway and Neve 1997; Schuck 1997; Crisp 2003), or to introduce a system of transfer contracts to redistribute refugees (so that each contracting state hosts its agreed quota) and compensate host countries, akin to the carbon credit system (Kremer, Bubb, and Levine 2011). However, such schemes have proven difficult to design in practice. Attempts to "allocate" refugees across countries also often run into a fundamental obstacle, which is that refugees are not objects but people.

Bibliography

Acket, S., et al. 2011. "Measuring and Validating Social Cohesion: A Bottom-up Approach." Working Paper 2011–08, Working Papers, CEPS INSTEAD, OECD. Available at: https://www.oecd.org/dev/pgd/46839973.pdf.

Adepoju, A., A. Boulton, and M. Levin. 2007. "Promoting Integration Through Mobility; Free Movement Under ECOWAS." *Refugee Survey Quarterly* 29 (3): 120–144.

Adhikari, P. 2011. "Conflict-Induced Displacement: Understanding the Causes of Flight." Dissertation. Albuquerque, NM: University of New Mexico.

———. 2013. "Conflict-Induced Displacement: Understanding the Causes of Flight." *American Journal of Political Science* 57: 82–89.

African Union. 2012. *Kampala Convention for the Protection and Assistance of Internally Displaced Persons in Africa*. Addis Ababa: African Union.

Aga Khan, S. 1983. "Mass Exodus: Root Causes and Prevention." Address by Sadruddin Aga Khan to the British Refugee Council.

Agblorti, S. 2011. "Refugee Integration in Ghana: The Host Community's Perspective." Research Paper 203. Geneva: UNHCR.

Aiyar, S., et al. 2016. "The Refugee Surge in Europe: Economic Challenges." IMF Staff Discussion Note, SDN/16/02. Washington, DC: International Monetary Fund.

Akerman, Sune. 1976. "Theories and Methods of Migration Research." In Harald Runblom and Hans Norman (eds.), *From Sweden to America: A History of the Migration*. Minneapolis, MN: University of Minnesota Press.

Alix-Garcia, J., A. Bartlett, and D. Saah. 2012. "Displaced Populations, Humanitarian Assistance and Hosts: A Framework for Analyzing Impacts on Semi-urban Households." *World Development* 40 (2): 373–386. http://doi.org/10.1016/j.worlddev.2011.06.002.

Alix-Garcia, J., and D. Saah. 2010. "The Effect of Refugee Inflows on Host Communities: Evidence from Tanzania." *The World Bank Economic Review* 24 (1): 148–170. Available at: http://doi.org/10.1093/wber/lhp014.

Aljuni, S., and M. Kawar. 2014. "The Impact of the Syrian Refugee Crisis on the Labour Market in Jordan: A Preliminary Analysis." Beirut, Lebanon: International Labour Organization Regional Office for the Arab States.

Allen, T., and H. Morsink. 1994. *When Refugees Go Home*. Geneva: UNRISD.

Allsopp, J., N. Sigona, and J. Phillimore. 2014. "Poverty among Refugees and Asylum Seekers in the UK: An Evidence and Policy Review." IRiS Working Paper Series 1 2014, University of Birmingham. Available at: http://www.birmingham.ac.uk/Documents/college-social-sciences/social-policy/iris/2014/working-paper-series/IRiS-WP-1-2014.pdf.

Amore, K. 2002. "Repatriation or Deportation? When the Subjects Have No Choice." *A European Journal of International Migration and Ethnic Relations* 39/40/41: 153–171.

Anderson, Martin. 2012. "The Cost of Living: An Analysis of the Time and Money Spent by Refugees Accessing Services in Nairobi." Geneva: UNHCR.

Apodaca, Clair. 1998. "Human Rights Abuses: Precursor to Refugee Flight?" *Journal of Refugee Studies* 11: 80–93.

Arias, M., A. Ibáñez, and P. Querubin. 2014. "The Desire to Return during Civil War: Evidence for Internally Displaced Populations in Colombia." *Peace Economics, Peace Science and Public Policy* 20 (1): 209–233.

Atlantic. 2013. "Syria Has a Massive Rape Crisis." Lauren Wolfe, April 3, 2013. Available at: http://www.theatlantic.com/international/archive/2013/04/syria-has-a-massive-rape-crisis/274583/.

Aydemir, A. 2011. "Immigrant Selection and Short-Term Labor Market Outcomes by Visa Category." *Journal of Population Economics* 24 (2): 451–475.

Aysa-Lastra, M. 2011. "Integration of Internally Displaced Persons in Urban Labour Markets: A Case Study of the IDP Population in Soacha, Colombia." *Journal of Refugee Studies* 24 (2): 277–303.

Azam, Jean-Paul, and Anke Hoeffler. 2002. "Violence Against Civilians in Civil Wars: Looting or Terror?" *Journal of Peace Research* 39: 461–485.

Baez, J.E. 2011. "Civil Wars Beyond Their Borders: The Human Capital and Health Consequences of Hosting Refugees." *Journal of Development Economics* 96 (2): 391–408.

Baines, D. 1994. "European Emigration: 1980–1930: Looking at the Emigration Decision Again." *Economic History Review, Economic History Society* 47(3): 525–544, 08.

Bakewell, O. 2000. "Repatriation and Self-settled Refugees in Zambia: Bringing Solutions to the Wrong Problem." *Journal of Refugee Studies* 13 (4): 356–373.

———. 2011. "Conceptualising Displacement and Migration: Processes, Conditions, and Categories." In Kalid Kosher and Susan Martin (eds.), *The Migration-Displacement Nexus, Patterns, Processes and Policies.* Oxford, U.K.: Berghahn Books.

———. 2014. "Encampment and Self-Settlement." In E. Fiddian-Qasmiyeh, G. Loescher, K. Long, and N. Sigona (eds.), *The Oxford Handbook of Refugee and Forced Migration Studies.* Oxford University Press. http://doi.org/10.1093/oxfordhb/9780199652433.013.0037.

Bakker, Linda, Godfried Engbersen, and Jaco Dagevos. 2014. "In Exile and in Touch: Transnational Activities of Refugees in a Comparative Perspective." *Comparative Migration Studies* 2 (3): 261–282.

Balcells, L. 2012. "Violence and Displacement in Civil War. Evidence from the Spanish Civil War (1936–1939)." Barcelona GSE Working Paper Series, Working Paper 603, Barcelona GSE.

Ballard, B. 2002. "Reintegration Programmes for Refugees in South-East Asia: Lessons Learned from UNHCR's Experience." UNHCR Evaluation and Policy Analysis Unit.

Banerjee, A., et al. 2015. "A Multifaceted Program Causing Lasting Progress for the Very Poor: Evidence from Six Countries." *Science* 348 (6263). Available at: http://science.sciencemag.org/content/348/6236/1260799.

Bangura, Z. 2016. Statement by United Nations Special Representative of the Secretary-General on Sexual Violence in Conflict, in connection with the agenda item "Women and peace and security," UN Security Council, 7704th meeting, June 2, 2016.

Banki, S. 2004. "Refugee Integration in the Intermediate Term: A Study of Nepal, Pakistan, and Kenya." Working Paper 108, New Issues in Refugee Research, UNHCR.

Bascom, J. 2005. "The Long, 'Last Step'? Reintegration of Repatriates in Eritrea." *Journal of Refugee Studies* 18 (2): 165–80.

Bastick, M., K. Grimm, R. Kunz. 2007. "Sexual Violence in Armed Conflict: Global Overview and Implications for the Security Sector." Geneva: Geneva Centre for the Democratic Control of Armed Forces.

Bauer, T., et al. 2013. "The Economic Integration of Forced Migrants: Evidence for Post-War Germany." *The Economic Journal* 123 (571): 998–1024.

Becker, G. 1975. "Human Capital: A Theoretical and Empirical Analysis with Special Reference to Education." New York: National Bureau of Economic Research.

Beerli, A., and G. Peri. 2015. "The Labor Market Effect of Opening the Border: New Evidence from Switzerland." Working Paper 21319, National Bureau of Economic Research, Cambridge, MA.

Beiser, M., and F. Hou. 2001. "Language Acquisition, Unemployment, and Depressive Disorder among South East Asian Refugees: A Ten-year Study." Social Science and Medicine, Pergamon.

Beissinger, M.R. 2007. "Structure and Example in Modular Political Phenomena: The Diffusion of Bulldozer/Rose/Orange/Tulip Revolutions." *Perspectives on Politics* 5 (2): 259–276.

Bell, Brian, Francesco Fasani, and Stephen Machin. 2013. "Crime and Immigration: Evidence from Large Immigrant Waves." *Review of Economics and Statistics* 95 (4): 1278–1290.

Bennett, C., et al. 2016. *Time To Let Go: Remaking Humanitarian Action for the Modern Era.* Humanitarian Policy Group, ODI. Available at: https://www.odi.org/hpg/remake-aid/.

Betts, A. 2009a. *Forced Migration and Global Politics.* Oxford, U.K.: Wiley-Blackwell.

———. 2009b. *Protection by Persuasion: International Cooperation in the Refugee Regime.* Ithaca, NY: Cornell University Press.

———. 2010. "*Survival Migration: A New Protection Framework, Global Governance.*" *A Review of Multilateralism and International Organizations* 16 (3): 361–382.

———. 2013. *Survival Migration: Failed Governance and the Crisis of Displacement.* Ithaca, NY: Cornell University Press.

———. 2014. "International Relations and Forced Migration Oxford." In E. Fiddian-Qasmiyeh, G. Loescher, K. Long, and N. Sigona (eds.), *The Oxford Handbook of Refugee and Forced Migration Studies* (pp. 1–11). Oxford University Press. http://doi.org/10.1093/oxfordhb/9780199652433.013.0004.

———. 2015. "The Normative Terrain of the Global Refugee Regime." *Ethics and International Affairs.*

Betts, A., L. Bloom, J. Kaplan, and N. Omata. 2014. "Refugee Economies: Rethinking Popular Assumptions." Oxford, U.K.: Refugee Studies Centre.

Bevelander, Pieter. 2011. "The Employment Integration of Resettled Refugees, Asylum Claimants, and Family Reunion Migrants in Sweden." *Refugee Survey Quarterly* 1, 22–43, Centre for Documentation on Refugees UNHCR/CDR, ISSN 1020-4067.

Bevelander, Pieter, and Nahikari Irastorza. 2014. "Economic Integration of Intermarried Labour Migrants, Refugees and Family Migrants to Sweden: Premium or Selection?" IZA Discussion Paper Series 8065. Bonn, Germany: Institute for the Study of Labor (IZA). Available at: http://ftp.iza.org/dp8065.pdf.

Bevelander, Pieter, and Christer Lundh. 2007. "Employment Integration of Refugees: The Influence of Local Factors on Refugee Job Opportunities in Sweden." IZA Discussion Papers 2551. Bonn, Germany: Institute for the Study of Labor (IZA).

Bevelander, Pieter, and Ravi Pendakur. 2011. "Citizenship and Employment: Comparing Two Cool Countries." Norface Discussion Paper Series 2011002, Norface Research Programme on Migration, Department of Economics, University College London.

———. 2014. "The Labour Market Integration of Refugee and Family Reunion Immigrants: A Comparison of Outcomes between Canada and Sweden." *Journal of Ethnic and Migration Studies* 40 (5): 689–709.

Bevelander, Pieter, and Justus Veenman. 2006. "Naturalisation and Socioeconomic Integration: The Case of the Netherlands." IZA Discussion Papers 2153. Bonn, Germany: Institute for the Study of Labor (IZA).

Bijl, R., and A. Verweij. 2012. "Measuring and Monitoring Immigrant Integration in Europe: Integration Policies and Monitoring Efforts in 17 European Countries." Available at: https://books.google.de/books/about/Measuring_and_Monitoring_Immigrant_Integ.html?id=xrmepwAACAAJandredir_esc=y.

Biswas, A., and C. Tortajada-Quiroz. 1996. "Environmental Impacts of Refugees: A Case Study." Impact Assessment, Third World Centre.

Black, R. 1994. "Refugee Migration and Local Economic Development in Eastern Zambia." *Journal for Economic and Social Geography* 85 (3): 249–62.

Black, R., and Koser, K., eds. 1999. *The End of the Refugee Cycle? Refugee Repatriation and Reconstruction*. Oxford: Berghahn Books.

Bloch, A. 2002. "Refugees' Opportunities and Barriers in Employment and Training." London: Goldsmiths University of London. Available at: http://icar.livingrefugeearchive.org/3297/research-directory/refugees-opportunities-and-barriers-in-employment-and-training.html.

Bohnet, H., F. Cottier, and S. Hug. 2013. "Conflict-induced IDPs and the Spread of Conflict." Paper prepared for presentation at the European Political Science Association (EPSA) in Barcelona, June 20–22, 2013. Available at: http://www.unige.ch/ses/spo/static/simonhug/ciasc/BohnetCottierHug2013_EPSA_Barcelone.pdf.

Bohra-Mishra, P., and D.S. Massey. 2011. "Individual Decisions to Migrate during Civil Conflict." *Demography* 48 (2): 401–424.

Boulton, A. 2009. "Local Integration in West Africa." *Forced Migration Review* 33.

Bozzoli, C., and T. Brück. 2009. "Agriculture, Poverty, and Postwar Reconstruction: Micro-Level Evidence from Northern Mozambique." *Journal of Peace Research* 46 (3): 377–397.

Bubb, R., M. Kremer, and D. Levine. 2011. "The Economics of International Refugee Law." *The Journal of Legal Studies* 40 (2): 367–404.

Bundervoet, T. 2006. "Livestock, Activity Choices and Conflict: Evidence from Burundi." HiCN Working Paper 24. Brighton, U.K.: Institute of Development Studies, Households in Conflict Network.

Buscher, D. 2009. "Women, Work, and War." In S.F. Martin and J. Tirman (eds.), *Women, Migration, and Conflict: Breaking a Deadly Cycle*. New York: Springer Publishing.

———. 2011. "The Living Ain't Easy: Urban Refugees in Kampala." Women's Refugee Commission.

———. 2011. "New Approaches to Urban Refugee Livelihoods." *Refuge* 28 (2): 17–29.

———. Forthcoming. *Refugees in the City: Promoting Resilience and Restoring Dignity*.

Buscher, K., and K. Vlassenroot. 2010. "Humanitarian Presence and Urban Development: New Opportunities and Contrasts in Goma, DRC." *Disasters* 34: S256–73.

Calderón-Mejía, V., and A.M. Ibáñez. 2015. "Labour Market Effects of Migration-related Supply Shocks: Evidence from Internal Refugees in Colombia." *Journal of Economic Geography*. Available at: http://doi.org/10.1093/jeg/lbv030.

Callen, M., M. Isaqzadeh, J. Long, and C. Sprenger. 2014. "Violence and Risk Preference: Experimental Evidence from Afghanistan." *American Economic Review* 104 (1): 123–48.

Campbell, E., J. Crisp, and E. Kiragu. 2011. "Navigating Nairobi: A Review of the Implementation of UNHCR's Urban Refugee Policy in Kenya's Capital City." Geneva: UNHCR. Available at: http://www.unhcr.org/4d5511209.pdf.

Card, D. 1990. "The Impact of the Mariel Boatlift on the Miami Labor Market." *Industrial and Labor Relations Review* 43 (2), 245–257. Available at: http://doi.org/10.2307/2523702.

Carrington, W. J., and P. J. De Lima. 1996. "The Impact of 1970s Repatriates from Africa on the Portuguese Labor Market." *Industrial and Labor Relations Review* 49 (2): 330–347.

Castles, S., and M. Miller. 1998a. *The Age of Migration: International Population Movements in the Modern World*. New York: Palgrave Macmillan Higher Education and Guilford Press.

———. 1998b. "New Ethnic Minorities and Society." In *The Age of Migration: International Population Movements in the Modern World*. New York: Palgrave Macmillan Higher Education and Guildford Press.

Cattaneo, C., C. Fiorio, and G. Peri. 2015. "What Happens to the Careers of European Workers when Immigrants 'Take Their Jobs?'" *Journal of Human Resources* 50 (3): 655–93.

Cebulla, A., M. Daniel, and A. Zurawan. 2010. *Spotlight on Refugee Integration: Findings from the Survey of New Refugees in the United Kingdom*. London: Home Office.

Center for Global Development and Social Finance. 2013. "Investing in Social Outcomes: Development Impact Bonds." Report of the Development Impact Bond Working Group. Washington, DC.

Cernea, M. 1997. "African Involuntary Population Resettlement in a Global Context." Environment Department Papers Social Assessment Series. Washington, DC: World Bank.

Chabaan, J., et al. 2010. "Socio-Economic Survey of Palestinian Refugees in Lebanon." Report published by the American University of Beirut (AUB) and the United Nations Relief and Works Agency for Palestine Refugees in the Near East (UNRWA). Available at: http://www.unrwa.org/userfiles/2011012074253.pdf.

Chambers, R. 1979. "Rural Refugees in Africa: What the Eye Does Not See." Disasters 3: 381–392.

———. 1986. "Hidden Losers? The Impact of Rural Refugees and Refugee Programs on Poorer Hosts." *International Migration Review* 20: 245–263.

Chan, et al. 2006. "Reconsidering Social Cohesion: Developing a Definition and Analytical Framework for Empirical Research." *Social Indicators Research* 75 (2): 273–302.

Chatty, D., and N. Mansour. 2011. "Unlocking Protracted Displacement: An Iraqi Case Study." *Refugee Survey Quarterly* 30 (4): 50–83.

Chen, M. 2007. "Rethinking the Informal Economy: Linkages with the Formal Economy and the Formal Regulatory Environment." New York: UNDESA.

Chin, A., and K. Cortes. 2014. "The Refugee/Asylum Seeker." Chapter prepared for *Handbook on the Economics of International Immigration*. Vol. 1. Elsevier.

Choi, S.W., and I. Salehyan. 2013. "No Good Deed Goes Unpunished: Refugees, Humanitarian Aid, and Terrorism." Conflict Management and Peace Science 30 (1): 53–75.

Clark, L. 1989. "Early Warning of Refugee Flows." Washington, DC: Refugee Policy Group.

Clemens, M. 2014. "Does Development Reduce Migration?" In R. Lucas (ed.) *International Handbook on Migration and Economic Development*. Cheltenham, U.K.: Edward Elgar Publishing.

Clemens, M., and J. Sandefur. 2015. *A Self-Interested Approach to Migration Crisis*. Foreign Affairs.

Cobb-Clark, D.A. 2006. "Selection Policy and the Labour Market Outcomes of New Immigrants." In D.A. Cobb-Clark and S. Khoo (eds.), *Public Policy and Immigrant Settlement*. Cheltenham, U.K.: Edward Elgar.

Coffé, H., and B. Geys. 2005. "Institutional Performance and Social Capital: An Application to the Local Government Level." *Journal of Urban Affairs* 27: 485–50.

Cohen, Roberta, and Francis Deng. 1998. *Masses in Flight: The Global Crisis of Internal Displacement*. Washington, DC: The Brookings Institution.

Cohen, S., and C.-T. Hsieh. 2000. "Macroeconomic and Labor Market Impact of Russian Immigration in Israel." Working Papers (October). Retrieved from http://ideas.repec.org/p/biu/wpaper/2001-11.html.

Coletta, N.J. 2011. "The Search for Durable Solutions: Armed Conflict and Forced Displacement in Mindanao, Philippines." Conflict, Crime and Violence Issue Note. Washington, DC: World Bank. Available at: http://documents.worldbank.org/curated/en/2011/03/14831170/search-durable-solutions-armed-conflict-forced-displacement-mindanao-philippines.

Coletta, N., and M. Cullen. 2000. *Violent Conflict and the Transformation of Social Capital: Lessons from Cambodia, Rwanda, Guatemala, and Somalia*. Washington, DC: World Bank.

Cortes, K. 2004. "Are Refugees Different from Economic Immigrants? Some Empirical Evidence on the Heterogeneity of Immigrant Groups in the United States." *The Review of Economics and Statistics* 86 (2): 465–480.

Couttenier, M., V. Preotu, D. Rohner, and M. Thoenig. 2016. "The Violent Legacy of Victimization: Post-Conflict Evidence on Asylum Seekers, Crimes and Public Policy in Switzerland." London: Centre for Policy Research. Available at: http://cepr.org/active/publications/discussion_papers/dp.php?dpno=11079.

Crawford, N., J. Cosgrave, S. Haysom, and N. Walicki. 2015. "Protracted Displacement: Uncertain Paths to Self-reliance in Exile." Humanitarian Policy Group and Internal Displacement Monitoring Center. Available at: http://www.odi.org/publications/9906-refugee-idp-displacement-livelihoods-humanitarian-development#downloads.

Crawley, H. 2009. "Understanding and Changing Public Attitudes: A Review of Existing Evidence from Public Information and Communication Campaigns." Swansea, U.K.: Centre for Migration Policy Research at Swansea University.

Crisp, J. 2003. "No Solution in Sight: The Problem of Protracted Refugee Situations in Africa." Working Paper 68. La Jolla, CA: University of California–San Diego, Center for Comparative Immigration Studies.

———. 2004. "The Local Integration and Local Settlement of Refugees: A Conceptual and Historical Analysis" New Issues in Refugee Research, Working Paper 102. Geneva: UNHCR.

Crisp, J., J. Janz, J. Riera, and S. Samy. 2009. "Surviving in the City: A Review of UNHCR's Operations for Iraqi Refugees in Urban Areas of Jordan, Lebanon, and Syria." Geneva: UNHCR.

Crush, J., and S. Ramachandran. 2009. "Xenophobia, International Migration, and Human Development." UNDP Human Development Reports. New York: UNDP.

Czaika, M. 2005. "A Refugee Burden Index: Methodology and its Application." *Migration Letters* 2 (2): 101–125.

———. 2009. "Asylum Cooperation among Asymmetric Countries: The Case of the European Union." *European Union Politics* 10 (1): 89–113.

Czaika, M., and K. Kis-Katos. 2009. "Civil Conflict and Displacement: Village-Level Determinants of Forced Migration in Aceh." *Journal of Peace Research* 46 (3): 399–418. Available at: http://doi.org/10.1177/0022343309102659.

D'Amuri, F., and G. Peri. 2014. "Immigration, Jobs, and Employment Protection: Evidence from Europe before and during the Great Recession." *Journal of the European Economic Association* 12 (2): 432–64.

Dadush, Uri, and Mona Niebuhr. 2016. "The Economic Impact of Forced Migration." OCP Policy Center, Research Paper, Carnegie Endowment for International Peace. Available at: http://carnegieendowment.org/2016/04/22/economic-impact-of-forced-migration/ixgz.

Damm, A.P. 2009. "Ethnic enclaves and immigrant labor market outcomes: Quasi Experimental Evidence." *Journal of Labor Economics* 27: 281–314.

Damm, A.P., and M. Rosholm 2003. "Employment Effects of Dispersal Policies on Refugee Immigrants, Part I: Theory." IZA Discussion Paper 924.

Danish and Norwegian Refugee Councils. 2013. "Durable Solutions: Perspective of Somali Refugees Living in Kenyan and Ethiopian Camps and of Selected Communities of Return." Available at: https://drc.dk/media/1311894/durable-solutions-perspectives-of-somali-refugees-2013.pdf.

Danish Refugee Council and Samuel Hall Consulting. 2013. "Designing Livelihood Programmes for Displaced Populations in Urban Settings in Afghanistan and Pakistan Labour Market Assessment in Kabul, Jalalabad, Herat, Kandahar, Charsadda, Mardan, and Peshawar." Commissioned by the Danish Refugee Council (DRC), Afghanistan.

Davenport, C.A., W.H. Moore, and S.C. Poe. 2003. "Sometimes You Just Have to Leave: Domestic Threats and Forced Migration, 1964–1989." *International Interactions* 29: 27–55.

De Haas, H., et al. 2014. "How Migration Transforms Societies." *In The Age of Migration: International Population Movements in the Modern World, Basingstone.* New York: Palgrave Macmillan.

Deininger, K. 2003. "Causes and Consequences of Civil Strife: Micro-Level Evidence from Uganda." *Oxford Economic Papers* 55 (4): 579–606.

Del Carpio, X., and M. Wagner. 2015. "The Impact on Syrian Refugees on the Turkish Labour Market." Policy Research Working Paper WPS 7402. Washington, DC.

Dennis, J.V. 1993. "Research for the Preparation of Environmental Assessment Guidelines." Geneva: UNHCR, PTSS.

Development Committee. 2016. "Forced Displacement and Development." Prepared by The World Bank Group for the April 16, 2016, Development Committee Meeting. Available at: http://siteresources.worldbank.org/DEVCOMMINT/Documentation/23713856/DC2016-0002-FDD.pdf.

Devictor, Xavier, and Quy-Toan Do. 2016. "How Many Years Do Refugees Spend in Exile?" Policy Research Paper 7810. Washington, DC: World Bank. Available at: http://documents.worldbank.org/curated/en/549261472764700982/pdf/WPS7810.pdf.

DeVoretz, D.J., M. Beiser, and S. Pivnenko. 2005. "The Economic Experiences of Refugees in Canada." In P. Waxman and V. Colic-Peisker (eds.) *Homeland Wanted: Interdisciplinary Perspectives on Refugee Settlement in the West*. New York: Nova Science.

De Vriese, M. 2006. "Refugee Livelihoods: A Review of the Evidence" Geneva: UNHCR.

De Vroome, T., and F. Van Tubergen. 2010. "The Employment Experience of Refugees in the Netherlands." *International Migration Review* 44: 376–403. doi: 10.1111/j.1747-7379.2010.00810.x.

Doerschler, Peter, and Pamela Erving Jackson. 2010. "Host Nation Language Ability and Immigrant Integration in Germany: Use of GSOEP to Examine Language as an Integration Criterion." *Democracy and Security* 6(2): 147–182.

Dolan, C. 1999. "Repatriation from South Africa to Mozambique: Undermining Durable Solutions." In R. Black and K. Koser (eds.) *The End of the Refugee Cycle? Refugee Repatriation and Reconstruction*. Berghahn: Oxford, U.K.

Duffield, M., K. Diagne, and V. Tennant. 2008. "Evaluation of UNHCR's Returnee Reintegration Program in Southern Sudan." Geneva: UNHCR Policy Development and Evaluation Services (PDES).

Durieux, J. 2009. "A Regime at a Loss?" *Forced Migration Review* 33.

Dustmann, C. 1997. "Return Migration, Uncertainty, and Precautionary Savings." *Journal of Development Economics* 52: 295–316.

Easterlin, R. 1961. "Influences in European Overseas Emigration Before World War I." *Economic Development and Cultural Change* 9 (3): 331–351.

Economist. 2015. "Leaving it Behind: How to Rescue People from Deep Poverty—and Why the Best Methods Work." December 12, 2015 Print Edition. Available at: http://www.economist.com/news/international/21679812-how-rescue-people-deep-poverty-and-why-best-methods-work-leaving-it-behind?utm_source=12%2F14%2F15+newsflashandutm_campaign=newsflash_12_8_15andutm_medium=email.

ECOSOC. 2015. "Report of Statistics Norway and the Office of the United Nations High Commissioner for Refugees on Statistics on Refugees and Internally Displaced Persons." Statistical Commission, Forty-Sixth Session E/CN.3/2015/9. New York: ECOSOC.

Edin, P-A., P. Fredriksson, and O. Åslund. 2004. "Settlement Policies and the Economic Success of Immigrants." *Journal of Population Economics* 17: 133–55.

Edwards, A. 2009. "Human Security and the Rights of Refugees: Transcending Territorial and Disciplinary Borders." *Michigan Journal of International Law* 30 (3): 763–807.

Engel, S., and A.M. Ibáñez. 2007. "Displacement Due to Violence in Colombia: A Household-Level Analysis." *Economic Development and Cultural Change* 55 (2): 335–365. http://doi.org/10.1086/508712.

Erlanger, S., and A. Smale. 2015. "Europe's Halting Response to Migrant Crisis Draws Criticism as Toll Mounts." *New York Times*. Available at: http://www.nytimes.com/2015/08/29/world/europe/europe-migrant-refugee-crisis.html.

Etang-Ndip, A., J. Hoogeveen, and J. Lendorfer. 2015. "Socioeconomic Impact of the Crisis in North Mali on Displaced People." Policy Research Working Paper 7253. Washington, DC: World Bank.

Eurostat. 2008. "European Union Labour Forced Survey Ad Hoc Module on the Labour Market Situation of Migrants and their Immediate Descendants." Available at: http://ec.europa.eu/eurostat/statistics-explained/index.php/EU_labour_force_survey_-_ad_hoc_modules.

Faini, R., and A Venturini. 1993. "Trade, Aid, and Migrations: Some Basic Policy Issues." *European Economic Review* 37 (2–3): 435–442.

FAO (Food and Agriculture Organization). 2014. "FAO/WFP Markets and Food Security Assessment Mission to the Central African Republic." Special Report. Rome: FAO.

FAO/WFP (Food and Agriculture Organization/World Food Programme). 2014. "Special Report. FAO/WFP Markets and Food Security Assessment Mission to the Central African Republic." Rome: FAO. Available at: http://www.fao.org/emergencies/resources/documents/resources-detail/en/c/232119/.

FOA, and V. Tanner. 2007. *All but Invisible: Internally Displaced Darfurians Outside Darfur.*

Farr, K. 2009. "Extreme War Rape in Today's Civil-War-Torn States: A Contextual and Comparative Analysis." *Gender Issues* 26 (1): 1–41.

Fawcett, John, and Victor Tanner. 1999. "A Report to USAID's Office of Foreign Disaster Assistance." Part of the OFDA Former Yugoslavia Review 1991–1997. Washington, DC.

Fearon, James D., and David A. Laitin. 2003. "Ethnicity, Insurgency and Civil War." *American Political Science Review* 97 (1): 75–90.

Ferris, E., et al. 2015. "Off To A Shaky Start: Ukrainian Government Responses to Internally Displaced Persons." Brookings-LSE Project on Internal Displacement, HIAS.

Fiala, A. 2002. "Terrorism and the Philosophy of History: Liberalism, Realism, and the Supreme Emergency Exemption." *Essays in Philosophy* 3 (3).

Fiddian-Qasmiyeh, E., G. Loescher, K. Long, and N. Sigona (eds.). 2014. *The Oxford Handbook of Refugee and Forced Migration Studies.* Oxford, U.K.: Oxford University Press. http://doi.org/10.1093/oxfordhb/9780199652433.013.0028.

Fielden, A. 2008. "Local Integration: An Under-reported Solution to Protracted Refugee Situations." New Issues in Refugee Research, Research Paper 158. Geneva: UNHCR.

Foa, R. 2011. "The Economic Rationale for Social Cohesion: The Cross-Country Evidence, Perspectives on Global Development." OECD Development Centre. Paris: OECD.

Foged, M., and G. Peri. 2015. "Immigrants' Effect on Native Workers: New Analysis on Longitudinal Data." Discussion Paper 8961. Bonn, Germany: Institute for the Study of Labor (IZA).

Francis, A. 2015. "Jordan's Refugee Crisis." Carnegie Endowment for International Peace. http://carnegieendowment.org/2015/09/21/jordan-s-refugee-crisis-pub-61338.

Frelick, Bill. 1992. "Preventative Prevention and the Right to Seek Asylum: A Preliminary Look at Bosnia and Croatia." *International Journal of Refugee Law* 4 (4): 439–454.

Friedberg, R.M. 2001. "The Impact of Mass Migration on the Israeli Labor Market." *The Quarterly Journal of Economics* 116 (4), 1373–1408. http://doi.org/10.1162/003355301753265606.

Fuller, S. 2015. "Do Pathways Matter? Linking Early Immigrant Employment Sequences and Later Economic Outcomes: Evidence from Canada." *International Migration Review* 49: 355–405. doi: 10.1111/imre.12094.

Fuller, S., and T.F. Martin. 2012. "Predicting Immigrant Employment Sequences in the First Years of Settlement." *International Migration Review* 46: 138–190. doi: 10.1111/j.1747-7379.2012.00883.

Gagnon, J., and D. Khgoudour-Casteras. 2011. "South South Migration in West Africa: Addressing the Challenge of Immigrant Integration." OECD Development Centre. Available at: http://www.oecd.org/dev/50251899.pdf.

GAO (Government Accountability Office). 2011. "Refugee Assistance: Little Is Known about the Effectiveness of Different Approaches for Improving Refugees' Employment Outcomes." Report GAO-11-369. Washington, DC. Available at: http://www.gao.gov/products/GAO-11-369.

Gelan, A. 2006. "Cash or Food Aid? A General Equilibrium Analysis for Ethiopia." *Development Policy Review* 24 (5): 601–624.

Geller, A., and M. Latek. 2013. "Returning from Iran." *Forced Migration Review* 46.

GHA (Global Humanitarian Assistance). 2014. *Global Humanitarian Assistance Report*. Available at: http://www.globalhumanitarianassistance.org/wp-content/uploads/2014/09/GHA-Report-2014-interactive.pdf

———. 2015. *Global Humanitarian Assistance Report*. Available at: http://www.globalhumanitarianassistance.org/report/gha-report-2015.

Ghanem, T. 2003. "When Forced Migrants Return Home: The Psychological Difficulties Returnees Encounter in the Reintegration Process." RSC Working Paper. Oxford, U.K.: University of Oxford.

Ghatak, S., and P. Levine. 1994. "A Note on Migration with Borrowing Constraints." *Scandinavian Journal of Development Alternatives* 13 (4): 19–26.

Ghosh, J. 2009. "Migration and Gender Empowerment: Recent Trends and Emerging Issues." Human Development Research Paper 04, United Nations Development Program, Human Development Report Office, New York.

Gibney, Mark, Claire Apodaca, and J. McCann. 1996. "Refugee Flows, the Internally Displaced and Political Violence (1908–1993): An Exploratory Analysis." In Alex Schmid (ed.), *Whither Refugee? The Refugee Crisis: Problems and Solutions*. Leiden: Ploom.

Gleditsch. 2007. "Transnational Dimensions of Civil War." *Journal of Peace Research* 44 (3): 293–309.

Global Development Index. 2014. *Measuring and Understanding the Impact of Terrorism*. Sydney, Australia: Institute for Economics and Peace.

———. 2015. *Measuring and Understanding the Impact of Terrorism*. Sydney, Australia: Institute for Economics and Peace.

Goenjian, A.K., A.M. Steinberg, L.M. Najarian, L.A. Fairbanks, M. Tashjian, et al. 2000. "Prospective Study of Posttraumatic Stress, Anxiety, and Depressive Reactions after Earthquake and Political Violence." *American Journal of Psychiatry* 157: 911–916.

Goodman, Sara Wallace, and Matthew Wright. 2015. "Does Mandatory Integration Matter? Effects of Civic Requirements on Immigrant Socio-economic and Political Outcomes." *Journal of Ethnic and Migration Studies* 41 (12): 1885–1908.

Goodwin-Gill, G. 1996. *The Refugee in International Law*. Oxford, U.K.: Oxford University Press.

Gorst-Unsworth, C., and E. Goldenberg. 1998. "Psychological Sequalae of Torture and Organized Violence Suffered by Refugees in Iraq. Trauma-related Factors Compared with Social Factors in Exile." *British Journal of Psychiatry* 172: 90–4.

Gottschang, T.R. 1987. "Economic Change, Natural Disasters, and Migration: The Historical Case of Manchuria." *Economic Development and Cultural Change* 35 (3): 461–490.

Gould, J. 1979. "European Inter-Continental Emigration 1815-1914: Patterns and Causes." *Journal of European Economic History* 8 (3): 593–679.

Government of Malawi, the World Bank, UNDP (United Nations Development Programme), and UNHCR (United Nations High Commissioner for Refugees). 1990. "Report to the Consultative Group of Malawi on the Impact of Refugees on the Government Public Expenditure." Lilongwe, Malawi.

Government of the United Kingdom. 2015. "UK-Somalia Safer Corridor Initiative." Summary Document, October 2015. London. Available at: https://www.gov.uk/government/uploads/system/uploads/attachment_data/file/471064/UK-Somalia_Safer_Corridor_Initiative.pdf.

Greenwood, M. 1969. "An Analysis of the Determinants of Geographic Labor Mobility in the United States." *The Review of Economics and Statistics* 51 (2): 189–94.

Grogan, L. 2008. "Universal Primary Education and School Entry in Uganda." *Journal of African Economies* 18 (2): 183–211.

Grun, R.E. 2008. "Household Investment Under Violence: The Colombian Case." Policy Research Working Papers 4713. Washington, DC: World Bank.

Gusmano, M. 2012. "Undocumented Immigrants in the United States: US Health Policy and Access to Care." Issue Brief. The Hastings Center.

Hakovirta, Harto. 1986. "Third World Conflicts and Refugeeism: Dimensions, Dynamics, and Trends of the World Refugee Problem." Helsinki: Finnish Society of Sciences and Letters.

Hammerstadt, A. 2014. "The Securitization of Forced Migration." In T*he Oxford Handbook of Refugee and Forced Migration Studies*. Oxford University Press.

Hammond, L. 1999. "Examining the Discourse of Repatriation: Towards a More Proactive Theory of Return Migration." In R. Black and K. Koser (eds.), *The End of the Refugee Cycle? Refugee Repatriation and Reconstruction*. New York, NY, and Oxford, U.K.: Berghahn.

———. 2014a. "Voluntary Repatriation and Reintegration." *Oxford Handbook of Refugee and Forced Migration Studies*. Oxford, U.K.: Oxford University Press.

———. 2014b. "History, Overview, Trends, and Issues in Major Somali Refugee Displacements in the Near Region." New Issues in Refugee Research. Geneva: UNHCR.

Harb, C., and R. Saab. 2014. *Social Cohesion and Intergroup Relations: Syrian Refugees and Lebanese Nationals in the Bekaa and Akka*. Beirut, Lebanon: Save the Children.

Hardgrove, A. 2009. "Liberian Refugees in Ghana: The Implications of Family Demands and Capabilities for Return to Liberia," *Journal of Refugee Studies.*

Harild N., A. Christensen, and R. Zetter. 2015. "Sustainable Refugee Return: Triggers, Constraints, and Lessons on Addressing the Development Challenges of Forced Displacement." Washington, DC: World Bank.

Harpviken, K.B. 2009. *Social Networks and Migration in Wartime Afghanistan*. New York: Palgrave Macmillan.

Harrigan, S., and N. Easen. 2001. Afghan Refugee Crisis Spreads, CNN. Available at: http://edition.cnn.com/2001/WORLD/asiapcf/central/09/20/ret.afghan.refugees/.

Hartog, J., and A. Zorlu. 2009. "Ethnic Segregation in The Netherlands: An Analysis at Neighbourhood Level." *International Journal of Manpower* 30 (1/2): 15–25.

Hathaway, James C., and R. Alexander Neve. 1997. "Making International Refugee Law Relevant Again: A Proposal for Collectivized and Solution-Oriented Protection." *Harvard Human Rights Journal* 11: 115–15.

Hatton, Timothy J. 2012. "Asylum Policy in the EU: The Case for Deeper Integration." NORFACE Migration Discussion Paper 2012–16. Available at: http://www.norface-migration.org/publ_uploads/NDP_16_12.pdf.

Hatton T., and J. Williamson. 1994. "What Drove the Mass Migrations from Europe in the Late Nineteenth Century?" *Population and Development Review* 20 (3): 533–559.

———. 2005a. *Global Migration and the World Economy: Two Centuries of Policy and Performance*. Cambridge, MA: MIT Press.

———. 2005b. "What Fundamentals Drive World Migration?" In G. Borjas and J. Crisp (eds.), *Poverty, International Migration and Asylum*. Helsinki: UNU WIDER.

———. 2011. "Are Third World Emigration Forces Abating?" *World Development* 39 (1): 20–32.

Haysom, S., and S. Pavanello. 2011. "Sanctuary in the City? Urban Displacement and Vulnerability in Damascus: A Desk Study." Working Paper, Humanitarian Policy Group ODI, London.

Hazlett, C. 2013. "Angry or Weary? The Effect of Personal Violence on Attitudes towards Peace in Darfur." Working Paper. Cambridge, MA: MIT.

Hercowitz, Z., and E. Yashiv. 2001. "A Macroeconomic Experiment in Mass Immigration." Discussion Paper Series 2983. London: Centre for Economic Policy Research.

Herszenhorn, D. 2015. "Many Obstacles Are Seen to US Taking in Large Numbers of Syrian Refugees." *New York Times*. Available at: http://www.nytimes.com/2015/09/05/us/many-obstacles-are-seen-to-us-taking-in-large-number-of-syrian-refugees.html.

Hiebert, D. 2009. "The Economic Integration of Immigrants in Metropolitan Vancouver" *Choices* 15 (7): 2–42.

Hinton, D., P. Ba, S. Peou, and K. Um. 2000. "Panic Disorder among Cambodian Refugees Attending a Psychiatric Clinic: Prevalence and Subtypes." *General Hospital Psychiatry* 22 (6).

Hinton, D., H. Chau, L. Nguyen, M. Nguyen, T. Pham, S. Quinn, et al. 2001. "Panic Disorder among Vietnamese Refugees Attending a Psychiatric Clinic: Prevalence and Subtypes." *General Hospital Psychiatry* 23: 337.

Hoerz, T. 1995. *Refugees and Host Environments: A Review of Current and Related Literature*. Eschborn: Deutsche Gesellschaft fur Technische Zusammenarbeit (GTZ).

Hoerz, T., and GTZ (Deutsche Gesellschaft für Technische Zusammenarbeit). 1995. "Refugees and Host Environments. A Review of Current and Related Literature." Oxford, U.K.: Refugee Studies Program, University of Oxford.

Hope Simpson, J. 1939. *The Refugee Problem, Report of a Survey*. Oxford, U.K.: Oxford University Press.

Hovil, L. 2014. "Local Integration." In *The Oxford Handbook of Refugee and Forced Migration Studies*. Oxford University Press.

Huddleston, Thomas, and Jasper Dag Tjaden. 2012. "Immigrant Citizens Survey: How Immigrants Experience Integration in 15 European Cities." May 2012. Available at: http://www.immigrantsurvey.org/downloads/ICS_ENG_Full.pdf.

Human Rights Watch. 2015. "When I Picture My Future, I See Nothing: Barriers to Education for Syrian Refugee Children in Turkey, Preventing a Lost Generation: Turkey." Washington, DC: Human Rights Watch. Available at: https://www.hrw.org/sites/default/files/report_pdf/turkey1115_reportcover_web.pdf.

Hunt, J. 1992. "The Impact of the 1962 Repatriates from Algeria on the French Labor Market." *Industrial and Labor Relations Review* 45 (3): 556–572.

IASC (Inter-Agency Standing Committee). 2007. "IASC Guidelines on Mental Health and Psychosocial Support in Emergency Settings." Geneva: Inter-Agency Standing Committee.

———. 2010. "IASC Framework on Durable Solutions for Internally Displaced Persons." The Brookings Institution–University of Bern Project on Internal Displacement, Inter-Agency Standing Committee. Available at: http://www.brookings.edu/~/media/Research/Files/Reports/2010/4/durable-solutions/04_durable_solutions.PDF.

Ibáñez, A.M. 2014. "Growth in Forced Displacement: Cross-Country, Sub-National and Household Evidence on Potential Determinants." In R.E.B. Lucas (ed.), *International Handbook on Migration and Economic Development*. Cheltenham, U.K.: Elgar.

Ibáñez, A.M., and A. Moya. 2006. "The Impact of Intra-State Conflict on Economic Welfare and Consumption Smoothing: Empirical Evidence for the Displaced Population in Colombia."

HiCN Working Paper 23. Brighton, U.K.: Institute of Development Studies, Households in Conflict Network.

———. 2010. "Vulnerability of Victims of Civil Conflicts: Empirical Evidence for the Displaced Population in Colombia." *World Development* 38: 647–663.

———. 2016. "Who Stays and Who Leaves during Mass Atrocities?" In Charles H. Anderton and Jurgen Bauer (eds.), *Economic Aspects of Genocide, Other Mass Atrocities, and Their Prevention*. New York: Oxford University Press.

Ibáñez, A.M., and C.E. Vélez. 2008. "Civil Conflict and Forced Migration: The Micro Determinants and Welfare Losses of Displacement in Colombia." *World Development* 36 (4) 659–676. http://doi.org/10.1016/j.worlddev.2007.04.013.

IDMC (Internal Displacement Monitoring Centre). 2013. "A Life of Fear and Flight: The Legacy of LRA Brutality in North-East DRC." Geneva: IDMC.

———. 2014. *Global Overview 2014: People Internally Displaced by Conflict and Violence*. Geneva: Internal Displacement Monitoring Centre. Available at: http://www.internal-displacement.org/assets/publications/2014/201405-global-overview-2014-en.pdf.

———. 2015. *Global Overview 2015: People Internally Displaced by Conflict and Violence*. Geneva: Internal Displacement Monitoring Centre.

———. 2016. *Global Report on Internal Displacement 2016*. Geneva: Internal Displacement Monitoring Centre.

IFRC (International Federation of Red Cross and Red Crescent Societies). 2012. *World Disasters Report 2012: Focus on Forced Migration and Displacement*. Geneva: IFRC.

ILO (International Labour Organization). 2003. "Preventing Discrimination, Exploitation and Abuse of Women Migrant Workers: An Information Guide." Geneva: International Labour Organization.

———. 2012. "Statistical Update to Employment in the Informal Economy." Geneva: ILO Department of Statistics. Available at: http://laborsta.ilo.org/applv8/data/INFORMAL_ECONOMY/2012-06-Statistical%20update%20-%20v2.pdf.

IMC (International Medical Corps). 2015. "Addressing Regional Mental Health Needs and Gaps in the Context of the Syria Crisis." Available at: http://internationalmedicalcorps.org/document.doc?id=526.

IMF (International Monetary Fund). 2014. "Article IV Consultation, Jordan." IMF Country Report 14/152. Washington, DC: IMF. Available at: http://www.imf.org/external/pubs/ft/scr/2014/cr14152.pdf.

———. 2015. "Article IV Consultation, Lebanon." IMF Country Report 15/190. Washington, DC: IMF. Available at: http://www.imf.org/external/pubs/ft/scr/2015/cr15190.pdf.

IOM. 2013. *Taking Action against Violence and Discrimination Affecting Migrant Women and Girls*. Geneva: International Organization of Migration.

———. 2014. *Global Migration Trends: An Overview*. Geneva: International Organization of Migration.

Irwin, M., C. Tolbert, T. Lyson. 1999. "There's No Place Like Home: Nonmigration and Civic Engagement." *Environment and Planning* A 31 (12).

Jacobsen, K. 1997. "Refugees' Environmental Impact: The Effect of Patterns of Settlement." *Journal of Refugee Studies* 10 (1).

———. 2001. "The Forgotten Solution: Local Integration for Refugees in Developing Countries." Working Paper 45. Geneva: UNHCR.

———. 2014. "Livelihoods and Forced Migration." In E. Fiddian-Qasmiyeh, G. Loescher, K. Long, and N. Sigona (eds.), *The Oxford Handbook of Refugee and Forced Migration Studies*. New York: Oxford University Press. http://doi.org/10.1093/oxfordhb/9780199652433.001.0001.

Jacobsen and Bakewell. 2013. *Inclusion Matters: The Foundations for Shared Prosperity*. New Frontiers of Social Policy. Washington, DC: World Bank.

Jaspars, S., and S. O'Callaghan. 2010. "Challenging Choices: Protection and Livelihoods in Conflict: Case Studies from Darfur, Chechnya, Sri Lanka, and the Occupied Palestinian Territories." Humanitarian Policy Group Report 31, Overseas Development Institute.

Jenson, J. 1998. "Mapping Social Cohesion: The State of Canadian Research." CPRN Study F/03, Ottawa, ON: Canadian Policy Research Networks.

JIPS (Joint IDP Profiling Service). 2011. Central African Republic. Available at: http://www.jips.org/system/cms/attachments/322/original_CAR_BaminguiBangoran_profile_at_a_glance.pdf.

———. 2012a. Afghanistan. Available at: http://www.jips.org/system/cms/attachments/277/original_Afghanistan_profile_at_a_glance.pdf.

———. 2012b. Profile at a Glance. Central African Republic Kabo. Available at: http://www.jips.org/system/cms/attachments/174/original_CAR_Kabo_profile_at_a_glance.pdf.

———. 2014. Ecuador: Quito. Available at: http://www.jips.org/system/cms/attachments/831/original_QuitoProfileAtAGlance.pdf.

Joona, A., and Eskil Wadensjö. 2009. "Being Employed by a Co-national: A Cul-de-sac or a Short Cut to the Main Road of the Labour Market?" SULCIS Working Papers 2009: 11. Stockholm: Stockholm University Linnaeus Center for Integration Studies (SULCIS).

Justino, P. 2009. "The Impact of Armed Civil Conflict on Household Welfare and Policy Responses." MICROCON Research Working Paper 12. Brighton, U.K.: Institute of Development Studies.

———. 2011. "War and Poverty." In M. Garfinkel and S. Skarpedas (eds.), *Oxford Handbook of Economics of Peace and Security*. Oxford, U.K.: Oxford University Press.

Kalyvas, S.N. 1996. *The Rise of Christian Democracy in Europe*. Ithaca, NY: Cornell University Press.

———. 1999. "Wanton and Senseless? The Logic of Massacres in Algeria." *Rationality and Society* 11 (3): 243–285.

———. 2006. *The Logic of Violence in Civil War*. New York: Cambridge University Press.

Kalyvas, S.N., and M. Kocher. 2007. "How 'Free' is Free Riding in Civil Wars? Violence, Insurgency, and the Collective Action Problem." *World Politics* 59 (2): 177–216.

Kamau, C., and J. Fox. 2013. "The Dadaab Dilemma: A Study on Livelihood Activities and Opportunities for Dadaab Refugees." Danish Refugee Council and UNHCR. Available at: https://drc.dk/media/1654297/dadaab_livelihood_study_-final_report.pdf.

Karasapan, O. 2016a. "Syrian Refugees: A Mental Health Crisis." Washington, DC: World Bank. Available at: http://blogs.worldbank.org/arabvoices/syrian-refugees-mental-health-crisis.

———. 2016b. *The Impact of Syrian Businesses in Turkey. Future Development*. Washington, DC: Brookings Institution.

Kasarda, J.D., and M. Janowitz. 1974. "Community Attachment in Mass Society." *American Sociological Review* 39 (3).

Kebede, E. 2006. "Moving from Emergency Food Aid to Predictable Cash Transfers: Recent Experience in Ethiopia." *Development Policy Review* 24 (5): 579–599.

Kelsey, T. 2011. "The Future is Open: Why Transparency Will Be the Organising Principle of 21st-Century Public Services." In *The Next Ten Years*. London, U.K.: Reform.

Kessler, R.C., et al. 1995. "Posttraumatic Stress Disorder in the National Comorbidity Survey." *Archives of General Psychiatry* 52: 1048–1060.

Khoo, S.E., C. Voigt-Graf, P. McDonald, and G. Hugo. 2007. "Temporary Skilled Migration to Australia: Employers' Perspectives." *International Migration* 45 (4): 175–201. doi: 10.1111/j.1468-2435.2007.00423.x.

Kibreab, G. 1985. *African Refugees: Reflections on the African Refugee Problem*. Africa Research and Publications Project.

———. 1990. *Wage-Earning Refugee Settlements in Eastern and Central Sudan: From Subsistence of Wage Labour*. Trenton, New Jersey: The Red Sea Press.

Kirchhoff, S., and A.M. Ibáñez. 2001. "Displacement Due to Violence in Colombia: Determinants and Consequences at the Household Level." ZEF Discussion Papers on Development Policy 41. Bonn, Germany: Bonn University.

Kjertum, J. 1998. "Repatriation and Reintegration of Mayan Indians Returning to Guatemala." Dissertation in partial fulfillment of the requirements for the M.Sc. in International Development Studies, Roskilde University.

Knack, S. 2002. "Social Capital, Growth and Poverty: A Survey of Cross-country Evidence." MPRA Paper 24893, University Library of Munich, Germany. Available at: https://ideas.repec.org/p/pra/mprapa/24893.html.

Kondylis, F. 2010. "Conflict Displacement and Labor Market Outcomes in Post-war Bosnia and Herzegovina." *Journal of Development Economics* 93 (2): 235–248. Available at: http://doi.org/10.1016/j.jdeveco.2009.10.004.

Korf, B. 2004. "War, Livelihoods and Vulnerability in Sri Lanka." *Development and Change* 35 (2): 275–295.

Koser, K., and R. Black. 1999. "The End of the Refugee Cycle?" In *The End of the Refugee Cycle? Refugee Repatriation and Reconstruction*. New York, NY, and Oxford, U.K.: Berghahn Books.

Koser, K., and A. Cunningham. 2015. *Migration, Violent Extremism and Terrorism: Myths and Realities*, Global Terrorism Index, Institute for Economics and Peace.

Kremer, Michael, Ryan Bubb, and David Levine. 2011. "The Economics of International Refugee Law." *Journal of Legal Studies* 40 (2): 367–404.

Kriebaum. 2016. "Their Suffering, Our Burden? How Congolese Refugees Affect the Ugandan Population." *World Development* 78: 262–287.

Landau, L. B. 2004. "Challenge without Transformation: Refugees, Aid and Trade in Western Tanzania." *Journal of Modern African Studies* 42 (1): 31–59.

Le Grand, C., and R. Szulkin. 2000. "Permanent Disadvantage or Gradual Integration: Explaining the Immigrant–Native Earnings Gap in Sweden." Scandinavian Working Papers in Economics 7/2000. Stockholm: Swedish Institute for Social Research.

Lehrer, K. 2010. "Economic Behavior During Conflict: Education and Labour Market Participation in Internally Displaced People's Camps in Northern Uganda." Doctoral Dissertation, University of British Columbia.

Lemaître, Georges. 2007. "The Integration of Immigrants into the Labour Market: The Case of Sweden." OECD Social, Employment and Migration Working Paper 48. Paris: OECD. Available at: http://www.oecd.org/els/38164205.pdf.

Lester, E. 2005. "The Right to Work and Durable Solutions: A Study on Sierra Leonean Refugees in the Gambia." *International Journal of Refugee Law* 17 (2): 331–393.

Liebig, T. 2009. "Jobs for Immigrants: Labour Market Integration in Norway." OECD Social, Employment and Migration Working Papers 94. Paris: OECD.

Lindley, A. 2009. "Leaving Mogadishu: The War on Terror and Displacement Dynamics in the Somali Regions." MICROCON Research Working Paper 15. Brighton, U.K.: Institute of Development Studies.

———. 2010a. "Leaving Mogadishu: Towards a Sociology of Conflict-Related Mobility." *Journal of Refugee Studies* 23 (1): 2–21

———. 2010b. *The Early Morning Phonecall: Somali Refugees' Remittances*. Oxford, U.K., and New York: Berghahn.

———. 2011. "Unlocking Protracted Displacement: Somali Case Study." Oxford, U.K.: Refugee Studies Centre, University of Oxford.

———. 2013. "Displacement in Contested Places: Governance, Movement and Settlement in the Somali Territories." *Journal of Eastern African Studies* 7 (2): 291–313.

Lischer, Sarah Kenyon. 2005. *Dangerous Sanctuaries: Refugee Camps, Civil War and the Dilemmas of Humanitarian Aid*. Ithaca, NY: Cornell University Press.

Lodovici, M.S. 2010. "Making a Success of Integrating Immigrants in the Labour Market." Discussion Paper. Brussels: European Commission Directorate-General for Employment, Social Affairs and Inclusion.

Loescher, G. 1992. *Refugee Movements and International Security*. Brasseys for the International Institute for Strategic Studies, London.

Long, K. 2009. "Extending Protection? Labour Migration and Durable Solutions for Refugees." New Issues in Refugee Research. Oxford, U.K.: Refugee Studies Centre.

———, K. 2014. "Rethinking Durable Solutions." In *Oxford Handbook of Refugee and Forced Migration Studies*. Oxford: Oxford University Press.

Lopez, R.C.V., C.I. Atehortua Arredondo, and J. Salcedo. 2011. "The Effects of Internal Displacement on Host Communities: A Case Study of Suba and Ciudad Bolivar Localities in Bogota, Colombia." Washington, DC, and London. Brookings Institute–London School of Economics Project on Internal Displacement.

Lozano-Gracia, N., G. Piras, A.M. Ibáñez, and G.J.D. Hewings. 2010. "The Journey to Safety: Conflict-Driven Migration Flows in Colombia." *International Regional Science Review* 33 (2): 157–180. http://doi.org/10.1177/0160017609336998.

Lucas, R. 2005. "International Migration and Economic Development." Cheltenham, U.K.: Edward Elgar Publishing, Number 3826.

Lundquist, Jennifer H., and Douglas S. Massey. 2005. "Politics or Economics? International Migration during the Nicaraguan Contra War." *Journal of Latin American Studies* 37 (1): 29–53.

Mabiso, A., J.-F. Maystadt, J. Vandercasteelen, and K. Hirvonen. 2014. "Refugees, Food Security, and Resilience in Host Communities." 2020 Conference Paper 2. Washington, DC: International Food Policy Research Institute.

Maier, G. 1985. "Cumulative Causation and Selectivity in Labour Market Oriented Migration Caused by Imperfect Information." *Regional Studies* 19 (3): 231–241.

Malikki, L. 1995. "Refugees and Exile: From 'Refugee Studies' to the National Order of Things." *Annual Review of Anthropology* 24: 495–523.

Mangala, J.M. 2001. "Prévention des déplacements forcés de population: possibilités et limites." *RICE* 83: 1067–1096.

Marc, A., et al. 2013. "Societal Dynamics and Fragility: Engaging Societies in Responding to Fragile Situations." Washington, DC: World Bank.

Markus, F. 2014. "Tanzania Grants Citizenship to 162,000 Burundian Refugees in Historic Decision." Geneva: UNHCR.

Marsden, P. 1999. "Repatriation and Reconstruction: The Case of Afghanistan." In R. Black and K. Koser (eds.), *The End of the Refugee Cycle? Refugee Repatriation and Reconstruction.* Oxford, U.K.: Berghahn.

Marshall, M.G., and T.R. Gurr. 2003. "Peace and Conflict 2003: A Global Survey of Armed Conflicts, Self-Determination Movements, and Democracy." College Park, MD: Center for International Development and Conflict Management, University of Maryland. Available at: http://www.systemicpeace.org/PC2003.pdf.

Martin, P.L. 1993. "Trade and Migration: NAFTA and Agriculture." Policy Analyses in International Economics 38. Washington DC: Institute for International Economics.

Martin, P.L., and J.E. Taylor. 1996. "The Anatomy of a Migration Hump." In J. E. Taylor (ed.), *Development Strategy, Employment and Migration: Insights from Models.* Paris: OECD.

Martin, S. 2004. "Women and Migration." Consultative Meeting on "Migration and Mobility and How This Movement Affects Women." Malmo, Sweden, December 2–4.

Martin-Rayo, F. 2011. "Countering Radicalization in Refugee Camps." Dubai Initiative Working Paper. Cambridge, MA: Belfer Center for Science and International Affairs, Harvard University.

Massey, D. 1988. "Economic Development and International Migration in Comparative Perspective." *Population and Development Review* 14 (3): 383–413.

Matthews, R.O. 1972. "Refugees and Stability in Africa." *International Organization* 26 (01): 62–83.

Maystadt, J.-F., and Verwimp, P. 2009. "Winners and Losers Among a Refugee-Hosting Population." HiCN Working Paper 60. Brighton, U.K.: Institute of Development Studies, Households in Conflict Network.

Mehta, Chirag, Nik Theodore, Iliana Mora, and Jennifer Wade. 2002. "Chicago's Undocumented Immigrants: An Analysis of Wages, Working Conditions, and Economic Contributions." Chicago, IL: Center for Urban Economic Development, University of Illinois at Chicago.

Melander, E., and M. Öberg. 2006. "Time to Go? Duration Dependence in Forced Migration." *International Interactions* 32: 129–52.

———. 2007. "The Threat of Violence and Forced Migration: Geographical Scope Trumps Intensity of Fighting." *Civil Wars* 9 (2): 156–73.

Merger, S. 2010. "Rape of the Congo: Understanding Sexual Violence in the Conflict in the Democratic Republic of Congo." *Journal of Contemporary African Studies* 28 (2).

Metcalfe, V., et al. 2011. "Sanctuary in the City? Urban Displacement and Vulnerability in Nairobi." Working Paper. London: Humanitarian Policy Group Overseas Development Institute.

Midtbøen, A.H. 2015. "The Context of Employment Discrimination: Interpreting the Findings of a Field Experiment." *The British Journal of Sociology* 66: 193–214. doi: 10.1111/1468-4446.12098.

Milner, C. 2013. "Declining Protection in Development Countries: Fact or Fiction?" *The World Economy* 36 (6): 689–700.

Mishra, N. 2012. *Displacement and Rehabilitation: Solutions for the Future.* Delhi, India: Gyan Publishing House.

Mkandawire, H. 2015. "Media Retaliation against the 2015 Xenophobic Attacks in South Africa: The Case of the QFM Radion in Zambia." *Global Media Journal*, African Edition 9 (2): 191–216.

Mollica, R.F., G. Wyshack, and J. Lavelle. 1987. "The Psychosocial Impact of War Trauma and Torture on South East Asian Refugees." *American Journal of Psychiatry* 114: 1567–1572.

Monsutti, A. 2006. "Afghan Transnational Networks: Looking beyond Repatriation." Kabul, Afghanistan: Afghanistan Research and Evaluation Unit.

Moore, W.H., and S.M. Shellman. 2004. "Fear of Persecution: Forced Migration, 1952–1995." *Journal of Conflict Resolution* 48: 723–745.

———. 2006. "Refugee or Internally Displaced Person? To Where Should One Flee?" *Comparative Political Studies* 39: 599–622.

Morrison, Andrew R., and Rachel A. May. 1994. "Escape from Terror: Violence and Migration in Post-Revolutionary Guatemala." *Latin American Research Review* 29: 111–133.

Mosel, I., and A. Jackson. 2013. "Sanctuary in the City? Urban Displacement and Vulnerability in Peshawar, Pakistan." HPG Working Paper, Humanitarian Policy Group.

Moya, A. 2015. "Violence, Psychological Trauma, and Induced Changes in Risk Attitudes in Colombia." Bogotá, Colombia: Universidad de los Andes. Available at: https://economia.uniandes.edu.co/files/profesores/andres_moya/docs/ViolenceRiskAversion_AndresMoya(1).pdf.

Moya, A., and M. Carter. 2014. "Violence and the Formation of Hopelessness and Pessimistic Prospects of Upward Mobility in Colombia." NBER Working Paper 20463. Cambridge, MA: National Bureau of Economic Research.

Mulvey, G. 2015. "Refugee Integration Policy: the Effects of UK Policy-making on Refugees in Scotland." *Journal of Social Policy* 44 (2).

Newland, K. 2015. *The U.S. Record Shows Refugees Are Not a Threat*. Washington, DC: Migration Policy Institute. Available at: http://www.migrationpolicy.org/news/us-record-shows-refugees-are-not-threat.

Newland, K., H. Tanaka, and L. Barker. 2007. "Bridging Divides: The Role of Ethnic Community-based Organizations in Refugee Integration." Chicago, IL: Migration Policy Institute and International Rescue Committee.

New York Times. 2015. "U.S. Soldiers Told to Ignore Sexual Abuse of Boys by Afghan Allies." Joseph Goldstein, September 20, 2015.

———. 2016. "On Perilous Migrant Trail, Women Often Become Prey to Sexual Abuse." Katrin Bennhold, January 2, 2016.

NORDECO. 2010. *In Search of Protection and Livelihoods: Socio-economic and Environmental Impacts of Dadaab Refugee Camps on Host Communities*. Copenhagen, Denmark: Nordic Agency for Development and Ecology.

Norwegian Refugee Council. 2014. "Living Conditions of Displaced Persons and Host Communities in Urban Goma, DRC." Report. Oslo, Norway. Available at: http://www.nrc.no/resources/reports/living-conditions-of-displaced-persons-and-host-communities-in-urban-goma-drc/.

OCHA (United Nations Office for the Coordination of Humanitarian Affairs). 1999. "Report on the Interagency Expert Consultation on Protected Areas." In *OCHA Orientation Handbook on Complex Emergencies*. New York and Geneva: United Nations Office for the Coordination of Humanitarian Affairs.

OECD (Organisation for Economic Co-operation and Development). 2008. *A Profile of Immigrant Populations in the 21St Century: Data from OECD Countries*. Paris: OECD. Available at: http://

www.oecd-ilibrary.org/social-issues-migration-health/a-profile-of-immigrant-populations
-in-the-21st-century_9789264040915-en.

———. 2015. *International Migration Outlook 2015.* Paris: OECD. Available at: http://
www.oecd.org/migration/international-migration-outlook-1999124x.htm.

———. 2016a. OECD Statistics Database. Available at: http://stats.oecd.org/.

———. 2016b. "Development Aid in 2015 Continues to Grow Despite Costs for In-Donor Refugees." The Development Assistance Committee. Paris: OECD.

———. 2016c. *Financing for Sustainable Development.* Paris: OECD. Available at:
http://www.oecd.org/dac/financing-sustainable-development.

———. 2016d. Making Integration Work: Refugees and Others in Need of Protection.
Paris: OECD. Available at: http://www.oecd.org/migration/making-integration-work
-humanitarian-migrants-9789264251236-en.htm.

Omata, Naohiko. 2011. "Repatriation Is Not for Everyone: The Life and Livelihoods of Former
Refugees in Liberia." *UNHCR New Issues in Refugee Research* 213.

———. 2012a. "Refugee Livelihoods and the Private Sector: Ugandan Case Study." Working
Paper Series 86. Oxford, U.K.: Refugee Studies Centre.

———. 2012b. "Struggling to Find Solutions: Liberian Refugees in Ghana." New Issues in Refugee Research, Research Paper 234. Geneva: UNHCR.

———. 2013. "Repatriation and Integration of Liberian Refugees from Ghana: The Importance
of Personal Networks in the Country of Origin." *Journal of Refugee Studies* 26 (2): 65–282.

Onoma, A. 2013. Anti-Refugee Violence and African Politics. Cambridge, U.K.: Cambridge
University Press.

ORSAM. 2015. "The Economic Effects of Syrian Refugees in Turkey" Report 196. Ankara, Turkey: ORSAM.

Ott, Eleanor. 2013. "The Labour Market Integration of Resettled Refugees." Evaluation Report
2013/6, United Nations High Commissioner for Refugees Policy Development and Evaluation Services.

Pantuliano, S., et al. 2008. "The Long Road Home: Opportunities and Obstacles to the Reinte-
gration of IDPs and Refugees Returning to Southern Sudan and the Three Areas, Report of
Phase II: Conflict, Urbanisation and Land." London: Humanitarian Policy Group, Overseas
Development Institute.

———. 2011. "City Limits: Urbanisation and Vulnerability in Sudan." London: Humanitarian
Policy Group, Overseas Development Institute.

Papademetriou, D.G., M. Sumption, and W. Somerville. 2009. "Migration and the Economic
Downturn: What to Expect in the European Union." Washington, DC: Transatlantic Council on Migration of the Migration Policy Institute.

Partridge, D. 2008. "We Were Dancing in the Club, Not on the Berlin Wall: Black Bodies, Street
Bureaucrats, and Exclusionary Incorporation into the New Europe." *Cultural Anthropology*
23 (4): 660–687.

Pavanello, S., S. Elhawary, and S. Pantuliano. 2010. "Hidden and Exposed: Urban Refugees in
Nairobi, Kenya." Working Paper. London: Humanitarian Policy Group, Overseas Development Institute.

Pavanello, S., and S. Haysom. 2012. "Sanctuary in the City? Urban Displacement and Vulnerability in Amman." Working Paper. London: Humanitarian Policy Group, Overseas Development Institute.

Phuong, Catherine. 2005. *The International Protection of International Displaced Persons*. Cambridge, U.K.: Cambridge University Press.

Pine, D.S., K. Mogg, B.P. Bradley, L. Montgomery, C.S. Monk, E. McClure, A.E. Guyer, M. Ernst, D.S. Charney, and J. Kaufman. 2005. "Attention Bias to Threats in Maltreated Children: Implications for Vulnerability to Stress-related Psychopathology." *American Journal of Psychiatry* 162 (2).

Pini, J. 2008. "Political Violence and the African Refugee Experience." *International Affairs Review*. Available at: http://www.iar-gwu.org/node/19.

Platts-Fowler, D., and D. Robinson. 2015. "A Place for Integration: Refugee Experiences in Two English Cities." *Population, Space, and Place* 21 (5): 476–491. doi: 10.1002/psp.1928.

Poptcheva, Eva-Maria, and Andrej Stuchlik. 2015. "Work and Social Welfare for Asylum-Seekers and Refugees: Selected EU Member States." Brussels: European Parliamentary Research Service. Available at: http://www.europarl.europa.eu/RegData/etudes/IDAN/2015/572784/EPRS_IDA(2015)572784_EN.pdf.

Porter, M., and N. Haslam. 2005. "Predisplacement and Postdisplacement Factors Associated with Mental Health of Refugees and Internally Displaced Peoples: A Meta Analysis." *Journal of the American Medical Association* 294 (5).

Putnam, R., R. Leonardi, and R. Nanetti. 1993. *Making Democracy Work: Civic Traditions in Modern Italy*. Princeton, NJ: Princeton University Press.

Raeymaekers, T. 2011. "Forced Displacement and Youth Employment in the Aftermath of the Congo War: From Making a Living to Making a Life." MICROCON Research Working Paper 38. Brighton, U.K.: Institute of Development Studies.

Ramcharan, B.G. 1989. "Early Warning at the United Nations: The First Experiment." *International Journal of Refugee Law* 1 (3): 379.

Rapoport, H., and J. Fernández-Huertas Moraga. 2014. "Tradable Refugee-admission Quotas: A Policy Proposal to Reform the EU Asylum Policy." RSCAS Working Paper 2014/101. Florence, Italy: European University Institute.

Ratha, Dilip, Supriyo De, Sonia Plaza, Kirsten Schuettler, William Shaw, Hanspeter Wyss, and Soonhwa Yi. 2016 "Migration and Remittances—Recent Developments and Outlook." Migration and Development Brief 26, April 2016. Washington, DC: World Bank.

REACH. 2014. *Access to Health Care and Tensions in Jordanians Communities Hosting Syrian Refugees*. Geneva: REACH.

Refugee Studies Centre. 2011. "Study on Impacts and Costs of Forced Displacement: State of the Art Literature Review." *The Journal of Development Studies* 49 (6): 772–784. Available at: http://dx.doi.org/10.1080/00220388.2013.777707.

Reid, Claire. 2005. "International Law and Legal Instruments." Available at: http://www.forcedmigration.org/research-resources/expert-guides/international-law-and-legal-instruments.

Riiskjaer, Maria Helene Bak, and Tilde Nielsson. 2008. "Circular Repatriation: The Unsuccessful Return and Reintegration of Iraqis with Refugee Status in Denmark." New Issues in Refugee Research. Research Paper 165. Geneva: UNHCR.

Rivera-Batiz, F. 1997. "Undocumented Workers in the Labor Market: An Analysis of the Earnings of Legal and Illegal Mexican Immigrants in the United States." *Journal of Population Economics* 12 (1) Special Issue on Illegal Migration: 91–116.

Rockmore, M. 2011. "The Cost of Fear: The Welfare Effects of the Risk of Violence in Northern Uganda." HiCN Working Paper 109. Brighton, U.K.: Institute of Development Studies, Households in Conflict Network.

———. 2012. "Living within Conflicts: Risk of Violence and Livelihood Portfolios." HiCN Working Paper 121. Brighton, U.K.: Institute of Development Studies, Households in Conflict Network.

Rogge, J., and B. Lippman. 2004. "Making Return and Reintegration Sustainable, Transparent, and Participatory." *Forced Migration Review* 21 (September 2004). Oxford, U.K.: Refugee Studies Centre.

Rowland, M., et al. 2002. "Afghan Refugees and the Temporal and Spatial Distribution of Malaria in Pakistan." *Social Science Medicine* 55 (11): 2061–72.

Ruiz, H. 2004. "Afghanistan: Conflict and Displacement 1978 to 2001." *Forced Migration Review* 13.

Ruiz, I., and C. Vargas-Silva. 2013. "The Economics of Forced Migration." *The Journal of Development Studies* 49 (6): 772–784. Available at: http://dx.doi.org/10.1080/00220388.2013.777707.

Sadiq, K. 2009. *Paper Citizens: How Illegal Immigrants Acquire Citizenship in Developing Countries.* Oxford University Press.

Salehyan, I. 2007. "Transnational Rebels: Neighboring States as Sanctuary for Rebel Groups." *World Politics* 59 (02): 217.

———. 2009. *Rebels without Borders: Transnational Insurgencies in World Politics.* Ithaca, NY: Cornell University Press.

Salehyan, I., and K. Gleditsch. 2006. "Refugees and the Spread of Civil War." *International Organization* 60 (2): 335–366.

Sambanis, N. 2002. "A Review of Recent Advances and Future Directions in the Quantitative Literature on Civil War." *Defence and Peace Economics* 13 (2): 215–243.

Schmeidl, Susanne. 1995. "From Root Cause Assessment to Preventative Diplomacy: Possibilities and Limitations of an Early Warning Forced Migration System." Unpublished dissertation. Columbus, OH: The Ohio State University.

———. 1997. "Exploring the Causes of Forced Migration: A Pooled Time-Series Analysis, 1971–1990." *Social Science Quarterly* 78: 284–308.

———. 1998. "Comparative Trends in Forced Displacement: Refugees and IDPs, 1964–96." In J. Hampton, (ed.), *Internally Displaced People: A Global Survey.* London: Earth Scan Publications.

Schuck, Peter H. 1997. "Refugee Burden-Sharing: A Modest Proposal, Fifteen Years Later." Faculty Scholarship Series Paper 1694. New Haven, CT: Yale Law School.

———. 2010. "Refugee Burden-Sharing: A Modest Proposal, Fifteen Years Later." Research Paper 480. New Haven, CT: Yale Law School, John M. Olin Center for Studies in Law, Economics, and Public Policy.

Schweitzer, R., F. Melville, Z. Steel. and P. Lacharez. 2006. "Trauma, Post-migration Living Difficulties, and Social Support as Predictors of Psychological Adjustment in Resettled Sudanese Refugees." *The Australian and New Zealand Journal of Psychiatry* 40 (2).

Shafy, S. 2013. "The Wave from Syria: Flow of Refugees Destabilizes Lebanon." Spiegel Online. Available at: http://www.spiegel.de/international/world/lebanon-faced-with-refugee-crisis-and-hezbollah-conflict-a-925767.html.

Shaver, A., and Y. Zhou. 2015. *Questioning Refugee Camps as Sources of Conflict.* Princeton, NJ: Princeton University.

Shinkman. 2013. "Syrian Refugee Crisis Destabilizes Jordan." *U.S. News and World Report.*

Singh, Kavita. 2001. "Forced Migration and Under-Five Mortality in Northwestern Uganda and Southern Sudan." Unpublished Dissertation.

Sinha, S., J. Gidwani, and N. Das. 2008. "Cost-Benefit Analysis of CFPR." Case Study. Gurgaon, India: EDA Rural Systems.

Sjaastad, Larry A. 1962. "The Costs and Returns of Human Migration." *Journal of Political Economy* 70 (Supplement): 80–93.

Smith, Ronald C. 2004. "Outsourcing Refugee Protection Responsibilities: The Second Life of an Unconscionable Idea." *Journal of Transnational Law and Policy* 14 (1): 137–153.

Srinivasa Murthy, R., and R. Lakshminarayana. 2006. "Mental Health Consequences of War: A Brief Review of Research Findings." *World Psychiatry* 5: 25–31.

Stanley, William. 1987. "Economic Migrants or Refugees from Violence? A Time Series Analysis of El Salvadoran Migration to the United States." *Latin American Research Review* 22 (1): 132–155.

Stark, O. 1984. "Rural-to-Urban Migration in LCDs: A Relative Deprivation Approach." *Economic Development and Cultural Change* 32 (3): 475–86.

———. 2006. "Inequality and Migration: A Behavioural Link." *Economics Letters* 91 (1): 146–152.

Stark, O., and D. Lehvari. 1982. "On Migration and Risk in LDCs." *Economic Development and Cultural Change* 31 (1): 191–196.

Stark, O., and J.E. Taylor. 1991. "Migration Incentives, Migration Types: The Role of Relative Deprivation." *Economic Journal* 101 (408): 1163–78.

Stark, O., J. Taylor, and S. Yitzhaki. 1986. "Remittances and Inequality." *The Economic Journal* 96: 722–740.

———. 1988a. "Migration, Remittances, Inequality: A Sensitivity Analysis Using the Extended Gini Index." *Journal of Development Economics* 28 (3): 309–322.

———. 1988b. "Labour Migration as a Response to Relative Deprivation." MPRA Paper 21670. Munich, Germany: University Library of Munich.

Steel, Z., T. Chey, D. Silove, C. Marnane, R.A. Bryant, and M. van Ommeren. 2009. "Association of Torture and Other Potentially Traumatic Events with Mental Health Outcomes Among Populations Exposed to Mass Conflict and Displacement: A Systematic Review and Meta-analysis." *Journal of the American Medical Association* 302 (5).

Steele, A. 2009. "Seeking Safety: Avoiding Displacement and Choosing Destinations in Civil Wars." *Journal of Peace Research* 46 (3): 419–430.

Stepputat, F. 2004. "Dynamics of Return and Sustainable Reintegration in a Mobile Livelihoods Perspective." DIS Working Paper 2004/10. Copenhagen: Danish Institute for International Studies. Available at: https://www.ciaonet.org/attachments/6674/uploads.

Stepputat, F., and N. Soerensen. 2001. "The Rise and Fall of Internally Displaced People in the Central Peruvian Andes." *Development and Change* 32 (4): 769–791.

Sturridge, C. 2011. "Mobility and Durable Solutions: A Case Study of Afghan and Somali Refugees." New Issues in Refugee Research. Research Paper 204. Geneva: UNHCR. Available at: http://www.unhcr.org/4d7657899.html.

Sussman, David D. Forthcoming. "The Integration of Refugees in Developed Economies." Report for the World Bank Global Program on Forced Development. Washington, DC: World Bank.

Taintor, Kit, and Gary Lichtenstein. 2016. "The Refugee Integration Survey and Evaluation (RISE) Year Five: Final Report A Study of Refugee Integration in Colorado." Denver, CO:

Colorado Office of Economic Security. Available at: https://cbsdenver.files.wordpress.com/2016/03/rise-year-5-report-feb-2016.pdf.

Talviste, V., J. Williamson, and A. Zeidan. 2012. "The ICRC Approach in Situations of Pre-Displacement." *Forced Migration Review* 41. Available at: http://www.fmreview.org/en/preventing.pdf.

Todaro, Michael P., and Lydia Maruszko. 1987. "Illegal Migration and US Immigration Reform: A Conceptual Framework." *Population and Development Review* 13 (1): 101–114.

Tomaske, J. 1971. "The Determinants of Inter-Country Differences in European Emigration 1881–1900." *The Journal of Economic History* 31 (04): 840–853.

Townsend, M. 2016. "10,000 Refugee Children are Missing, Says Europol." *The Observer*. Available at: https://www.theguardian.com/world/2016/jan/30/fears-for-missing-child-refugees.

Turner, B.L., et al. 2003. "A Framework for Vulnerability Analysis in Sustainability Science." *Proceedings of the National Academy of Sciences* 100 (14).

Turton, D., and P. Marsden. 2002. "Taking Refugees for a Ride? The Politics of Refugee Return in Afghanistan." Issue Paper Series. Kabul, Afghanistan: Afghanistan Research and Evaluation Unit. Available at: http://areu.org.af/Uploads/EditionPdfs/208E-Taking%20Refugees%20for%20a%20Ride-IP-web.pdf.

UCDP/PRIO (Uppsala Conflict Data Program/Peace Research Institute Oslo). 2015. "Armed Conflict Dataset." Uppsala, Sweden: Uppsala Universitet, Department of Peace and Conflict Research. Available at: http://www.pcr.uu.se/research/ucdp/datasets/ucdp_prio_armed_conflict_dataset/.

Uhlenberg, P. 1973. "Noneconomic Determinants of Nonmigration: Sociological Considerations for Migration Theory." *Rural Sociology* 38 (3): 296.

UN (United Nations). 2002. "Monterrey Consensus on Financing for Development." International Conference on Financing for Development, Monterrey, Mexico, March 18–20. Available at: http://www.un.org/esa/ffd/monterrey/MonterreyConsensus.pdf.

———. 2016. *Regional Refugee and Resilience Plan (2015–2016), In Response to the Syria Crisis.* The 3RP. Geneva and New York: UNHCR and UNDP.

UNCEB (United Nations System Chief Executives Board for Coordination). 2015. "United Nations System Chief Executives Board for Coordination (CEB) Retreat Session." Discussion Paper, November 2015. Geneva: UNCEB.

UNEP (United Nations Environment Programme). 1999. *Global Environmental Outlook* 2000. Nairobi, Kenya: UNEP.

UNFPA (United Nations Population Fund). 2006. "State of World Population: A Passage to Hope. Women and International Migration." New York: UNFPA.

UNGA (United Nations General Assembly). 1993. Resolution 48/116. Available at: http://www.un.org/documents/ga/res/48/a48r116.htm.

UN Global Pulse. 2014. "Estimating Migration Flows Using Online Search Data." Global Pulse Project Series 4. Available at: http://www.unglobalpulse.org/sites/default/files/UNGP_ProjectSeries_Search_Migration_2014_0.pdf.

UNHCR (United Nations High Commissioner for Refugees). 1951. *Convention and Protocol Relating to the Status of Refugees.* Geneva: UNHCR. Available at: http://www.unhcr.org/en-us/3b66c2aa10.

———. 1991. "Note on International Protection, A/AC.96/777." Geneva: UNHCR.

———. 1996. "Follow Up to ECOSOC Resolution 1995/96: UNHCR Activities in Relation to Prevention." EC/46/SC/CRP.33. Geneva: UNHCR.

———. 2000. *The State of the World's Refugees 2000: Fifty Years of Humanitarian Action*. Geneva: UNHCR. Available at: http://www.unhcr.org/en-us/publications/sowr/4a4c754a9/state-worlds-refugees-2000-fifty-years-humanitarian-action.html.

———. 2004. *Afghanistan: Challenges to Return*. Geneva. UNHCR.

———. 2008. *Syria Public Information Unit Assessment on Returns to Iraq Amongst the Iraqi Refugee Population in Syria*. Geneva: UNHCR. Available at: http://www.unhcr.org/48185fa82.pdf.

———. 2009. *UNHCR Policy in Refugee Protection and Solutions in Urban Areas*. Geneva: UNHCR.

———. 2011. "General Principles on the Criteria for the Determination of Refugee Status, Article 28." *Handbook on Procedures and Criteria for Determining Refugee Status under the 1951 Convention*. Geneva: UNHCR.

———. 2012. "Population Profiling, Verification and Response Survey of Afghans in Pakistan 2011." Final Report. Geneva: UNHCR. Available at: http://unhcrpk.org/wp-content/uploads/2012/11/PPVR-Report.pdf.

———. 2013. "Syrian Refugees Living Outside Camps in Jordan: Home Visit Data Findings 2013." Geneva: UNHCR. Available at: https://s3.amazonaws.com/unhcrsharedmedia/urban-refugees-in-jordan/HVreport_09MarCS6_smallsize.pdf.

———. 2014a. *UNHCR Policy on Alternatives to Camps*. Geneva: UNHCR.

———. 2014b. *Global Strategy for Livelihoods: A UNHCR Strategy 2014–2018*. Geneva: UNHCR.

———. 2014c. "Figures at a Glance." Geneva: UNHCR. Available at: http://www.unhcr.org/figures-at-a-glance.html.

———. 2014d. "Inter-agency Multi-Sector Needs Assessment (MSNA) Phase One Report: Secondary Data Review and Analysis." Geneva: UNHCR.

———. 2015a. *Statistical Yearbook*. Geneva: UNHCR. Available at: http://www.unhcr.org/statistical-yearbooks.html.

———. 2015b. "Addressing Security Concerns Without Undermining Refugee Protection: UNHCR's Perspective. Revision 2." Geneva: UNHCR. Available at: http://www.refworld.org/docid/5672aed34.html.

———. 2015c. "Global Trends: Forced Displacement in 2014: World at War." Geneva: UNHCR. Available at: http://www.unhcr.org/statistics/country/556725e69/unhcr-global-trends-2014.html.

———. 2015d. *Vulnerability Assessment of Syrian Refugees in Jordan 2015*. UNHCR, WFP, and UNICEF.

———. 2015e. *Operational Guidelines on the Minimum Criteria for Livelihoods Programming*. UNHCR/OG/2015/4.

———. 2015f. *Guidelines on International Protection No. 11: Prima Facie Recognition of Refugee Status*. HCR/GIP/15/11. Available at: http://www.refworld.org/docid/555c335a4.html.

———. 2015g. "Durable Solutions." Geneva: UNHCR. Available at: http://www.unhcr.org/pages/49c3646cf8.html.

———. 2015h. "Living in the Shadows. Jordan Home Visits Report 2014." UNHCR, Geneva. Available at: http://www.unhcr.org/54b685079.pdf.

———. 2015i. "Worldwide Displacement Hits All-Time High as War and Persecution Increase." Press release, June 18, 2015. Geneva: UNHCR. Available at: http://www.unhcr.org/558193896.html.

———. 2016a. *UNHCR Mid Year Trends 2015.* Geneva: UNHCR.

———. 2016b. *UNHCR Global Trends 2015.* Geneva: UNHCR.

———. 2016c. *Population Statistics Database.* Available at: http://popstats.unhcr.org/en/overview.

UNRWA (United Nations Relief and Works Agency for Palestine Refugees in the Near East). 2016. *Historical Refugee Registration Data from Year 1952–2015.*

Uzonyi, G. 2014. "Unpacking the Effects of Genocide and Politicide on Forced Migration." *Conflict Management and Peace Science* 31 (3): 225–243.

Valentino, Benjamin, Paul Huth, and Dylan Balch-Lindsay. 2004. "Draining the Sea: Mass Killing and Guerrilla Warfare." *International Organization* 58: 375–407.

Van Damme, W. 1995. "Do Refugees Belong in Camps: Experiences from Goma and Guinea." *Lancet* 346 (8971): 360–62.

Van Damme, Wim, Vincent De Brouwere, Marleen Boelaert, and Wim Van Lerberghe. 1998. "Effects of a Refugee-assistance Programme on Host Population in Guinea as Measured by Obstetric Interventions." *The Lancet* 351 (9116): 1609–1613.

Vanderkamp, J. 1971. "Migration Flows, Their Determinants, and the Effects of Return Migration." *Journal of Political Economy* 79 (5): 1012–31.

Van der Kolk, B. 1996. "Trauma and Memory." In B. Van der Kolk, A. McFarlane, and L. Weisaith (eds.), *Traumatic Stress: The Effects of Overwhelming Experience on Mind, Body and Society.* New York: Guilford Press.

Van Hear, N. 2003. "From Durable Solutions to Transnational Relations: Home and Exile Among Refugee Diasporas." New Issues in Refugee Research. Working Paper 83. Copenhagen, Denmark: Centre for Development Research and UNHCR Evaluation and Policy Analysis Unit.

———. 2009. "Managing Mobility for Human Development: The Growing Salience of Mixed Migration." UNDP Human Development Research Paper 2009/20. New York: UNDP. Available at: http://hdr.undp.org/en/ reports/global/hdr2009/papers/.

Verme, P., et al. 2015. *The Welfare of Syrian Refugees: Evidence from Jordan and Lebanon.* Washington, DC and Geneva: World Bank Group and UNHCR. Available at: http://reliefweb.int/sites/reliefweb.int/files/resources/9781464807701.pdf.

Verwimp, P. 2005. "An Economic Profile of Peasant Perpetrators of Genocide: Micro-Level Evidence for Rwanda." *Journal of Development Economics* 77 (2): 297–323.

Verwimp, P., and J. Maystadt. 2015. "Forced Displacement and Refugees in Sub-Saharan Africa: An Economic Inquiry." Policy Research Working Paper Series 7517. Washington, DC: World Bank.

Vinck, P., et al. 2007. "Exposure to War Crimes and Implications for Peace Building in Northern Uganda." *Journal of the American Medical Association* 298: 543–554.

Weiner, Myron. 1996. "Bad Neighbors, Bad Neighborhoods: An Inquiry into the Causes of Refugee Flows." *International Security* 21: 5–42.

Werker, E. 2007. "Refugee Camp Economies." *Journal of Refugee Studies* 20 (3): 461–480.

WFP (World Food Programme). 2014. "Vulnerability Assessment of Syrian Refugees (VASyR) in Lebanon, 2014." Available at: http://reliefweb.int/sites/reliefweb.int/files/resources/VASyRexecsum2015.pdf.

Whitaker, B.E. 1999. "Changing Opportunities: Refugees and Host Communities in Western Tanzania." *Journal of Humanitarian Assistance* 4 (1):1–23.

———. 2002. "Refugees in Western Tanzania: The Distribution of Benefits and Burdens among Local Hosts." *The Journal of Refugee Studies* 15 (4).

———. 2003. "Refugees and the Spread of Conflict: Contrasting Cases in Central Africa." *Journal of Asian and African Studies* 38 (2–3): 211–231.

Wiesbrock, A. 2011. "The Integration of Immigrants in Sweden: A Model for the European Union?" *International Migration* 49: 48–66.

Williams, N.E. 2008. "Betting on Life and Livelihoods: The Role of Employment and Assets in the Decision to Migrate during Armed Conflict." PSC Research Report 09-679. Ann Arbor, MI: University of Michigan, Population Studies Center.

———. 2013. "How Community Organizations Moderate the Effect of Armed Conflict on Migration in Nepal." *Population Studies* 67 (3): 353–369.

Wilson, K., D. Cammack, and F. Shumba. 1989. *Food Provisioning amongst Mozambican Refugees in Malawi: A Study of Aid, Livelihood and Development.* Oxford, U.K.: Refugee Studies Programme.

Wood, R.M. 2010. "Rebel Capability and Strategic Violence against Civilians." *Journal of Peace Research* 47 (5): 601–614.

Woods, N. 2008. "Whose Aid? Whose Influence? China, Emerging Donors and the Silent Revolution in Development Assistance." *International Affairs* 84 (6): 1205–1221.

Worbs, S., and E. Bund. 2016. "Asylberechtigte und anerkannte Flüchtlinge in Deutschland: Qualifikationsstruktur, Arbeitsmarktbeteiligung und Zukunftsorientierungen." Edition 1/2016 of the Short Analyses of the Research Center on Migration, Integration, and Asylum of the Federal Office for Migration and Refugees (BAMF). Nuremburg, Germany: BAMF.

World Bank. 1999. *The Economic Consequences of the Kosovo Crisis: A Preliminary Assessment of External Financing Needs and the Role of the Fund and the World Bank in the International Response.* Washington, DC: World Bank.

World Bank. 2006. *Global Economic Prospects: Economic Implications of Remittances and Migration.* Washington, DC: World Bank.

———. 2009. *World Development Report: Reshaping Economic Geography.* Washington, DC: World Bank.

———. 2010. *System of Cities: Harnessing Urbanization for Growth and Poverty Alleviation.* Washington, DC: World Bank. Available at: http://siteresources.worldbank.org/INTURBANDEVELOPMENT/Resources/336387-1269651121606/FullStrategy.pdf.

———. 2011a. *World Development Report: Conflict, Security, and Development.* Washington, DC: World Bank.

———. 2011b. *Azerbaijan: Building Assets and Promoting Self Reliance: The Livelihoods of Internally Displaced Persons.* Washington, DC: World Bank.

———. 2012. "Managing Risk, Promoting Growth: Developing Systems for Social Protection in Africa, The World Bank's Africa Social Protection Strategy 2012–2022." Washington, DC: World Bank.

———. 2013a. "Forced Displacement of and Potential Solutions for IDPs and Refugees in the Sahel: Burkina Faso, Chad, Mali, Mauritania and Niger." Washington, DC: World Bank.

———. 2013b. "Lebanon: Economic and Social Impact Assessment of the Syrian Conflict." Policy Note 81098, Volume 1. Washington, DC: World Bank.

———. 2013c. *Building Resilience: Integrated Climate and Disaster Risk into Development.* Washington, DC: World Bank.

———. 2013d. *Inclusion Matters: The Foundation for Shared Prosperity.* New Frontiers of Social Policy. Washington, DC: World Bank.

———. 2013e. "Crowdfunding's Potential for the Developing World 2013." infoDev, Finance and Private Sector Development Department, Washington, DC: World Bank.

———. 2014. "Invisible Wounds: A Practitioners' Dialogue on Improving Development Outcomes through Psychosocial Support." Washington, DC: World Bank.

———. 2015a. "Turkey's Response to the Syrian Refugee Crisis and the Road Ahead." Washington, DC: World Bank.

———. 2015b. "Rise of the Anatolian Tigers: Turkey Urbanization Review." Report 87180-TR. Washington, DC: World Bank.

———. 2015c. "Sustainable Refugee Return: Triggers, Constraints and Lessons on Addressing the Development Challenges of Forced Displacement." GPFD Issue Note Series. Washington, DC: World Bank.

———. 2015d. *East Asia's Changing Urban Landscape: Measuring a Decade of Spatial Growth.* Washington, DC: World Bank. Available at: http://www.worldbank.org/content/dam/Worldbank/Publications/Urban%20Development/EAP_Urban_Expansion_full_report_web.pdf.

———. 2015e. *World Development Report: Mind, Society, and Behaviour.* Washington, DC: World Bank.

———. 2015h. *Examining Recovery and Peacebuilding Needs in Eastern Ukraine.* Washington, DC: World Bank.

———. 2016a. *Women, Business, and the Law.* Washington, DC: World Bank.

———. 2016b. *Doing Business 2016: Measuring Regulatory Quality and Efficiency.* Washington, DC: World Bank.

———. 2016c. *Global Monitoring Report 2015/2016: Development Goals in an Era of Demographic Change.* Washington DC: World Bank. Available at: http://www.worldbank.org/en/publication/global-monitoring-report.

———. 2016d. *An Assessment of Uganda's Approach to Refugees.* Washington, DC: World Bank.

———. 2016e. World Development Indicators Database. Available at: http://data.worldbank.org/data-catalog/world-development-indicators.

———. Forthcoming. *Stocktaking of Global Forced Displacement Data.* GPFD.

World Bank and UNHCR (United Nations High Commissioner for Refugees). 2011. *Research Study on IDPs in Urban Settings: Afghanistan.* Available at: http://siteresources.worldbank.org/EXTSOCIALDEVELOPMENT/Resources/244362-1265299949041/6766328-1265299960363/WB-UNHCR IDP_Full-Report.pdf.

World Bank and WHO (World Health Organization). 2016. *Out of the Shadows: Making Mental Health a Global Development Priority.* Available at: http://www.who.int/mental_health/advocacy/wb_background_paper.pdf.

Xue, L. 2007. "Portrait of an Integration Process: Difficulties Encountered and Resources Relied on by Newcomers in Their First Four Years in Canada." Research Working Paper, Citizenship and Immigration Canada.

———. 2008. "Social Capital and Labour Market Outcomes of Recent Immigrants to Canada: Employment Entry, Wages and Duration of Access to the First Job in Intended Occupation." Ph.D. Dissertation. Ottawa, ON: University of Ottawa, Department of Economics.

Yehuda, R. 2002. "Post-Traumatic Stress Disorder." *New England Journal of Medicine* 345: 108–114.

Young, H., K. Jacobsen, and A.M. Osman. 2009. *Livelihoods, Migration and Conflict: Discussions of Findings from Two Studies in West and North Darfur, 2006–2007*. Boston, MA: Feinstein International Center.

Yu, S., E. Ouellet, and A. Warmington. 2007. "Refugee Integration in Canada: A Survey of Empirical Evidence and Existing Services." *Refuge* 24 (2): 17–34.

Zapater, J. 2010. "Prevention of Forced Displacement: The Inconsistencies of the Concept." UNHCR Research Paper 186. Geneva: UNHCR.

Zelinsky, W. 1971. "The Hypothesis of the Mobility Transition." *Geographical Review* 61 (2): 219–249.

Zetter, R., and G. Deikun. 2010. "Meeting Humanitarian Challenges in Urban Areas." *Forced Migration Review* 34 (Urban Displacement).

Zetter, R., A. Purdekova, and A.M. Ibáñez. 2013. "Violence, Conflict, and Mobility: A Micro Level Analysis." In T. Brück, P. Justino, and P. Verwimp, (eds.), *A Micro-Level Perspective on the Dynamics of Conflict, Violence, and Development*. Oxford, U.K.: Oxford University Press.

Zetter, R., and H. Ruaudel. Forthcoming. *Assessing Refugees' Right to Work (R2W): Law, Policies, Socio-economic Conditions and Outcomes*. Global Knowledge Partnership on Migration and Development (KNOMAD).

Zetter, R., and C. Vargas-Silva. 2011. *Assessing the Impacts and Costs of Forced Displacement*. Volume I. Oxford, U.K., and Washington, DC: Refugee Studies Centre and World Bank.

Zolberg, Aristide R., Astri Suhrke, and Sergio Aguayo. 1989. *Escape from Violence: Conflict and the Refugee Crisis in the Developing World*. New York: Oxford University Press.

FORCIBLY DISPLACED